The Indians' Last Fight

Dennis Collins

The Indians' Last Fight
or The Dull Knife Raid
Recollections of the Western American Frontier

Dennis Collins

The Indians' Last Fight or The Dull Knife Raid: Recollections of the Western American Frontier
by Dennis Collins

Leonaur is an imprint of Oakpast Ltd

First published under the title
The Indians' Last Fight or The Dull Knife Raid

Material original to this edition and presentation of the text in this form copyright © 2011 Oakpast Ltd

ISBN: 978-0-85706-759-3 (hardcover)
ISBN: 978-0-85706-760-9 (softcover)

http://www.leonaur.com

Publisher's Notes

The views expressed in this book are not necessarily those of the publisher.

Contents

Preface	7
General Conditions	11
Santa Fe Trail	14
The Freight Outfit on the Trail	17
First Settlers	22
The Round-Up	25
The Vigilantes	27
Wild Horses	38
Why I Came West	47
The Character of the Cowboy	56
Entertaining a Hobo	62
The Man From Missouri	68
Indian Scares	72
Hard Times	84
Returning to Kansas	111
The Race for Land	121
An Arkansaw Traveller	127
Savages on the Warpath	146
The Whirlwind Raid	164
The Sun Dance	171
The Adobe Wall Raid	183
The "Dull Knife" Raid	201
Buffalo Hunters	229
Custer's and the Indians	235
Sheridan's Camp	241
Expedition to Panhandle	247
Murder of a Freighter	255
Custer's Massacre	262
Trouble With the Northern Cheyennes	272
Ben Clark & General Creel	281
Afterword	286

Preface

The work of writing a book is one that requires a vast amount of knowledge, natural ability and educational advantages, to produce something that is reliable, as regards information imparted, unimpeachable authority, and, at the same time, a power of expression that will present the matter to the reader in a manner that will convey the proper meaning of the author. I would not have undertaken the present work, were it not that I was encouraged by the friends of former days who felt confident in my ability to portray the scenes to be depicted in a fitting manner. I should probably be able to perform the task before me with greater success if I had some of the advantages of what is called higher education, but, I set out on my journey through this new domain, encouraged particularly, by a statement made by a certain ex-president, that he did not believe in all the "Phs", and "Chs", that are in common use in our language; that he believed in a plain, intelligent expression of ideas that conveys the full meaning of the speaker or writer, without any unnecessary verbiage.

My own personal qualifications for undertaking the task before me, might be considered too inadequate to many. True, I have not had the advantage of a university education, but with a solid foundation of learning laid in the little school of boyhood in Canada, supplemented by a wide course of reading through all the years I have spent in the west, I feel that the difficulties before me are not too great to be overcome, especially as I have the example of so many men before me who have become self-educated by an earnest application of time and energy to the opportunities presented.

If I have developed any facility of expression, I must attribute it to the wealth of good books I have had the good fortune to have at my disposal at various times.

Another motive that has impelled me to undertake the task of presenting the "west" to the general reader, is that there has been so much written about it that is not veracious, and that many have a false notion of what the term really means. I shall endeavour to set before the public a true account of many of the recent happenings in the vast country that lies west of the Mississippi, that they may have a better idea of its history and its people. I have read in numerous magazines and journals, accounts of the habits and customs of the western people in general, and of the cow-puncher in particular, with a full description of the Indian at peace and at war, that, from the reality, it would be impossible to recognize any of them. I am quite satisfied that the authors of the so-called narrations did not have an opportunity of studying the subject at close quarters, and, consequently, were not in a position to do the topic justice. As a consequence of this unreliable mode of narration, people who do not know, imagine that the cow-puncher was half-man and half-horse, or, if not so bad as that, pictured him as a ranting, roaring, rollicking, bloodthirsty, oath-emitting, unconstrained son of perdition, whose chief occupation was murder and rapine, and whose avocation was herding cattle. As for the Indian, he was supposed to have no other qualification for attention than murder and pillage, totally depraved, and beyond the scope of all civilizing influences. Such ideas are based on imaginary authority, and are as far from the truth as it is possible for any narrative to be. I shall endeavour to set before the reading public a proper appreciation of both the Indian and the cow-puncher. Both had faults, but, in view of their surroundings and circumstances of life, they both will bear comparison with those who have had all the advantages of the higher education, and the influence of civilization. One thing that will always stand in their favour is that they were "men," and played the game of life, in "man" fashion. Smallness, or rather, pettiness of character was entirely lacking in their general scheme of life; that remained in the big cities of the east.

Having spent more than thirty years among the cow-men and the Indians of the different tribes, from the Dakota line to the Panhandle of Texas, I feel that I am not presuming when I say that in that time I have acquired considerable knowledge of both classes of men, their habits, and ideals, and I trust that the present narrative may be interesting to all my old comrades of the "Plains" as well as instructive to the friends of my boyhood days in the "Land of the Maple Leaf." I have the further hope, that if any of the readers of this little work contemplate coming west to grow up with the country, they may find the difficulties of the way overcome, and the rough places made smooth. They will find a generous welcome awaiting them from the whole-souled men of the great west, and will discover that their lot has fallen on pleasant places.

The Author

Chapter 1

General Conditions

Someone has said, and I think very truthfully, too, that one-half of this world doesn't know how the other half lives, and if he had added that one-half did not care, he would have hit the nail on the head. In order to verify this statement, go to the frontier of any new country, and you will readily see that the progressive, or producing class, is too busy and too much interested in trying to make a little home, and in providing the necessaries of life, for himself and family, to stop and inquire into the cause of such conditions which surround him. He is busy, very busy, with his own affairs. He must dig a well, build a dugout, and plough the sod to roof it. He must make a storm cave, as it is one of the essentials in Oklahoma and in Kansas, as a cyclone is liable to make a visitation, and he himself and all that he has, may very likely be nothing more than a memory. A storm cave is a very valuable asset, as it gives the family a place of safety in storms, and is a very great factor socially, as the neighbours, if there be any close enough, are most likely to drop around should there be a threatening cloud in the sky, for the sake of mutual encouragement and consolation. I have seen twenty-two persons in one cave that was no larger than eight by ten feet, and all seemed to be satisfied; at least I was.

At one time, of the early settlement of western Kansas, Indian Territory and western Texas, there were no mail routes established except between the military posts, Fort Dodge, Kansas, Fort Elliot, Texas, Camp Supply, Fort Reno and Fort Sill, I.T. About this time, 1870, Dodge City, Kansas, sprang into existence, and became the Mecca for the cowmen of the southwest, and like Rome, all roads led to it. If mail was wanted, or trading was necessary, one had to go from fifty to seventy-five miles for the purpose, and in no case less than twenty, as the S. F. R. R. had a land grant of twenty miles on each side of the roadway, and one could not homestead inside of that limit more than eighty acres, and that is why settlers who wanted 160 acres went farther out.

In making those trips two neighbours usually went together, leaving their families in one place until their return. Their outfit for the journey consisted generally of a few blankets, a shot gun, a Winchester, a coffee pot, a frying pan, tow lariat ropes to picket out the horses, and a box of axle grease. The time required for the trip from three to five days and sometimes longer, owing to the distance and condition of the roads. There were no hotels on the way. In fact, there was nothing but the open prairie, and when it came to camping out time they picketed out the horses, gathered some buffalo chips for a fire, made coffee and flapjacks, fried some bacon and then satisfied their appetites with the fare at hand. Supper over, they discussed prospects for the future and then rolled up in their blankets for a good sound sleep with nothing to disturb them but the howling of the coyotes that were around looking for something to eat. At times something would stampede a herd of antelopes and in their mad flight they would create a noise like the roll of distant thunder. One thing that was in the favour of the camper-out was that it seldom rained and any dust that was made on the trail was blown away, leaving the way as clean as a pavement. The wind generally blew from the south for four days at a time, or thereabouts, at a rate of about forty miles an hour, and then returned at the same rate from the north.

On a trip of this kind, one became the messenger and delivery boy for all the neighbours. It was mail for one, paregoric for another, Epsom Salts for a third, and tobacco, coffee, sugar and other commodities which they were in need of at the time the journey was undertaken. The return of the expedition was looked forward to with as much interest and anxiety as is the return of the Cunard steamer at the port of New York. Each day found the children on the hillside watching and waiting for the return of the dear ones, and night was made hideous by the howling of the family watchdog wailing over the absence of his master.

The neighbours, too, shared the general feeling and called several times a day to see if any tidings had been received of them, or if there was anything they stood in need of.

The next step in the way of progress was to sink a well. This was a necessity of the first degree, as the early settlers were compelled to haul water from the distant creeks, or rivers, in barrels, and the quality of the supply was not very high class. The presence of a well near at hand would solve the problem and at the same time save a lot of time which would naturally be required to bring it from a distance. The task was the work of two men, as the well had to be sunk from one hundred to one hundred and twenty-five feet before water could be found that would meet the needs of the situation. One man could not do the work alone, so a neighbour lent his assistance. By means of a derrick and a cheap mule purchased for the purpose they raised the water when the well was dug. The animal was left at the well and each man that went to draw water was to see to it that his muleship did not suffer from want of attention.

The above were only a few of the difficulties that the pioneer encountered in his endeavour to get a start in life. Those who came to the country in '79 or the early 80s found difficulties in abundance. As it rained very little during those years, their means were soon exhausted, and a great many were forced through necessity to abandon their claims and return east in search of employment. All would have been compelled to go were it not for the carcasses left by the buffalo hunters who had taken nothing but the hide and the hump. Buffalo bones were worth about $14 per ton, and the pioneers that remained gathered them up and hauled them to market at Dodge City. It took from eight to ten days to gather and market a load of bones. This source of revenue, while not very remunerative, served as an opportunity for them to keep body and soul together. By the time the bones began to disappear entirely, they had succeeded in getting some land in a state of cultivation and raised a fair crop of millet, sorghum and Kaffir corn, crops adapted to the dry climate. Besides these things, a few chickens and a cow or two relieved the situation a great deal. Most of the old-timers who had the courage to stay, or rather lacked the means of getting away, are today in good circumstances, and the land that was then almost a desert, is now as productive as any in the United States.

CHAPTER 2

Santa Fe Trail

The man who enlists in the army under the influence of patriotic speeches delivered by some great orator, accompanied by a brass band, has no conception of the nerve, energy and enterprise that was required of the first man who popped his bull-whip over the backs of his oxen at little old Westport on the banks of the Missouri River, and shouted to his men, "Come on, boys, we are bound for Santa Fe." There were no mile posts before him to direct him on his way, and no scouts in advance to warn him of impending dangers. There was nothing before but the open prairie, trackless as the ocean, but onward he pressed across the unmarked plains, over hills and canyons, across creeks and rivers, until he reached his destination. His whole route lay through dangers from hostile tribes who, if not on the warpath one day, were liable to be on the next. Everybody was supposed to sleep with one eye open, otherwise he would be likely to wake up in an unknown land, while his poor habitation of clay would be left minus part of its thatch. Such were the conditions confronting the heroes who opened up the trail and made it possible for the immigrants to take Horace Greeley's advice to "Go west and grow up with the country." It is true that there was a great profit in the freighting business in the early days, but the difficulties and dangers were proportionally great. The Indian was not the only risk—there was the prairie fire, the Texas fever, and numerous other dangers confronting one at every step. When the Texas fever seized the cattle, as the ox teams were called, the game was up. I knew one man who drove into Dodge City with over a hundred head of fine work oxen, and in less than six weeks he did not have enough stock left to pull the empty wagons out of town, such was the fatal results of the Texas fever.

The prairie fire could be handled in most cases if it caught in the short prairie or buffalo grass. All that was necessary was to start a back fire, drive onto the burned space and wait until the head fire had passed. But if it caught one in the river, or creek bottoms, where the grass grew from four to six feet high, the only hope lay in flight with the chances very much against one.

Such were the principal difficulties to be encountered on the trail. There were others of a less serious nature, but, nevertheless, very irksome and sometimes dangerous, such as bogging down in the quicksand while crossing a river, or creek. If the sand was not thoroughly packed by driving the cattle back and forth over it before driving into it with a wagon, one was liable to lose a wagon or two, and possibly the entire outfit.

Freighting soon became quite an important industry. New trails were laid off from the little towns that sprang up along the Santa Fe trail to the different ranches in the territory and Texas. The price paid for freighting was at one time two to three dollars per hundred pounds, to the Panhandle ranches. I have seen a train of wagons half a mile long going to the Panhandle. It was about this time that the great American promoter, or capitalist, came out of the jungles with a railroad scheme, went before Congress and begged assistance for the infant industry. The idea was to build the Santa Fe R. R. westward from Kansas City, and they could not afford to do it without a land grant. It is needless to say that they received it. It consisted of each alternate section for twenty miles on each side of the track. The same railroad at about the same period gave birth to another railroad (they came near being twins.) That is the branch that runs southward through Kansas and the Indian Territory, through the richest oil field in America. It is needless to say that they got this grant through Congress also. I may here remark that I have watched our legislators for a number of years and have never seen them make any special effort to protect the farmer's infant industry, though the farmer outnumbers the promoter and the capitalist five hundred to one. The same can be said of the mechanic's infant industry.

Moreover, it is to be noted that in a time of national distress, it is the farmer and the mechanic who take their places in the ranks of the army to fight the battle of the country. I have seen Congress take a hand in the protection of the cattlemen in the Cherokee Strip, but at the same time there was a certain Senator from Kansas who had interests there and who wished that tract of land to remain a sort of "No Man's Land" for the sole benefit of himself and the Cattle Syndicate in which he was very much interested. This condition endured for fourteen years. During this time Payne and Couch organized a colony of settlers or "Nesters" as they were called, and set a movement on foot to take up some of that land, and establish their homes. Although it was unclaimed land, as soon as the settlers had their little homes built and things in shape to take up the burden of their lives, the soldiers through the influence of the Cattle Syndicate swooped down upon them, arrested the settlers, tore down their houses, and drove the offending parties back across the Kansas line. Through all these discouraging conditions the settlers maintained the fight and finally won out against the powerful Syndicate, but at what a cost! Payne was arrested and taken to Fort Smith, handcuffed like a criminal, and was held there for a long time but was not given a trial, as there were no legal grounds for his arrest. Poor Payne did not live to enjoy the fruits of his labours for the early settlers, but he made it possible for them to make homes for themselves and enjoy them in peace, unmolested by the powerful Syndicate and those who were in league with them. Were it not for the fight put up by Payne and Couch, the land now occupied by homes of thousands of happy and contented farmers would now be the grazing ground of cattle owned by the Syndicate. Verily the wheels of Justice move slowly when the interests of the poor man are at stake.

CHAPTER 3

The Freight Outfit on the Trail

The freighter's team was composed of from four to six yokes of oxen, sometimes more, driven by one man called a "bullwhacker." The train consisted of a "lead" wagon and one or two "trail" wagons. The "lead" wagon, being the heaviest and largest, usually carried a load of about five tons. The "trailers" were loaded considerably lighter, carrying about two or three tons each. In ascending steep hills, or crossing streams, the "trail" wagons were usually "dropped" if the conditions of the road demanded it. If the river crossing was quicksandy the cattle were taken out and driven back and forth across the stream until the quicksand was packed sufficiently to be considered safe. This decision was left to the judgment of the foreman, or the "boss" of the train. Then the wagons were taken across one by one until the whole outfit was landed safely on the opposite side.

The old-time freighter invariably crossed the streams in the afternoon or evenings, for two reasons. First, the teams, whether oxen or mules, would pull much better in the evening than when hitched up fresh in the morning as they usually had sore shoulders, and in the morning were very reluctant to go against the yoke or collar in a very heavy pull. Secondly, it might rain during the night and the rivers or streams would become so swollen that passing would be impossible, and they would be compelled to remain in camp until the streams returned to their usual shallow condition.

The foreman always kept one or two saddle horses, a pair of forty-five six-shooters, a Winchester, and a slicker, as it was one of his duties to ride a few miles in advance of the train to pick out the crossings and to avoid all difficulties of the journey, and to keep the teamsters posted on the best route to follow. Very frequently the foreman kept the commissary department of the train supplied with fresh meat, as deer, antelope and other large game were plentiful, and the prairie was literally covered with buffalo. It was no difficult matter to kill such game, as they were unacquainted with the sound of a gun, or the sight of man, which condition changed as they soon learned that the proximity of a man spelled danger and consequently they became very wild. When a buffalo or deer was killed, it was skinned and the hide salted and taken along for use, or to sell. The hide of the antelope was considered worthless. The meat that was not intended for immediate use was cut into strips, dipped in salt water and hung on a line or the wagon bows to dry and was then preserved for future use. Flies never bothered meat treated in this manner. Such meat was said to be "jerked," and would remain in good condition for use for over a year.

The outfits usually made a journey of about twelve miles a day, as it was impossible to carry enough feed along for the stock and have at the same time room enough for the freight. Consequently, it was necessary to graze the stock, which required a considerable time and caused much delay. It was necessary also to have the cattle graze during the daytime owing to the fact that the Indians had a penchant for stampeding a herd at night and running it off to parts unknown for their own use. As a result of this condition, what travelling was done was accomplished in one shift, as it would require too much time and trouble to hitch up twice in the same day. At times, when the grazing was exceptionally good, the freighter remained in such a place for some time, as some of the stock would be footsore and besides the wagons needed greasing, the harness and the rest of the outfit had to be examined and repairs made where needed, sore shoulders had to be given medical treatment, and, in fine, everything had to be done to keep the expedition in proper shape. The teamsters particularly spent considerable of their spare time in looking after their own accoutrements, as it was a matter of pride with a teamster to have his implements in proper condition. The whip to the teamster was the same as the rifle to the soldier. It had to be looked after with care. New tips, called "poppers," or "crackers," had to be provided. The lash, usually about twelve feet in length, required considerable skill in the handling of it. A green hand was as likely to wrap it around his own neck as to hit the object intended to receive the blow. The whip in the hands of an expert was a different weapon, and he could perform wonders with it. I have seen drivers wrap the tip of their whip around the neck of a prairie chicken or a grouse and jerk it into the wagon without leaving their seats. If it were necessary some of them could tear a patch of hide off the side of a refractory mule with the deftness of a surgeon.

In going into camp there was one rule that the old-timers always lived up to rigidly, and that was to form a corral by driving one part of the wagons to the right and the other part to the left, making the two lead wagons meet and forming a circle with the trail wagons six or eight feet apart. The space thus left open served the purpose of a gate, and they usually made their beds inside the corral. The stock was usually held inside the corral for the night, or if permitted to graze were driven in to be hitched. If any of them proved unruly, they were usually roped and drawn up to the wagon while being yoked and harnessed. In case of an attack by the Indians the corral offered a good protection for the men as well as the stock.

The third trail wagon attached to some of the teams was never as heavy nor loaded as heavily as the others, but was used as a sort of trap-wagon or "catch-all" for all the extras that were brought along to supply the place of any of the parts that were broken or suffered damage. Each man looked after his traps and particularly his own bed, consisting of a blanket. When not in use it was rolled up and carried in the trap wagon.

With each large outfit there was a night herder, or a horse wrangler. It was his duty to go out with the stock during the night and bring them into the corral in the morning. In case the Indians were on the warpath or were reported near at hand, he had to stand guard over the outfit, as the stock in such a case would be left in the corral until daylight. This system was maintained by all outfits, whether they drove oxen or mules.

The cowman's outfit was entirely different. He never used more than two wagons, one the lead wagon, and the other the trail, to carry his supplies and cooking utensils. He always used mules or horses in preference to oxen, as oxen were too slow for the needs of his business. The trail wagon was used principally for carrying bedding. In the rear of it there was a cupboard, or grub box, built about three feet in height and fastened to the wagon by means of bolts. The door of the cupboard, instead of swinging as in ordinary articles of the kind, swung downwards and was used as a dining table. The interior of the cupboard was so arranged that the dishes could be safely stored away together with some canned goods, if it were possible to obtain the latter, as they were seldom seen in the early days along the trail. Outside of the necessary articles required for the journey, nothing else was carried, so that the cowman and his party had little opportunity to enjoy any luxuries. As supply points were few and far between, the price of goods, especially bacon, baking powder, salt, tobacco and other essentials was very high. The lead wagon was used for general supplies, and it required an abundance of the same to carry the outfit from one replenishing point to another. I am speaking here of what is called "through herds," that is, herds on the way to market.

While provisions were scarce and difficult to obtain, it is a remarkable fact that the ranchers never tried to improve the situation in any appreciable degree. They never planted a garden. No vegetables ever appeared at mess excepting, once in a while, potatoes and onions. Nevertheless, all kinds of garden produce might have been had at a very small outlay, and with very little labour, but the average, and you might say, all the cowboys had an aversion for anything that had the appearance of farming, which they considered degrading. I have been at a number of ranches that maintained from twenty-five to thirty thousand head of cattle and did not see a pound of butter or a drop of milk on the table. Eggs, chickens and fresh pork were unknown to them. In fact, they produced nothing but cattle and considered everything else unimportant.

When the railroad was extended to Dodge City, that place became the shipping point for the beef-cattle of the whole southwest. When that assembling point was established to supply the eastern market, it relieved the tedium and difficulties of an overland journey to Kansas City. As a consequence of this, the cattle industry in Indian Territory received an impetus, and many cattlemen moved into that district from Colorado and Texas, and established themselves along the North and South Canadian Rivers and their tributaries. Quite a number of them became very wealthy in a few years owing to the rise in the price of beef and the low cost of production. While some of them grew wealthy through taking advantage of the natural resources, others lost all they possessed owing to the severe winters, lack of protection for their stock and an insufficient supply of food for their herds. The result of their misfortune was that they slipped back among the vast army of the luckless ones and were seldom heard of, while those who had the foresight to provide against all the contingencies of the uncertain climate by putting up hay in the summer time and protecting their ranches from the destructive prairie fires, prospered handsomely.

CHAPTER 4

First Settlers

About the year 1878, as the last buffalo was about to disappear, the hunters were compelled to seek some new field of labour, or devote their attention to some other occupation. It was about this time that the first house was erected in what is now called Beaver City, the county seat of Beaver county, Oklahoma. At that time the county was unsurveyed, and a man's possessions were limited to what land he could use, or furnish cattle to graze upon, as there was plenty for everybody, and no need of disputing ownership.

I shall briefly mention a few of the earliest settlers.

Two ex-hunters, Jim Lane and Nels Cary, brought their families and built a sod house. With an eye to business, they put up hay and built corrals for the accommodation of freighters and cattlemen. Seeing their way open to further development, they put in a stock of groceries and provisions of all kinds, and were soon doing a flourishing business by providing for the wants of man and beast.

The Healy Brothers came from Galveston with their herds of cattle, and located their ranch on the north bank of Beaver Creek, where their efforts were crowned with success.

The Kramer Brothers, Lou and Frank, with a brother-in-law, Mr. Hooker, established a ranch west of Beaver City and also another one on Clear Creek, where they devoted their time and attention to the improvement of their stock by raising thoroughbred cattle.

The Cader Brothers, formerly engaged in the hunting business, chose for themselves a ranch on Paladuro Creek and met with great success, if rumour is to be believed.

Colonel Hardesty, more familiarly known as Old Jack, established two ranches, one in Beaver county and another on the Cimarron River, which were known as the "Hardesty" and "Smith" ranches, and at one time claimed to have forty thousand head of cattle.

Another successful ranchman of those early days was John George, who is still residing in the district where he met with such success. After the opening of Oklahoma Territory for settlement, he was chosen to represent his district in the Oklahoma legislature, and was one of the very few members thereof who gave complete satisfaction to his constituents. He was a staunch Democrat, an honest and upright man, just the kind that was sorely needed in the Territorial Legislature at that time, and of which there was a lamentable scarcity.

Fred Tainter, of Boston, Massachusetts, established a ranch on Cottonwood Creek, and bred a fine grade of stock. He remained in those parts for years. There were many others who succeeded in attaining success in the business of raising cattle, but I mention only a few of the most successful ones.

I here mention another branch of the ranching business that met with great difficulties in its day and which, to the cowman, was most unwelcome. The Tarbox Brothers, Rufe and Wall, moved in with a drove of sheep from Colorado and settled on the Cimarron River. A sheepman is always received with scant courtesy in a cattle country. There has always been ill feeling between the sheepman and the cattleman, and in the trouble that generally ensued on their meeting, the sheepman was the one to move to other quarters. In fact, even if the cattlemen were left out of consideration, the sheepmen would be compelled to move by force of circumstances, as sheep are very destructive feeders, and soon ruin the range for themselves as well as for the cattle. In a very short time after their arrival, every vestige of grass will disappear from the range, and the prairie will be converted into a desert. The reason lies in the fact that the sheep crop the grass into the ground and cut up the soil with their hoofs so that the high wind which invariably blows drives the sand before it, cutting off the new grass that may spring up. This, together with the long dry periods, soon kills out the roots, and the prairie is left a waste. Moreover, cattle will not eat off the range that has been grazed over by sheep, so of the two industries it was a case of the survival of the fittest.

The struggle between the cattlemen and the sheepmen was little, if any, short of war. This condition existed for many years in Texas, Indian Territory, western Kansas, Wyoming, Montana, the Dakotas, and in all of the states adapted to the raising of stock. The usual arguments advanced by both sides of the question, in order to determine who was to hold any particular section, generally sounded like the exhausts of a few racing automobiles. One of the sufferers of misfortune due to the habitual state of hostility between the two industries was the firm of Tarbox brothers, who gave up the business of raising sheep, moved to Dodge City, Kansas, where Rufe was afterwards elected mayor.

As the most desirable location for the establishment of a ranch was along the creeks and rivers, through the necessity of having plenty of water for the stock, and as the rivers and creeks were few and far between, all the choice sections were soon taken up.

As none of the ranchers cared to venture into the semi-arid plains that lay between the far distant sources of their water supply, and being equally unwilling to depend upon the deep wells that would be required if they would branch out into the open flat lands around them, they left that part of the prairie for the small farmer, or the "nester," as they called them.

Each cattleman had his own private brand which was duly registered and was known to every other cattleman in the entire west. They were, also, very careful to employ the said brand on all cattle, mules and horses, and any young stock that had been weaned and was not running with the mother was classified as a maverick and belonged to the first man who put his brand upon them.

There were many men who became very wealthy in the cattle country, whose sole assets in the beginning were, a branding iron, a rope, a pony and a saddle. They branded mavericks, and the natural increase of their original find belonged to them also. In this way, in a very short time, they accumulated quite a herd. Then, by establishing their headquarters somewhere, they became full-fledged ranchers without the outlay of any capital whatever. This was successful as long as they were not caught, but woe to the man whose brand was upon a calf that was running with a cow that carried another brand. The meanest way such men had of carrying on their nefarious trade was to kill the mother cow after the calf was old enough to live on grass, brand the calf and run it off to another part of the range.

CHAPTER 5

The Round-Up

Every spring and fall occurred the general round-up, which consisted of all the cattlemen in the country, who assembled all the cattle found on the ranges in which they were interested. They rounded them up, or bunched them at a common centre in different districts, each ranch being represented at each place. All the increase was branded and marked by the owner, the ownership being decided by the brand borne by the mother cow. The beef-cattle were cut out and shipped. Here occurred at times a combination of forces. Ranchers two or more in number lumped their herds together, and drove them to market, each one bearing his proportion of the expense, and receiving his proceeds in accordance with the number of cattle in his part of the drove.

Between round-ups it was surprising how the cattle would drift. Even though the cowboys took all precautions, when the round-up came there was always a great mix-up in the brands, some of the stock having wandered as far as two hundred miles from its own ranch. These, when found, were separated and thrown back on their own range. During the summer while the cattle were grazing, the rancher usually put up hay for the season when the grass would be covered with snow. As soon as the fall round-up was completed, sheds were erected and windbreaks made to protect the stock from the inclemency of the "northers" as the storms were at that time called.

A few buffalo that had escaped the hunters still remained on the range, and frequently furnished diversion for the cowboy during the dull season. It was his sport and, at the same time, a test of his skill, to rope a buffalo calf and bring it to the ranch to be mothered by an old cow that already was devoting her time and energy to raising a young one of her own. Then was displayed the motherly instinct for the protection of one's own. As soon as the young buffalo was introduced to his foster-mother there ensued a vigorous protest against the additional burden imposed upon her by the scheming of others. Strenuosity was displayed at all angles, particularly fore and aft, in her efforts to rid herself of the new-found charge. She kicked and hooked and kicked again till kicking was a failure. The more she objected, the more the self-adopted buffalo persisted in devoting his time and attention to her. Once he had a taste of that cow's milk he hung to her with all the persistency and tenacity of an Oklahoma office-seeker, and she finally submitted with more or less bad grace to the inevitable, and consented to act as mother to the mascot of the ranch.

CHAPTER 6

The Vigilantes

About the year 1876, if I remember rightly, the U. S. Government made an appropriation to have Beaver county surveyed. The contract was let and the county divided up into sections or townships, each six miles square, and zinc monuments were erected at the corners of each, but as the appropriation was insufficient to meet the costs of the survey, the work was abandoned for a considerable time, and it was not till some years later that the completion of the undertaking took place.

It soon became known that there was no law in that section of the country; nor had the U. S. Government any control over, nor authority to arrest criminals, nor even to prosecute them there. Consequently it soon became the dumping grounds for fugitives from justice and criminals of all kinds. Saloon men who had been paying license for the sale of intoxicating liquors, ceased contributing to the general fund, but continued to deal out their wares with impunity. One man built a still and manufactured his own whiskey and did a flourishing business, although he had to freight his corn from Kansas to produce his wares. To give honour where honour is due, I must confess that he produced a very good quality.

There was considerable immigration into this county in '79 and '80, as most of the desirable land in Kansas had been pre-empted. Hundreds of good men and women came in and selected homes, and those who could not find locations along the water courses went out into the flat prairie lands, erected houses, fenced their fields to protect them against the range cattle, broke up as much land as they could conveniently handle, and made what improvements their means would permit. As soon as the neighbours became acquainted with one another, they organized Sunday Schools, held meetings at some convenient place weekly, divided the districts into school sections and built schools. Each school house served the purpose of a meeting house for Sunday services as well as for any other business that required a meeting of the people. In a short time the county began to develop the earmarks of civilization.

Following in the footsteps of those law-abiding citizens came a class of criminals who migrated from their native heaths expecting immunity from the punishment due to the crimes they had committed, and which caused their departure to this haven of refuge. Nor did they abstain from their criminal pursuits while in this *refugium peccatorum*, or asylum of the wicked. As soon as they had become familiar with the topography of the county, and, as they were too lazy to work, they soon took up their old practice of lying in wait for the unsuspecting and carrying off his goods when possible. They usually drifted from one ranch to another pretending to look for work, and imposed upon the hospitality of the rancher, who provided for their wants free of charge as long as they cared to remain. I may here remark that the hospitality of the western people has never been surpassed, and I may say, never equalled. A cowman considered himself insulted if one should leave or pass his ranch at meal time without partaking of his hospitality. Not only this, but as nothing was ever locked up, it was considered the proper etiquette if no one were at home, to enter and help oneself to his supplies and to make oneself perfectly at home. No one was ever asked whence he came or whither he was going. If he volunteered the information without being asked, it was received, and if not given the result was the same, namely, no questions asked. In this way it was a very easy matter for the criminal to gain an intimate knowledge of conditions, which they used to their own advantage later on to the detriment of people generally. They did not confine their depredations to Beaver county only, nor to No-Man's Land, but thoroughly organized themselves into bands and extended their nefarious business to western Kansas, Indian Territory, and west Texas. Those who actually stole stock from the farms and ranches, usually took them a few miles and passed them on to their companions in crime, so that no familiar face was absent from the scene of the theft, and thus they avoided suspicion. When a settler's stock was stolen, he very seldom had the slightest idea of the direction to be taken to recover them, and in most cases was financially unable to make an extended search in any direction. Many a time the loss of a few head of cattle meant all that he had, wiping out his whole accumulation of years of hard work and privation and just at a time when he began to see better times ahead as he was getting something to work with. This condition of affairs could not be permitted to continue, and while the means employed by the settlers to terminate this organized pilfering, and at the same time make some return to the culprit for the wrongs suffered at his hands, may seem hard to the people who were never subjected to conditions such as prevailed in that country, they were as a matter of fact nothing more nor less than cold-blooded Justice. Those who are ignorant of the conditions must remember that the loss of a *milch* cow meant the principal part of his family's support, and his wife and children were thus put in a state of actual want thereby, and as there were no means of obtaining legal redress for such losses, they had the law of self-preservation to guide them and from it there was no appeal.

At this point the idea forced itself upon the settlers that they must organize, as it was a physical impossibility to combat a well-regulated band of outlaws single-handed; so, after calling a meeting of the best citizens and discussing the matter carefully, it was decided to organize a vigilance committee and see what effect the hanging of a few of the "rustlers" would have upon the remainder of them, and at the same time how it would affect the welfare of the settlers. The moral effect of the organization of the committee resulted in checking to a certain degree the depredations of the criminals, but it did not wipe it out entirely. A great many of the more timid ones abandoned their evil ways, but the more daring were willing to take a chance and abide by the consequences, which several of them experienced. The vigilantes occupied the positions of Sheriff, Judge, Jury and Executioner, and when a culprit was caught red-handed his case was summarily disposed of in about thirty minutes, except for the funeral and burial services, which were left usually for anybody that cared to participate in them.

I had a ranch in Texas during those troublous times, and was one time wintering a herd of cattle near Fowler City, Kansas. Consequently I had to make a number of trips through that unsettled district, sometimes on horseback and at others in a buckboard, and it seemed almost invariably my good or bad fortune, as you wish to call it, to enter some place or other at a time when a tragedy was being enacted.

I was once crossing in a buckboard in the direction of Englewood, Kansas, with a consignment of eggs that were beginning to suffer breakage owing to the roughness of the journey, and I began to look for a place to dispose of them to some settler. I soon reached a place that bore the sign, "Groceries," and there sold my eggs, bought some tobacco and a few other necessaries. While talking to the store-keeper, I noticed a group of men at another sod building, and I inquired of him what they were doing.

"Oh, nothing much. They have just been hanging a man over there."

I asked him what the unfortunate had done.

"Well," said he, "he has been stealing horses."

I went out to water my horses just as a part of the group were passing. Recognizing two of them I inquired of them what the fellow had done and where they had arrested him. They replied he had been stealing horses both in the neighbourhood and in Clark county, Kansas. The sheriff had followed his trail and caught him south of where we were then, and was taking him back to Kansas. He was bringing him through that section and they took him away from the sheriff and hanged him. I asked him if he did not think the punishment rather severe. He replied that he did not think so, and besides there was no use of letting the sheriff take all the trouble of bringing him back to Kansas where the judges would turn him loose in ninety days and then he would be back at his criminality again. Mike Shrugrue was the name of the sheriff who had the prisoner in charge, and a braver man was not to be found in the State of Kansas, but he could not stand off the vigilantes. To attempt anything of the kind was to invite disaster. It would be only throwing away another life needlessly, as the one was doomed under any circumstances.

The difference between the vigilantes and a mob must be thoroughly understood to be appreciated. The one stood for law and order, was organized from necessity, as there was not any law than theirs, and was approved of by the residents of the country in which they operated in the interests of justice; the other, the mob, is a hot-headed, angry, or rather frenzied crowd that usually defeats the claims of justice by taking the law into its own hands in most cases where the law would handle the case in a more satisfactory manner, if allowed to take its course. This mode of procedure is always condemned by the better class of citizens, while the actions of the vigilantes, who were, with few exceptions, of the better class, were performed usually through stern necessity, rather than from anger. The trial given was usually very short. In most cases the guilt was very clear, as the criminal was nearly always taken manifest, as he was usually taken in the act of committing a crime. If the prisoner had a plausible story to tell, it was investigated before any further proceedings took place. If he happened to be one of the notorious class of criminals, which was commonly the case, the culprit was given short shrift. Neither mode of procedure is to be recommended as the safest course to attain the ends of justice.

The greatest difficulty to be met with in the interest of justice, was in handling the cases of "rustlers," as there were always some of the same ilk on hand to prove a complete alibi. Fifty men could be assembled on a day's notice to prove that the accused was a hundred miles away from the scene of the crime when it was committed. As a consequence of this, most of the accused were released, or, if caught red-handed in their rascality, were admitted to bail, which was furnished by their companions in crime, and then they forfeited the bail and took leave to parts unknown.

My next experience occurred not long afterwards while making a trip from Timms City, Texas, across the country to the Fred Taintor ranch. On this occasion my family accompanied me in the then up-to-date means of travel, namely, a lumber wagon. The trail was in good condition and we were making good time. One day, about dinner time, I was keeping a lookout for a good camping place for the purpose of supplying the needs of both the family and the cattle. It was impossible to build a fire, as the wind was blowing a gale, and the prairie was very dry and a fire would likely spread and lay waste the whole county. Seeing the impossibility of camping, though I had found a suitable place, I determined to push on to some ranch where our wants would be supplied. I knew where a man by the name of Kingston, from Illinois, had put up a small frame building and had laid in a stock of groceries. I finally reached the object of my search and when approaching the store I had to pass another building occupied by a family. As I was passing a woman stepped out and asked me if I was going to the store. I replied that I was, and told her what my business was there. She informed me that it was of no use as Mr. Kingston had been murdered the evening before. She showed me where they were burying him at that moment. She also informed me that one of the bullets fired at Mr. Kingston had passed under the cow she happened to be milking at the time. It is needless to say that I did not tarry long in that neighbourhood, but went on until I finally reached the Taintor ranch, where the latch string always hung on the outside of the door. The reception we had and the supper provided soon made us forget that we had had no dinner. After a good night's rest we proceeded on our way to sunny Kansas.

In the meantime I had learned the circumstances leading up to the Kingston tragedy. It appeared that Mr. K—had received through the mail a draft for several hundred dollars and the postmaster had mentioned the fact to a neighbour. The conversation had been overheard by two cut-throats who waited until they thought it had been cashed and then hatched up a plan to murder him for his money. It seemed from the appearance of things inside the house that they had intended to hang him so as to give it the appearance of suicide and then get away with the cash. The room was not ceiled and a rope was found hanging over a joist with a noose in one end. While making their preparations it seemed that he had broken away from them and had reached the prairie in front of the store, where they shot him.

Someone has said that the way of the transgressor is hard, and in this instance it proved undoubtedly correct, for the vigilants set out after those men, ran them down in the brakes of a creek and sent sixteen bullets through one of them; the other escaped and made his way to Dodge City, Kan., where he proceeded to fill up on whiskey and made other arrangements to take in the town. The City Marshall's opinion was that the town was too small for two men to run at the same time, especially as one was a stranger who had not been duly elected for the position. As a result, a gun argument was introduced to settle the question and the bad man was killed in the first round. His funeral occurred next day with all the ceremonies befitting a man of his calling and he was interred on "Boot-hill" without flowers on his casket, or tears shed over his demise. It turned out afterwards that Mr. Kingston had not cashed the draft, so all the money that the rogues obtained by murder and robbery was what was in the cash drawer at the time.

The vigilants, for the time being, performed valuable services for the settlers and were largely instrumental in driving out of that country a lot of thugs, thieves, and cut-throats, who were preying upon the people. But, strange to say, time proved that some of themselves were not entirely above suspicion, as the following incident will show. One day as I was riding along the divide between Kiowa Creek and the Beaver, I met a man whom I recognized to be Jake Smith. I use the name Smith for convenience, as that was not his name, and I do not care to use his rightful cognomen as he left that country shortly afterwards, went over to Kansas, married a nice girl, went into business and became a leader socially and a pillar in the Church, is generally respected and is living an upright life. Knowing him well, I hailed him.

"Well, Jake," I said, "your horse looks pretty well jaded, you must have had a long ride."

Said he, "Oh, that's nothing. I must ride to Alpine tonight as there is to be a meeting of the vigilants at eight o'clock and I want to be there."

"Do you belong to the vigilants?" I asked.

"Why, yes," he replied. "I was one of the first to join them and have been working with them ever since."

"Well, Jake," said I, "you're a jewel, a regular diamond. You know that you have been stealing cattle and branding 'mavericks' ever since you landed in this country, and all the old-timers know it, and now you are running your horse to death to catch a rustler. That is a great joke!"

"I see plainly that you do not understand," said he. "The situation is this: I had to join them for self-protection and also to look after the interests of my friends. Talk of running my horse to death! I have just been returning a favour. I have just been up to the head of Clear Creek to tell Slim Jim to skip, because if they catch him he will stretch hemp for stealing Old Dusenberry's mules, and besides, Slim ain't no bad fellow when he has a good paying job."

I have never had the pleasure of meeting Jake since, but if I ever visit Kansas I shall be certain to call and see him to find out how he managed to keep from stealing his own goods and hiding them out in the canyons, through force of habit after having resolved to leave other men's chattels alone.

It seemed to be the custom whenever a small settlement was formed, for some one to put up a grocery store, locate a post-office and call it by some high-sounding title and establish the nucleus of a city. For instance, there was Boyd City, Beaver City, Benton City, Alpine City, Neutral City, and Gate City, mostly located on the divides, or flat prairie lands on the established trails. "Sod Town," whose name was not so high-sounding as descriptive, soon sprang into existence as the Monte Carlo, or sporting centre of the whole country. It was there at round-up time, each spring and fall, that the boys were accustomed to meet and run their horses, discuss matters of common interest, and, in general, to have a good time. As nearly every ranch had a fast horse or two, also a prize roper, whenever the convention took place, things were bound to be lively and at times quite a little money changed hands on the result of a horse race, or other contest of skill.

Among the famous horses of that day that I recall, were "Old Pumpkin," a general favourite, "Stick-in-the-Mud," "Greasy Heels," "Wobble Shanks," and "Sore Toes" with a dozen or so of others to select from, and each and every one had its backers and admirers.

Frank Biggers, Jim Mahoney, Sour-dough-Charlie, Heel-Fly Bill, Snake Eater, and Bull Joe were generally the leading spirits at the race course, and as Frank Biggers was a lover of fair play, he was usually chosen to act as judge; besides, he had a manner of enforcing his decisions which commanded respect and the compliance of the wildest and woolliest of the assembly.

For the benefit of the readers who are unaccustomed to the ways and phrases of the western people, I shall here state that the nicknames of a great many of them were acquired from their calling, or from some incident or occurrence on the range. If one were to drop into the Panhandle country and inquire for

Mr. Chas. Deitrich, Mr. Joseph Parish, or some others who were mostly known by nickname, I doubt very much if the inquirer would find his man, but if he were to ask for Sour-dough Charlie, or Bull Joe, any one could tell them at once where to find them or what their business was. Some of the names allotted to individuals may seem rude to the elite of the east and give the impression of vulgarity and rudeness, but on acquaintance one would find them good, kind, and obliging men as ever saddled a bronco or branded a maverick. The congregation at Sod Town was composed of men who knew one another and any money won or lost was taken as a matter of course, and there was no grief over spilt milk. Theirs was a vigorous life and healthy outdoor sport appealed to them. When their sport was over, they were off to the ranch again in good spirits.

Among the early settlers of Sod Town were two young men, named Ellis and Fiske, who opened a Grocery and Supply store. They kept a large stock of provisions, as well as, boots, shoes, slickers, and other articles adapted to the trade of the cattlemen. In a short time they built up a good trade and were liked by all. One night, two bad men, or would-be road agents, called at the store and rapped for admission. This was not at all out of the ordinary as the cattleman's business kept him at all hours. It was nothing unusual for him to rout out the store-keeper at any hour of the night and have his wants supplied. On the night in question, when Ellis heard the rapping, he donned his trousers and fortunately had his six-shooters in his waistband. As soon as he opened the door of his store he was commanded to put up his hands. He proceeded to do so, but in the act of raising his hand he drew his gun and shot one of the bad men, wounding him badly. Both turned to flee. Ellis pulled down on them in their flight, and by the aid of light from a prairie fire that was burning at the time, fired at the fleeing bad men and killed outright the man he had wounded at the door. The other villain made his escape into the darkness. Of course, Ellis was arrested and taken before the U. S. Court for that district and was honourably discharged. He should not have been arrested for a case of that kind, but there were mileage fees to be considered, and the marshal seldom if ever overlooked an opportunity of the kind for increasing his wealth.

I have never heard of any other bad men calling on Ellis and Fiske in search of assistance in a financial way, especially in the manner mentioned above.

Sour-dough Charlie had a little ranch of his own on Wolf Creek where he kept a few horses. He raised a few colts each year, and to fill in his odd time he tanned deer skin, made gloves for the cow punchers, and at times used to cook for a round-up as he was an artist in that line of work as well as being a very entertaining fellow. His chief work of art was the construction of sour dough bread and he had the reputation of being a master in the work. One afternoon a cow-puncher pulled up to the wagon and called for his chuck-a-way, and said he wanted it at once as he had to return to the herd and stand guard while his partner came for his supply. The cook told him he would have to wait for awhile as he did not have things in shape to get an extra meal. Without further parley and without any warning the puncher picked up a crock full of sour dough and struck the cook over the head with it. The contents spilled over his head and ran down into his eyes and mingled with his whiskers. Right then and there was originated and conferred upon him the title of "Old Sour-dough Charlie," a name that will remain with him as long as he lives.

Nicknames and titles, in this county, amount to about the same thing although conferred in different ways according to conditions. The man who succeeded in accumulating a herd of cattle amounting to one or two hundred was given the name of captain. If he acquired five or six hundred, he was addressed as major, and a man who through good management and perseverance numbered his stock by thousands became the "Old Colonel." There was one very noticeable change in the habits, manners, customs and character of the men who had acquired the title of captain, major, or colonel, and that was shown in their dress. The styles of their garments differed, they dispensed with the snake-skin band, they changed their underwear, frequently had their whiskers trimmed and hair cut, and occasionally became a power in local politics. The question was never asked when and how these men became possessed of such large herds in such short time, but to the old-timer it was plain that the Old Colonel was a great business man, or was an expert with the lariat and an artist with the branding iron.

How different is the conferring of titles in foreign lands, especially in Great Britain, where titles have to be ratified by supreme authority and approved of by local potentates, and even there we find some titles resting on tottering foundations and others hang by a very slender thread which is liable to part at any time and leave the possessor in a pitiable mass of social wreckage. The ceremonies on such occasions are calculated to dazzle the eye and deceive the judgement of the spectator. The sleight-of-hand performer and the street *fakir* practice the same system and the man with the three-shell game and the three card monte man are all on the same level, but royalty claims age and dignity wherever you find it. When Capt. Drake returned to England after his expedition of murder, plunder, and piracy, and his arrival was announced to the Good Queen Bess who was on the throne at the time, she at once called for a royal banquet to be held on board his vessel. After rounding up all her royal roustabouts, flunkeys, and followers, she proceeded direct to the ship where she was going to preside in state until she had knighted the capt., whose hands were still red with the blood of his murdered victims. When the time for the ceremony was at hand, at a motion of her magic wand the captain dropped to his knees at her feet to receive the power and authority to take and keep any property on the seas that he felt like confiscating; which meant any that he might be able to lay his hands on. The ceremony consisted of laying the sword of authority across his bald pate and telling him that henceforth he was at liberty to do as he pleased and that he should remain her loyal subject. She then commanded him to arise and he did so, but was so dazzled with the great honour conferred upon him that I do not suppose he could tell whether he was a duck or a drake.

A prince can make a belted Knight,
A Marquis, duke, and a' that,
But an honest man's aboon his might,
Good faith he muna fa' that.

The price of titles, like other commodities, depends greatly upon the locality where they are granted. In England, the title cost Sir W. Raleigh his head; in Texas, a title cost Sour-dough Charley but a few loaves of bread. Imagine the difference.

Chapter 7
Wild Horses

My experience has taught me that there has not been another animal on the plains as inquisitive and suspicious as the wild horse, or mustang, as it is called. The early horse hunter took advantage of this characteristic inquisitiveness to approach sufficiently close to effect his capture. This was done by placing a wagon sheet, or a bed quilt on a stake and then hiding in the bushes or grass in the vicinity. The hunter was compelled to remain perfectly quiet in his lair as the slightest sound at times would stampede the horses and render his quest futile. The mustangs, on discovering the strange object in their neighbourhood would commence to run round and round in circles, reducing the radius of the circle each time until finally they were within a distance of about two hundred yards of the object of their curiosity. Then they would stand perfectly still and that was the time there was need of caution on the part of the hunter, as the breaking of a twig, the sound of a voice, or any slight noise that would be likely to reach their ears, would start them off in wild affright to return no more as long as there were any indications of disturbance in the neighbourhood. If the hunter remained quietly in hiding and gave no sign of his presence in any manner, their curiosity would bring them back again to make a further exploration of the strange phenomenon. In this manner the old horse-hunter used to entice them close enough to "crease" one of them, as it was called. This "creasing" consisted in taking a very careful and deliberate aim with a rifle and shooting the horse in front of the withers, through the top of the neck close to the spinal cord. This stunned or shocked him so that he would fall in his tracks, paralyzed for the time being, giving the hunter time, if he moved swiftly, to run from his hiding place with his hobble-rope and hog-tie him before he recovered. It frequently happened that the hunter arrived there too late as the horse often recovered from his shock and was up and away before his arrival; or, the shot being badly aimed, reached a vital spot and the horse would be dead before he could get the hobbles on him. If everything worked out satisfactorily, and the mustang was secured, he would place a *hackamaw* on his head in such a way that it could not be shaken loose in the struggle that was bound to follow. I shall here explain that a *hackamaw* is a sort of halter, or headstall, made of the end of a lariat rope and put on in such a manner that it holds the head of the mustang firmly without the danger of choking the animal. When the animal was secured, the hunter gave his partner a signal to bring up the saddle horses that were held at a distance and out of sight so as not to scare the herd before capture. The fun commenced in earnest when the hobbles were removed and the captured mustang was permitted to rise. The first thing on the program was to try to escape back to the herd. That failing, he would go on the war-path and it took a skilful horseman and active ponies to bring him under subjection. It usually required, at least, two, each with his lariat attached so as to prevent the mustang's reaching the other. Several hours of hard fighting then ensued, but in the end when the mustang was conquered he made the toughest and wiriest of cow-ponies.

It very frequently happened that two of these bands of wild horses met and then trouble began. Every herd was headed by a stallion that exercised supreme authority over the whole band at all times, and never allowed any intruder to trespass on his rights and privileges. As a result, when two herds encountered each other, war was at once proclaimed by the two stallions for the complete control and management of both herds. Never did knights of old covered with armour, go forth to battle with more dignity and determination to protect their lady loves, or to maintain the honour of their own good names, than was displayed by those mustang stallions. With ears turned back and their noses to the ground, they dashed forth to the deadly conflict. The meeting of the two champions was of the fiercest nature. At times they fought standing on their hind feet with their teeth sunk in each others neck, and at others they waged their mortal combat standing on their fore feet using their hind feet as weapons of offence. Sometimes these battles terminated fatally to one or both of the contestants, but more frequently ended when one of the struggling brutes became so exhausted that he was unable to continue the fight, and acknowledged defeat by retreating to the protection of some canyon or sand hill with his little band of mares and colts, provided the other stallion did not have sufficient energy left to run them into his own harem leaving his defeated adversary to a lonesome existence on the bleak prairie.

I had an old friend at one time who followed up the pursuit of catching wild horses for a living, and for patience and perseverance he never had an equal among his contemporaries. He met disaster and disappointment with unflinching energy and returned to the conflict with unabated courage. Though the remuneration was small, there was a fascination about the work that he could not resist. Before entering upon an expedition of this kind, he fitted up a camping outfit consisting of a few blankets, a tarpaulin, slicker, coffee pot, skillet, knife, fork, hobble ropes, a supply of lariat ropes, a Winchester, six-shooters, and some bacon, the latter being taken along for grease to be used in cooking, as fresh meat was to be had at all times. The prairies were alive with antelope, turkey, deer, and occasionally a stray buffalo was discovered. Such buffalo, deer, and wolves as were taken, were skinned and the hide salted for sale on the market. He used no wagons in his business, but took two mares with him, one to be used as a saddle pony and the other for the purpose of serving as a pack animal. His favourite pony was called Topsy, and was the mascot of the expedition. He had raised her and trained her from colthood and she was trained to such a degree of perfection that she would obey the sound of his voice, whistle, or signal given by the waving of his hat, and never did a railway engineer, or brakeman respond with greater promptness than did Old Topsy when she received the signal from her master. At the word of command she would lie down or rise, and owing to this peculiarity of her training she was frequently used as a wind shield during a cold storm from the north, her master making his bed beside her for protection.

Preparations for these trips were usually made in the early autumn, during the month of September, as the heat of the summer was somewhat lessened by that time, and he generally managed to set out when the moon was new so as to travel by night if necessary. He was so thoroughly acquainted with the country that he knew every creek, and canyon, every spring and waterhole where the mustangs were accustomed to get water. He was not compelled to scour the country for his quarry as every wild horse within a range of five miles seemed to know by instinct the arrival of his pack animals and ponies. Such uncertainty of knowledge did not satisfy them, but to satisfy their curiosity they came along on the run to make an investigation into the character of the intruders who had so unceremoniously intruded into their domain. By the time the huntsman had unpacked, had his camp-fire built, and was preparing his meal, they would be encircling his camp, running, romping, and playing. The stallion usually took the lead in these diversions with the mares and young colts by their side trying to keep up to his advance. Finally they would come to a standstill and remain perfectly quiet until some noise would startle them and off they would go pell-mell only to return and repeat their investigation into what was the new element that was disturbing the peaceful possession of their range. This hunter's method was different from what was usually followed by others. It was not his intention to excite or disturb the wild horses in any way; on the contrary his object was to get them accustomed to his presence, get them acquainted with the domestic mares, and render them peaceful and quiet. In a few days his object would be accomplished, and then he proceeded to set the herd in motion to drive them back to the settlements where they could be corralled and handled. He never permitted them to get a moment's rest, day or night, once he had them in motion, and as little chance to graze as possible. In the mean time he saw to it that his own mares had every advantage possible. In a few days, such a system could not but have its effect on the mustangs and they would as a consequence become more docile. Gradually he got closer to them without the danger of stampeding them, until within the course of ten days or two weeks they showed unmistakable signs of weariness and weakness which allowed him to get in closer touch with them. In fact, so much was he in their presence that they came to look upon him as one of the herd. Then took place the working out of his design. He headed Old Topsy for home over the hills, through the canyons and creeks, never stopping for anything, gradually moving along, slowly and quietly nursing them into captivity. Such was the care that he exercised that he made no more than five or ten miles a day on his straight course. At times, before the herd became too wearied, the flight of a bird or the barking of a coyote would stampede them and thus he would lose five or ten miles that he had gained with so much difficulty. On he went after them, doing over again all that had been done before. In case there were no unforeseen difficulties, or accidents, he would finally drive them into the neighbourhood of some good strong corral where, with the permission of the proprietor, he would run them in until such time as he would be able to hobble the leaders, which usually required a week or more.

A mustang is so sensitive and observing that I sometimes thought he could count the buttons on one's clothes. In fact, I know, that should one change his clothing while breaking one of them, he would have all the work to do over again until the mustang became accustomed to the change. He received everything with suspicion and even a fence-post would call for an investigation. The corral was a new world entirely for him and it took days of patience and perseverance to induce him to enter it. Old Topsy would go in and out and make herself at home, but not so with her associates, at least for quite a long time. Finally they would venture in little by little, the hunter permitting them to pass in and out several times before putting up the bars on them. As soon as the mustangs found themselves unable to get out they became badly frightened and excited, especially during the absence of the hunter. His return seemed to pacify them very much. He had to manage them with great judgement until he managed to hobble the leaders, which, as I said before, took days to accomplish.

It is true that he could have roped and hobbled them in a short time once he had them in the corral, but this was not the way with my friend. He said often times that once he had gained their confidence, he could not betray it. After the mustangs had been corralled for some time and had grown accustomed to the presence of men, then the interesting work took place. They had to be broken to the saddle and bridle and ridden by somebody, and I wish to state that it was a work that required an expert, all green-horns and tenderfeet barred. Around all ranches was to be found a man whose sole occupation was to do this work. He offered to accomplish the task of reforming the wild mustang at from two to five dollars a head, and he usually had the work assigned him. By the time they were broken they were usually sold at a fair price for that class of stock while the hunter made preparations for returning to the plains for another lot of mustangs, a work which he seemed to enjoy.

These mustangs did not command a very high price as most of them were too small for cow-work, and too light for single drivers. Sometimes one could pick up a team of these ponies and find them the toughest and wiriest animals that were ever hitched to a buckboard. They could travel from sunrise to sunset at ten miles an hour and never turn a hair. But viewed from all angles the business was not a financial success and the men engaged in it never cleared up any great amount of money, as I proved to my own satisfaction later on. Before what is now called Meade County was established, there was nothing there but the open prairie. A fence was an unknown thing except where some settler had built one around a stack of hay to protect it from the range cattle that were roaming the plains in great numbers in those days. It was necessary for him to do this as a small stack of feed would be a tempting morsel, in cold weather, to the thousands of cattle wandering loose and in search of fodder. In case they did succeed in reaching the tempting supply, it lasted about as long as a water melon at a negro picnic. It had been reported on what I considered reliable authority that there was a black stallion running on the flat between Crooked and Sandy Creeks, about nine miles southeast of the present county seat of Meade county, Kansas. The cowboys had often tried to capture him, but in every instance failed. He was described to me as standing about fifteen hands high, which was exceptionally large for a mustang, with long flowing mane and tail, and he could trot faster than any cow-pony could run. After weighing the matter carefully for some time I decided to go out and capture him. From the description given, he was just what I wanted for a saddle horse. I determined to have him provided I could enlist the services of G. W. Brown, an old Indian scout, and former companion of the buffalo range. He was, moreover, an expert with the lariat rope and was considered one of the best trailers in the country. The other man I wanted, and whom I finally succeeded in getting, was C. M. Rice, formerly of Jasper, Ind., a veteran of the Civil war, an old and experienced plainsman who knew every creek and trail in the country. After discussing the matter carefully in all its different aspects, we decided to capture him regardless of trouble and expense attached to the undertaking, even though it took all summer. We had to take a camp wagon, grain and provisions enough to last several weeks, as we would not be able to return for more if we happened to run short. We took our favourite saddle ponies and started early so as to get in operation as soon as possible. It was our intention to locate him early in the morning and have the whole day for the first run. We were fortunate in finding him shortly after daybreak, but his looks were rather disappointing as he did not seem as large as he had been pictured to me by the cowboys. However, we were there to capture him and determined to do so. One thing favoured us and that is one of the peculiarities of the mustang, he will not leave his range unless driven from it. He will take his departure very reluctantly and will return at the earliest opportunity.

Our first night was one of rest, with nothing to disturb us but the howling of the coyotes and the bawling of the cattle. Morning found us up early and ready for the chase. We knew it would be useless to try to catch him on a straight run as he would have, at least, half a mile start on us. We decided to run him in a circle, keep inside of his course, and keep him on the run until he became jaded and exhausted and then let him get a chance to drink his fill of water as he would surely be very thirsty after a long gallop. The consequence of this strategy would be that the mustang would become stiffened and it would be easy to run him down and rope him. After making the first large circle, C. M. Rice, seeing his horse lathered with perspiration that trickled down from the flanks of his horse, his favourite Old Tom, decided to return to camp and prepare something to eat for himself and us on our return. If we did not return by night-fall he was to keep the camp-fire burning to act as a beacon for our guidance. In order to save our horses, Brown and I decided that one of us should keep on the chase whilst the other rested his horse. This gave each of us chance to refresh our mount with water and grass until it came his turn to take up the pursuit. In the meantime the mustang was not allowed to have a respite from his exertions, but was kept on the move until about three or four o'clock in the afternoon. Nature asserted herself in his case and frequently, after that time, he would stop to look around and see if his pursuers were likely to give him a chance to rest and refresh himself. It was plainly evident that the pace was telling on him, but he found that his pursuers gave him no opportunity to rest his weary legs. Closely and more closely they came in spite of all he could do to ward off their unremitting pursuit. The moments he took to stop and look around offered us an opportunity to draw closer. Then we both took up the chase at the same time. We divided our forces, one going on one side of him and the other on the opposite. By this time we were within twenty rods of him. By this strategy we headed him for Gypsom Creek in the hope that when he reached it he would stop and drink his fill. That would give us an opportunity of roping him. Everything worked out as we had planned. When the thirsty brute reached the water he drank abundantly of the refreshing fluid. It seemed as though he would never stop. When finally he had his fill we ran him off to the mouth of a canyon where, if once we could get him to enter, there would be no opportunity of his escape as there was no outlet at the other end. I say none, or rather should have said there was one but it was practically out of the question for him to make it. It was about a mile away and the road was filled with boulders and sand heaps and was up hill all the way, and we knew that in his present condition his wind would be gone before he could again reach the open prairie. Now came the opportunity to rope him if he was to be captured at all, as there was nothing left for him to do but choose between the rough boulders and ledges of the other end of the canyon, or strive to evade us by seeking safety in the way he entered. Brown went around and awaited his arrival, while I followed as best I could until I saw him disappear at the head of the canyon. Then I retraced my way and rode around on the divide so as to be in on the final chase. When I came in sight of Brown, I saw that he had him roped securely, but on reaching him I discovered that he had captured him in a prairie-dog town and in the struggle that followed the roping he had jumped into one of the holes and broke his leg between the knee and the fetlock, and the bones were protruding through the flesh. Under those conditions, as he would be of no value to me, and also, as it would be inhuman to turn him loose to suffer and starve, or become the food of mountain lions, or coyotes, I thought it best to end his misery without further delay. This being done, we tightened up our saddle cinches and returned to camp very weary and much wiser than when we set forth in the morning. Thus ended my first, last, and only chase after a wild mustang stallion on the plains of Kansas. As per agreement, Rice had kept the camp fire burning and had, moreover, prepared a supper of hot beans, biscuits, antelope steak, and coffee, which was a feast fit for a king and one which I think no guest of Delmonico ever appreciated more.

The next morning we arose and went to look after our ponies. What a pitiful sight we beheld when we came upon them in the secluded place where we had tethered them! They were gaunt, covered and caked with perspiration and dust of the preceding day's chase.

We gave them a good rub-down and plenty of food and water, which refreshed them very much. After a good breakfast, we took a farewell look at the camp and returned to the ranch. The black stallion with his flowing mane and tail became a matter of past history of the plains. In conclusion I shall say that my two companions of the chase of thirty-two years ago are still both hale and hearty business men in the Queen City of the Canadian, El Reno, Okla.

CHAPTER 8

Why I Came West

When commencing to write this semi-historical work, it was my intention to confine myself to the early settlement of "No-Man's-Land," but find that I must include the Panhandle to Texas and the south-western part of Kansas, as the soil, climate, and social conditions were almost identical. The industries of all three localities were very much the same, excepting that the Panhandle was much better adapted to cattle raising than to agriculture. In fact, farming was looked upon by cattlemen as too menial an occupation for them to engage in, and, consequently, they knew little about it and cared less. Their indifference to agriculture was such that they would prefer literally to starve to death than endeavour to gain subsistence from the soil. The difference between the old-time cow-puncher and the Cheyenne Indian as agriculturists was very little. The former might do a little at farming if he knew how, and the latter might know how if he would only do a little at it. It seemed to be the height of the average cow-puncher's ambition to ride on a fifty-dollar saddle, wear a ten-dollar Stetson hat, a pair of silver mounted spurs, a pair of ten-dollar high-heeled boots, leather leggings, a slicker and a forty-five calibre white handled six-shooter. This made a complete outfit to suit his vanity. Riding broncos, roping wild cattle, running races, and branding mavericks were his principal business and amusement. Attending the spring and fall round-ups, and driving beef stock to market rounded out his season's work.

It is true that there are some exceptions to the general rule. As an example, about twenty-eight years ago I became acquainted with a green cow-puncher, fresh from some Texas town, a tall, fair-haired lad, who was rather reticent, but very punctual in his work. He was the first out in the morning, last in at night and was ready for anything that was to be done in the meantime. His manner lacked the boisterousness of the swaggering swearing, blow-hard that was very frequently encountered in the days work. It was apparent to all that he was a man of reliability and integrity. He was employed by R. M. Wright and Martin Culver to superintend the "W-L" ranch. He was successful in his management and at the same time displayed an honesty that was something new to some of the settlers in his neighbourhood. He never permitted a man to rope an animal until he was certain of the brand, and knew to whom the property belonged. Such a man was certain to rise in the world and today one would find it difficult to recognize in Mr. R. A. Harper, president of the First National Bank, Meade, Kansas, the stripling greenhorn of thirty years ago. Another of the old-time successful cow-punchers, who fought the battle of life alone and single-handed as cowmen, farmer, merchant, sometimes overtaken by adversity but never discouraged, who plodded on until he reached the top of the financial ladder beyond the reach of want, is Mr. C. M. Rice, of El Reno, Okla.

The majority of the early settlers who stayed throughout the first hard times, managed to do fairly well, accepting the changed conditions as law and order moved in, while a few developed foolish notions about the curtailment of their freedom, as they called it, and resented the encroachment and manifested their disposition by holding up trains, or other depredations. Such a course of conduct invariably proved a failure and brought disaster upon the defenders of such a cause. The state prisons are still harbouring some of those misguided men, protecting them from themselves as well as defending society at large from their peculiar notions. It may seem strange to the reader, but the greater part of the so-called bad men of this country came from the east where they first conceived a false impression of the wildness of the west. The origin of their idea arose from the reading of a poor class of literature. Such reading created in their young minds the idea of being "bad men of the west" and they were not long in putting the idea into practice. Just to mention a few of the most notorious, I shall set down the names of Billy the Kid, from New York, Dutch Henry from Michigan, Sam Bass from Indiana. I might mention dozens of others whose careers of iniquity did not last as long as those mentioned above. As for the real western-bred bad men, they were very few in number and were usually driven to it by being credited with the crimes of others.

One of the principal causes of the development of the outlaw was, as I said above, the publication of fiction and falsehood in such papers as the *New York Weekly* and dime novels. These were scattered broadcast over the country in cheap editions and the result was the creation of false impressions of the west, and at the same time inflamed the imagination and corrupted the minds of many of the then rising generation.

Well do I remember my introduction to the name of Buffalo Bill. It was in the columns of the New York Weekly, in 1874, when in a lumber camp in northern Michigan, that I read of his alleged engagement with the chief of the tribe of the Sioux Indians. It ran as follows, as near as I can remember it: "They met on the plains and each measured his chances to overcome his adversary, etc." It would take no great philosopher to tell that the Indian with no weapon but the bow and a bunch of arrows, stood but a very meagre chance with Bill armed with two six-shooters and a Winchester. "At the first crack of Bill's trusty rifle the wily savage toppled over and fell to the ground. Then, as if by magic, about fifty braves galloped out of a canyon and set out to capture the heap-big pale face who had slain their chief. That purpose was more easily planned than accomplished, for at the psychological moment Bill was re-enforced by his favourite scouts, Little Buckshot and Hotfoot John. After a brief engagement in which they killed about fifteen warriors, they retreated to headquarters for more re-enforcements." This is but a sample of the lies that filtered through the columns of the eastern papers regarding the Indian outbreaks of the west, and the worst part of it was that such trash was believed by thousands, myself among the number.

Whenever I read of the hair-breadth escapes of "Dare-devil Dick," "Shuffle-foot Sam," "Moccasin Mike," and "Goodeye, the Scout," I felt that I would like to take a hand in some of those adventures, having had a rather fair training in Canada by attending the county fairs, and having had the advantage of a course of training in collar-and-elbow wrestling under Prof. John Lennon. Besides these advantages I was rather proficient in the hop-sted-and-leap, high jumping, high kicking, foot racing, but not in shin kicking.

Shin kicking was introduced into Canada by Cornishmen. As I have never seen it practiced in this country I shall endeavour to describe it for the advantage of the reader. Like all games of competition it had its champions. On occasions of merriment it was customary to indulge in this sport, though I do not think that everyone will agree with me that it was a sport. When the crowd had assembled and some preliminary feats of skill were performed, then a man with a voice on him like the Bashan bull would announce in stentorian tones that the champion shin-kicker was requested to appear. A ring was immediately formed by the bystanders locking arms. Into this ring so formed the champion threw his hat as a challenge to all and each. After fifteen minutes delay if no one appeared to take up the challenge, the champion retained his title by default, and to add to the occasion a prize of some kind was added as a reward for his willingness to entertain them by his skill. If an opponent stepped into the enclosure, judges were chosen and preparations made for a battle royal. First, the shoes of the contestants were examined by the judges to see that there were no spikes, nor toe-plates, and to see that the shoes were the common clog type. Then their trousers and drawers were rolled back above the knees leaving the leg bare from the knee cap to the shoe top. Things were then ready for the performance. They caught each other by the shoulders and at the dropping of a hat, or other signal, the battle was on. Kicking as high as the knee was called a foul and judgement rendered accordingly. It required great skill and agility to take part in a contest of the kind. From what I can hear, the game has fallen into oblivion as times have changed the notions of games of the kind. For myself I did not indulge in it very freely as I felt that my legs lacked sufficient side action to permit me to become sufficiently expert at it, to issue a challenge to the champion.

Returning to the thread of my story, I must say that after reading several numbers of the *New York Weekly*, I came to the conclusion that Buffalo Bill was getting short handed, and that unless he received some help rather soon the Indians would drive him out of the country and the advantages already gained by his prowess would be lost to succeeding generations. With such ideas running through my head, I bought a railway ticket and started west to look over the field and see for my own satisfaction how things were getting along. I stopped off at Leavenworth and made the acquaintance of several military men stationed at the fort. They seemed to know nothing of the Indian troubles as published in the eastern papers. Thinking, perhaps, that they might not be well informed on the matter, I left that place and set out for Topeka. I was certain that the officers there would know something definite about affairs of the kind. I made inquiries and soon found that they, like all politicians, were too busy fixing political fences to pay any attention to such matters. The nearer I approached the seat of war, the less I heard about it. I continued my journey and finally reached Dodge City, Kansas, and secured lodging in the Western Hotel, managed by a genial host, Dr. Gallard.

As I arrived there after dark I did not venture out until I had a good night's rest and a hearty breakfast. Next morning I took up my position on the porch to take in a view of the surroundings, and I confess they looked strange and weird to me. I had been told that Dodge City was the ante-chamber of the Infernal Regions; that the temperature began to rise at Great Bend and did not return to normal until one crossed the Colorado line; that the population was made up of cut-throats and thieves; that vice and crime walked brazenly in the streets, while virtue and innocence were unknown in that region of iniquity. Funerals were reported to me to be held every morning, to bury those killed during the preceding night. The cemetery where the unfortunates were to find their last resting place was called "Boot Hill," because those who were buried there were laid to rest with their boots on. The above impression is only a sample of what I had gleaned from the eastern journals. From where I took my stand I could see thirty or forty cow-ponies tied to the hitch racks. Each pony wore a good saddle with a Winchester in a scabbard hanging at the side. After viewing the situation for some time, and not hearing any shooting, nor seeing any funerals, as everything appeared peaceful and quiet, I decided to take in the sights, although I confess I had a rather creepy feeling when I ventured out. I felt somewhat encouraged, as I remembered

I was wearing a Stetson hat, and a pair of high-heeled boots, which, from the reports I had received, were considered the passport to the best society in those days. I crossed the railroad tracks which ran up Main street, and took my course along the sidewalk, encountering in my way men with their pant-legs in their boots, wearing wide-leafed sombreros with snakeskin bands around them, with wide cartridge belts around their waists supporting six-shooters large enough to kill a buffalo. Everyone I met seemed to be peaceable. The only representative of the weaker sex I encountered was a lady dressed in fine style with her face painted and powdered, her hair done up *a la mode*, and decked out in a Mother Hubbard large enough to cover a corn shock.

To my great surprise I spent the first day in Dodge City without any evidence of shootings or funerals, and in my meanderings about the place formed the acquaintance of men who afterwards proved themselves to be as high-principled as could be found in the whole country.

The horses that I had seen hitched to the racks, were all ridden across the river to the different herds to stand guard over the cattle and prevent stampedes. Some of the herds were waiting to be shipped, while others were rounded-up to drive them to the branding pens, after which they would be turned back to the range. In this way the natural increase of the herd was maintained for the owner.

Next morning I set out with a better opinion of the town and of its inhabitants. I found the same ponies tied to the same racks, and the streets full of wagons, some loading for the different ranches, others at the shop for repairs. I found the river banks on both sides lined with campers, a mixed lot of immigrants, looking for land, freighters resting their stock, horse traders, Mexicans, and a multitude of others with their old-time prairie schooners. Everybody was busy, some greasing their wagons, others mending harness, repairing ox yokes, or oiling and refitting six-shooters and Winchesters. The stock had all been turned loose in the care of herders who remained with them to keep them from straying off, and who would bring them in when they were required. The old familiar camp kettle and coffee pot were kept simmering over a slow fire so as to have everything hot at meal time. When the noon hour arrived, the tail gate of the wagon, which was the door of the grub-box, was let down to form a table. Each man found for himself a plate, knife, fork, and tin cup to help himself when the meal was ready. As soon as dinner was over, they scattered again through the town, some to the saloon, others to the dance-halls, others to their trading, or to make arrangements for their next load of freight. After spending some time in observing all that was to be seen, I returned again to the town. As I was walking up the street I overheard a conversation between two cow-punchers whom I afterwards found to be known as "Bronco Jack" and "Slim Jim." They were arguing about Slim's ability to ride a bronco called "Gabe," that Jack had brought to camp that morning. This argument led to the general result—not a fight, as I supposed it would, but to a bet. The conversation ran about as follows:

S. J.—Say, Jack, I see you bringing in Old Gabe this morning. What are you dragging that old skate around for? Why don't you shoot him, or don't you want to waste a cartridge? Going to sell or trade him?

B. J.—Oh, I just brought him in, as I thought some tenderfoot might want to take his lady-love out for a ride, and Gabe would afford some fun.

S. J.—You don't suppose any tenderfoot, nor anybody else wants to be seen riding that old crow-bait around with a young lady? He can't travel fast enough to work up a sweat.

B. J.—Can't he? He has enough life and vinegar in him to throw any puncher on the "81" ranch, and don't you forget it!

S. J.—Oh, pshaw! Jack, you talk like an old parrot my mother used to have down in San Antonio. He would repeat anything he heard and when he could not hear anything, he talked to himself.

B. J.—Money is what talks in Dodge City, and I'll bet you five dollars you can't ride that bronco two blocks without getting thrown.

S. J.—I'll take that bet if you'll make it three blocks. I don't care about short rides. Why, I can ride all over the old goat and make cigarettes while doing it.

B. J.—Say, Slim; that old horse will throw you so high that the sparrows will build nests in your leggings before you come down.

S. J.—That will be all right! Where have you got that old mouse-coloured critter, and where do you want the money put up?

B. J.—He's around here in Cox's corral, and we can put the money up in Kelly's hands.

S. J.—All right! Let's go and put the money up and get down to business.

I went along to see the fun, and especially to see how it would terminate. We entered a saloon finely furnished, with a mirror behind the bar that cost more than the average 160-acre farm in that country. We approached a big, two-fisted, well-dressed man who stood before the bar. Jack addressed him as Mr. Kelly, the man decided upon to hold the stakes. He explained his mission and asked him to hold the money pending the test of horsemanship. Mr. Kelly replied, "I'll hould anything yese give me, but I would loike to know what will be done with the money in case the young man is kilt." "Oh," says Jack, "just treat the crowd and let the balance go to the house." "All right," said Kelly. Slim agreed to the proposal.

B. J.—Well, Slim, you had better take a cold drink before you start, or make arrangements to have some one throw you a bottle of water, as the old pony will throw you so high that you may die of thirst before you come down.

S. J.—Never mind! I'll take that drink after the job is done. Let's go and get busy.

By this time quite a crowd had collected and set out to see the fun. I joined them for the same purpose. It was but a short distance to Cox's corral. When we arrived there, Slim said to Jack, "Go in and rope your old dry land turtle. Bring him out here and I'll see what I can do for him."

Jack went in and pitched his rope on a sleepy-looking, pot-bellied, dun-coloured pony that would weigh in the neighbourhood of eight hundred pounds, and led him into the street. Slim procured his saddle, bridle, and blanket, and proceeded to saddle him. He first put on the bridle and then put a gunny-sack over it. The purpose of this was to blindfold him till the saddling was complete. When the saddling began, Old Gabe stood perfectly quiet, except to take a few short steps, apparently to make sure that all of his four feet and legs were there. As soon as he was saddled, Slim said to Jack, "When I crawl his hump, you take off the gunny-sack and I will take a little ride." As soon as the sack was removed, Old Gabe put his nose to the ground and went to bucking and bawling like an old cow. He bucked about six or eight rods, but found he could not throw Slim in that manner. Then he stood straight up on his hind feet and fell over backwards. As soon as he struck the ground, Slim was standing beside him. When he regained his feet Slim was on his back, and then the bucking and bawling began in earnest. He did the figure eight several times, jumped up and turned halfway 'round and repeated the same, going in the opposite direction, alternately. When he found that this was not successful he headed for an alley close by, bucking and bawling all the time. He worked like a cyclone among a lot of oil barrels and dry goods boxes, wheel-barrows, and obstacles of all kinds that littered the alley. He drove his way through that strange assortment of difficulties until he reached the open street. Then Slim, by means of the application of spurs and quirt got him into a gallop. Then I knew that the battle was over and Old Gabe had met his master. Slim rode back to the crowd and dismounted, and he and Jack went over to Kelly's to collect the wager. Then the bantering was continued, as follows:

B. J.—Well, Slim, how does it go?

S. J.—Oh, not bad. I guess I'll take that cold drink you spoke of. I feel a little thirsty.

B. J.—Yes, and I reckon you feel a little bit sore, too.

S. J.—Oh, shucks! he was a little bit fussy, but he is nothing like those outlaw horses on the 81 ranch.

Chapter 9

The Character of the Cowboy

Next day I began to breathe easier as I had not witnessed any shooting scrapes, nor funerals, so I felt rather safe in walking the streets, although I was rather suspicious of anybody I met wearing a six-shooter. Nevertheless, I kept on the move, endeavouring to find where I could locate a good homestead, as that country was nearly all open and unsettled. In my wanderings I happened into Cox's feed yard where Bronco Jack kept his horses. I entered the camp house and found Jack and Slim Jim sitting on a bench and there was every evidence to show that they had been indulging too freely in "Kelly's Sovereign Remedy for a Sour Disposition." They seemed very confidential in their conversation, and I could not help overhearing it. It ran about as follows:

S. J.—Jack, do you know that old nester that settled on the flats out on Crooked Creek?

B. J.—No, I don't know him, but I heard there was a fellow out there going into farming and raising fine stock.

S. J.—Well, he's there all right, and has two of the prettiest daughters I ever saw.

B. J.—What has that to do with you?

S. J.—It has this to do with me. I am done ranching. I am going to drop off this old bronco and will step right in between the old man's plough handles and there I'll stay until removed by death, or the County Sheriff.

B. J.—Have you had any introduction to those young ladies, or what is the matter with you? Have you taken leave of your senses and gone wild?

S. J.—I never had an introduction to them, but I met them at the post-office and they had a nosebag full of letters and a wheelbarrow full of papers and books. Oh, I tell you they are educated, or what would they want with all that printed stuff. I am going farming, that is what I am going to do.

B. J.—Now I know you are daffy. Talk about farming, don't you know it has not rained out there in the last eighteen months. I met a travelling evangelist the other day who told me that he almost had to forego the pleasure of immersing a class of six cow-punchers for want of sufficient water to perform the ceremony. He was afraid that if it did not soon rain he would lose them sure as he would not be able to get them again if they went back to the ranches before they received his ministrations.

S. J.—Oh, that is all right about the rain! The old man does not need rain. He has a wind-mill and a trough to water his stock, and I can tell you that his stock is first class. I saw some of them and the *milch* cows had bags on them the size of washtubs and the teats hung down like baseball bats. He is well fitted in every way. He has a top buggy with a high back and a low seat all for himself. He wears a white shirt just as some folks do in Texas when they are running for office. I met his boy on the train a day or so ago and he shows good raising. He had shoes and stockings on, and he is no more than fifteen years old. He also had on a collar and tie and did not swear once while I was talking to him. I asked him where his pa had got the big stock and he said that they came from Ohio, and that they were Poland China or something like that.

B. J.—Let me tell you, Slim, if that old man is from Chicago and is a Republican, he has no use for a cow-puncher or a Democrat, no more than a pig has for side pockets. He would not want you to picket your horse on the trail in front of his place, nor to holler in his rain barrel, much less going to call on one of his daughters. Why, they scare the children back there and compel them to be good by telling them that the nasty, old, long-haired cow-puncher will take them away to the ranch where there is nothing but wild cattle, cow-punchers, tarantulas and centipedes, and a lot of other reptiles.

S. J.—Well, I have to leave you Jack, and the next time I see you I shall be on my honeymoon trip. I am now on my way to the farm to see the lady that I expect to soon be Mrs. Slim Jim.

Cheyenne Indian girl

B. J.—Good-bye, Jim. Good luck to you!

About two weeks afterwards, Bronco Jack and I were seated on the bank of Crooked Creek discussing the situation, whether the opportunities for making money were better in hunting or picking bones, catching mustangs, or blacksmithing. I came to the conclusion that the last was the most conducive to wealth just then, and later on opened up a shop there. During our conversation Slim Jim rode up. Throwing the reins over his pony's head, he dismounted and shook hands. Slowly he rolled a cigarette and began to unbosom himself to Jack.

"Say, Jack," said Slim, "you remember what you told me in the camphouse in Dodge City the day I left you. You recollect saying what a consarned fool I was about that young lady, and what you thought of the old man? Say, I hope to die and go to heaven if every word of what you told me was not true. I have ridden for two days to tell you what kind of a durn fool I am. You are a fortune teller, a prophet, a prognosticator. I had not ridden out to Five Mile Creek until he got to soliloquizing with myself. You know all cow-punchers do that out on the prairie! Well, I got to fixing up how to act, what to do and say when I got out there where the young lady lives. I had read a society book that some fellow from back east had left at the ranch once. There was some of it torn out, but there was a lot of it left and I learned a whole lot out of it, and I was going to govern myself accordingly. It said that a young man in company after taking his seat, should sit erect and throw his head back, keep his knees close together, and that chewing tobacco or smoking cigarettes was not good form. Under no circumstances should the young man wear spurs, carry a gun, especially in the company of the young lady with whom he is anyways intimate. I guess that book was written for the Texas trade, as there was a proviso that gun-wearing would be permissible if there were other gentlemen present. If there was anything about the disposal of the hands, it must have been torn out or I forgot it. It was most likely torn out, as that crowd of boys at the ranch would tear the leaves out of their mother's Bible to make a cigarette. I can ride a horse or throw a rope, but what to do with my hands when I entered the house was beyond me. I knew how to hold my head, chest, and knees, but I could not for the life of me figure out what to do with those hands. I felt as if each hand was as big as a ham and the nearer I approached the house, the larger they seemed to grow. I felt pretty much like a Hottentot. He is usually pictured with a very depleted wardrobe. He has no books of instruction on the art of going into society, and I am of the opinion he had just as much trouble with his hands as I had. I guess he just folded his hands across his manly chest and backed in. By the time I arrived at the Mulberry Ranch I had decided to do all I knew and trust to luck for the rest. When I had staked out my pony, I went in and slicked up some. I washed, combed my hair, brushed my clothes, and then took about three fingers of old Tom Duggan's best bourbon, not as a stimulant, but to put some colour in my cheeks. As soon as the bourbon began to show some of its efficacy, I put on a couple of rings I had bought in Dodge and headed for the old man's ranch, letting my hands take care of themselves. In my generosity of feeling I pictured myself being invited to supper and perhaps even being requested to spend the night at the old man's. With an eye to putting an appearance on things I was going to try to trade some long-horned stock for some of his short-horns. I was in terror lest the young lady I was yet to choose, would smell my breath, and if the old man and his family were prohibitionists, I knew it would be all up with my chances. However, I was encouraged in the knowledge of the fact that this was to be my first call and I was not likely to get within breath-smelling distance of the lady of my choice. Regardless of consequences, I turned in and rode up to the hitching post, dismounted, took off my spurs and my gun, and then set out for the house. It seemed miles from that hitching-post to the front door. I finally covered the distance and rapped gently on the panel as I did not want them to think I was one of those rough, roaring, cow-punchers—the kind you mentioned. I listened attentively for one of those gentle footfalls, or the sound of an angelic voice bidding me to enter. I imagined once I heard the rustle of a silk dress but I am satisfied now that I was mistaken as I believe the sound was caused by the girls husking roasting ears for supper. You know that husking green corn makes a kind of squeaking noise. I did not have long to wait as I heard the sound of footsteps—the kind a bull moose makes when in trouble. The door was thrown open savagely and I was confronted by an old man who weighed about two hundred and fifty pounds. He had a face like a full moon with side whiskers to match and a moustache that resembled a second-hand shoe brush. He wore a white shirt with a home-made collar that reached to his ears. I tell you he was a fierce looking object. He stared me straight in the eye and said, "What can I do for you?" Now, Jack, you know that I am a fairly good talker, but right there my voice failed me. I could not utter a word if my life depended upon it. To make matters worse, he kept those two big eyes on me just like a dog setting a quail. My throat became all tied up in a knot, but after a pause I pulled myself together and asked him if he was bothered by any range cattle breaking through his fences. I thought I would get him into conversation in that way, and said that the range foreman had asked me to make the inquiry. He turned and slammed the door in my face. My love that a few moments before threatened to burn a hole in my shirt, was turned to hate. I detest that old man, and what makes my hatred more intense is the fact that when I was riding away I saw the girls laughing and making fun of me. I have come to the conclusion that I had better stick to the ranching as I never did care much for farming anyway. As for society and things like that, I abominate them."

CHAPTER 10

Entertaining a Hobo

About the year 1877, an extensive sheep ranch was established in the Panhandle by a Mr. Southerland. He came from California and bought up the range in the neighbourhood of the Adobe Walls, for the purpose of transferring his flocks from that far off State, where the grazing was getting very scarce, to the northern part of Texas, where there abounded better opportunities for pasturage. He was not the only one to cast a longing eye upon that territory, for many cattlemen from the same State as Mr. S—, also visited the Panhandle district looking for grazing grounds. As Mr. S. was the first to acquire rights there, the story in this chapter will deal with his men and his flocks.

When he returned to California after securing the title to the property, he sent his step-son, Bill Anderson, in charge of the drive from his native State to the new range. Besides the thousands of sheep that were in his care he brought along a few hundred head of horses and burros with enough Mexican help to make the drive successful. Of course, there was quite an outfit of mules and wagons to transport the equipage of an expedition of this kind. There was no opportunity of going to the corner grocery for supplies, nor was there any chance of securing them along the way, as the journey led over hills, mountains and canyons, amongst wild tribes of Indians, from California to Texas. It was a tremendous undertaking, but Bill was equal to the occasion.

He was a man of iron nerve, a good shot with either six-shooter or Winchester and his skill and daring in roping wild animals excited the admiration of even the hardiest of his followers. It was a common thing for him to ride into a herd of buffalo, rope and hog-tie one, and then turn him loose again, just, as he used to say, to show the boys how it was done. Along with his great physical courage and fortitude, there existed another quality often found in men of rugged health and spirits. Bill was a practical joker, and in the pursuit of his endeavours to provoke a laugh he spared neither age, sex, nor previous condition of servitude. It seems to me that I can hear his merry laughter ringing in my ears though many years have passed since I had the pleasure of being in his company. His was a sunny disposition and the dark side of a cloud never appealed to him. He saw the brightness ahead long before it was visible to others. Such was the leader of the expedition that set out from California, and many a merry yarn or joke lessened the burden of the long drive.

At the outset of the journey, the Mexican herders were started off with a supply of bacon and coffee, besides having burros laden with bedding and other utensils. He divided the whole flock into smaller sections, each with a herder in charge. They moved along in close proximity to one another for the sake of company as they would likely be out on the road for weeks, and would return to camp only when in want of provisions. If fresh meat were wanted, all they had to do was to kill a lamb, or procure some of the wild game that infested the way, such as antelope, wild turkeys, prairie chickens, quail and other game. Their horses did not require much attention as there was plenty of grass and water was easily located.

Thus they kept on their way during the long weeks, day succeeding day with the same monotonous routine. Finally they reached their range in safety, glad that the long and tedious journey was completed. Here they made their first improvements in the way of a settled habitation. They constructed a dugout and covered it over with poles and willows. On these they piled a layer of soil to turn the rain. The furnishing of the dugout was of the simplest kind. A split log to sit on, a table made in the same way with saplings for legs, was all they had in the way of household furniture. Their bedchamber consisted of the open prairie with the blue sky above them for a canopy. This done, they were at home for friends and neighbours.

Among the members of the outfit that followed Anderson from

California, was a faithful and trusted employee named James Farrell. He had been with them for years and was one of the family. He was a shrewd man and one hard to deceive. One thing he felt proud of was that Bill Anderson never succeeded in working off a practical joke at his expense. He boasted of the fact that Bill had often tried, but always failed and he felt confident that he would never succeed. And thereby hangs the following tale:

One day as Bill was sitting in front of the dugout doing nothing in particular and having lots of time to do it in, he spied a man in the distance coming toward him on foot. This was something very unusual in those days, as a man on foot in the prairie is very much like a man in the middle of the Atlantic, he feels as though he is twenty miles from nowhere and does not know how to get there. Bill came to the conclusion that the man afoot was some cow-puncher that had been thrown from his horse. He soon discovered his mistake, for the stranger proved to be a veritable hobo. He gave no information regarding himself, and it was impossible to find out anything about him, whence he came, or what profession he followed to gain a livelihood. He manifested an interest in only one thing and that was when meal time came. Then he was a whirlwind of energy. He had been invited to take a supper with the outfit, and Bill even went so far as to divide his blanket with him, favours which the hobo appreciated so much that he continued to stay for meals and share the proprietor's blanket. Time passed on, as time usually does, and the sign of taking his departure. In fact he seemed so much at home that it seemed impossible to drive him away. Weeks went by, but still the hobo was not accused of showing any inclination to work except when the table was to be cleared of provisions. However, all good things come to an end, and Bill felt that he had done all that the laws of western hospitality required and felt impelled to do something to rid himself of his unwelcome guest. He thought the matter over carefully. If he offered the hobo a job, the latter turned the subject of conversation into politics or something else. It was useless to hint to the star boarder that the climate of other localities might be better for his health. He seemed proof against hints, invitations, or even mildly expressed wishes that he would take his departure. Nothing but personal violence would rid them of his company, and they were loath to do that. Bill began to worry over the matter. He went around with a thoughtful look as though he had something serious on his mind. Finally he determined to lay the matter before Jim to see if he could not suggest some way to be rid of a guest, who was not only a burden but a nuisance. After some reflection, it was decided that Jim was to act crazy, and some time or other when all were assembled at the table, at a given sign, he was to give a jump, knock over the table, stick his dirk into one of the rafters of the dugout, and grab his gun and begin to shoot up the place. Of course, he was not to kill anybody, but the purpose was to stampede the hobo and set him on his way over the hills to other localities where he might have an opportunity of showing his staying qualities.

The next day it happened that Bill and the hobo were down at the corral to brand some colts. It dawned upon the proprietor that right here was a brilliant opportunity for a practical joke and at the same time put an end to Jim's assertions that he could not be tricked by any practical jokesmith on either side of the Rockies. It made Bill smile. He took a look around to see if Jim was in the neighbourhood and found him sitting at the door of the dugout braiding a lariat. With an air of simplicity, and trustfulness he told the hobo that he had something to tell him; that he was thinking of telling it to him some time ago, and that was as good an opportunity as would present itself to him to do so. "You know," said he, in a guileless manner, "Jim has been with me for a number of years and I have found him one of the best fellows that I have ever known. He is trusty, and is a good judge of stock. I can rely on him at all times and he takes as much interest in the work and the ranch as I do myself. However, he has been a cause of much worry to me. I do not like to tell my troubles to others but I find I must tell it to someone. I have taken quite a shine to you and I feel that the confidence I place in you will not be abused. Well, to bring the matter to a focus, I must tell you that Jim is subject to spells, and when in that condition is likely to be quite dangerous. The cause of his condition is this. A few years ago, out in California he was thrown from his horse and in falling his head struck a stone. He was quite delirious for a long time. He grew out of his condition after a year or so, but at certain periods he has a return of his old illness and is likely to turn things topsy-turvy before we can get him quieted. We have tried everything in the medical line, but it was no use. We found out by accident, one day, that the only thing that would restore him to his senses was a jar on the head. He had one of his spells and made an attack on one of the hands with a knife. The man in desperation let fly at Jim with his fist and knocked him senseless for about ten minutes. When he recovered from the blow, he was as rational as any of us. I know it is painful for us to have to lay violent hands on the poor fellow, but it must be done, and besides, Jim is very thankful for our doing it, as he has a very tender heart and would not for anything in the world be the cause of injury to anyone. The reason I am telling you this is that I may have to be away some time or other and as you are pretty well acquainted with the run of things around the ranch, you will know what to do if the poor fellow has one of those sudden attacks. You may not feel like doing it, but he will thank you for it when he has recovered, and besides, Jim thinks a lot of you. When I was leaving California I promised my poor old mother that I would look after Jim and see that no harm came, to him on account of his weakness."

When Bill returned to the dug-out, it would not take a mind-reader long to figure out that there was something going to happen. He kept his face straight, but he could not conceal the merry twinkle of his eye. He kept the cause of his merriment to himself, but frequently he would take a look out of the corner of his eye at Jim and if Jim was not looking, a smile would spread over his countenance. The thought of working a practical joke on Jim was too much for him at times and he would have to go outside to conceal his feelings.

Things went along thus for a few days, but the tension became too great for him to control himself any longer. One day, at dinner he gave the pre-arranged signal to Jim. With a yell Jim jumped up upset the table and spilled the contents all over the floor of the dug-out, grabbed his dirk and stuck it into the rafter of the dug-out, then pulled his six-shooter and let blaze. He ploughed up the earthen floor with some of the bullets, others he sent flying through the roof. All the while he was yelling like a Comanche Indian on the warpath. By the time he had emptied his gun, the place was filled with smoke. At the first shot Bill and the others filed through the door, or rather threw themselves through it, but the hobo mindful of the instructions given him some time before, worked his way around through the smoke until he came within arm's length of Jim. He summoned up all his strength and let fly one of his fists. It was a mighty blow, delivered with care. It landed on the side of Jim's head and sent him reeling and senseless into a pile of gunny-sacks lying in the corner. With an eye to the necessity of further ministrations if necessary, he stood looking at the poor fellow lying there. In a minute or more, Jim opened his eyes and reached for his gun. It was empty of course, and he reached for his cartridge box also. Bill looked in through the door when he heard no noise. He saw what Jim was doing and also noted by the flare in his eyes that there was going to be moments of activity there as soon as he succeeded in getting the chambers of his 45 filled. He took one look at the hobo, and uttered the word "run." Without waiting any further instructions, the hobo fairly flew through the door and bounded away like a cat pursued by a bull dog. Jim dashed for the door with his weapon ready for vengeance. He saw the fleeing figure bounding over the prairie and let fly at him with the six-shooter. Happily for all concerned, he was too excited to take aim, and consequently all of his shots went wild. Every shot seemed to increase the speed of the swiftly running hobo. He was over the hill and far away in about the shortest time he ever made. Jim looked around the end of the dug-out and found Bill and his companions rolling on the ground and holding their sides with laughter. He realized immediately that there was something strange about the whole affair. It seemed more than he could stand. "Bill Anderson," said he, "I believe you are at the bottom of all this. If I were certain of it I would send you back to California on a pair of wooden legs, but out of respect for your good old mother whose feeling I would not like to hurt on account of a 'bloody spalpeen' like you, I want to warn you never to do the like of it again." Jim never afterwards made the boast that he could not be tricked by any one on either side of the Rockies.

Bill sold out the ranch sometime afterwards for $125,000, and the last I saw of him he was setting out for Old Mexico.

If Jim ever had any more crazy spells, I never heard of it.

CHAPTER 11

The Man From Missouri

While out hunting one day, about 18 miles south of Dodge City, I chanced to meet a stranger who inquired the way to the nearest horse corral. In the twinkling of an eye I took an inventory of his outfit, and I must say that it was good. He had a fine team of young mules, a three seated spring wagon covered over, harness all covered over with brass mountings. His wife and children who were with him were well-dressed and he himself showed traces of being well bred and was rather a good talker. His conversation showed refinement, though at times he sandwiched in a mild cuss-word to emphasize his statements. From his bearing I could see that he was rather high-strung. Before giving the required information I ventured to ask if he was going to take up land for the purpose of farming. He said that that was his intention. I looked the family over and felt sorry for them, knowing what they would have to endure on a claim. I had not the same regrets for proprietor of the outfit as I felt that a little experience and exposure was what was needed to round out his character. The more I explained the general conditions of the neighbourhood of his destination, the more he seemed determined to go. I explained to him that others from the different states of the east had tried to raise crops and made a failure of the venture, and returned to their several homes disgusted with the west. "Oh, pshaw!" said he, "I have heard that same tale of woe more than a dozen times during the last three days, and the land-agents in Dodge City told me that yarn was fabricated expressly by the cow-men to discourage the farmers from settling on the range and cutting off their supply of pasture." "Moreover," said he, "I have a little provision made for the future and can stand it as long as any of them."

During my interview with that gentleman, I learned that his name was Waugh, that he was a native of Pennsylvania, and had been living in Missouri on a rented farm during the preceding two years. He had become dissatisfied with the state and had come farther west to improve his fortunes. I ask him if he did not think it better to return to Missouri where his children would have the advantage of schools, and he and his wife would be able to enjoy some society rather than establish a home on a raw prairie. He replied, "I see, stranger, that you have never lived in Missouri. I tell you those folk back there don't know the war is over yet, and besides one's standing in society depends upon how many hounds one keeps and, also, on the length of one's whiskers. Why, don't you know that there was only one razor in the neighbourhood where I lived and that was owned by the school teacher. He was some up on social niceties. Once in awhile he used to go to St. Joe to have his hair cut and the back of his neck shaved and this caused some of the patrons of the school to threaten to take their children away from him if he did not stop such unwarranted proceedings. I am sure they would have done so if they had known that he used to go down to the creek every Saturday night to take a bath. No Siree, I do not want any more of Missouri in mine. The first year I worked there I did fairly well. I made about half a crop. The next year was a complete failure. I raised nothing, absolutely nothing, and when I saw the hens bringing leaves from the timber to build nests, I told Hannah to put out the fire and call the dog and we would start for Kansas."

The next time I met Mr. Waugh was one afternoon about three months later. I noted that his mules had fallen away in flesh, and on inquiring about his general condition, he stated that things were in poor condition. He said the grass had been poor and that it was impossible to procure corn for the cattle. In fact he had not ploughed nor put in any crops. He informed me that it had not rained since he had taken up his claim and to plough was out of the question. The only line of work open for him was to gather buffalo bones. He said that things had come to such a pass that he had to exchange some of his belongings for others not as good. His spring wagon had to go for an old lumber-wagon as he could not use the spring affair in the work of gathering the bones. In this trade he received a cow to boot.

When next I met him he had traded off his mules and brass-mounted harness for a one-eyed mule and a pony, receiving boot on that occasion also in the shape of a sewing machine and a shot gun, with a set of chain harness thrown in for good measure. He said he preferred the chain harness as the dry weather did not affect the corn-husk collars and if it rained he could throw it on the ground and it would suffer no injury from the moisture. Shortly after this he came to my blacksmith shop to have the wheels of his wagon set. Before that he used to soak them in the bed of the creek, but as the water in the creek bottom failed, he had to bring them to me to set them.

The last time I had the opportunity of meeting Mr. Waugh, he was camped at the creek with his family. He was busy at the camp-fire cooking his meal at the time. After the usual greetings, I ventured to ask him how he liked farming. He seemed very despondent. "Don't talk to me about farming in this desolate country," said he. "It has not rained enough between here and the head of the creek since I have been here to wet a postage stamp. Moreover, there are skunks enough up there to drive the Standard Oil Co. out of business, and coyotes without number. They gave us no rest. They would steal a chicken out of the pot while it was boiling on the fire." "Why," he continued, "You know old man Spriggins up there? Well, only last week his chickens got so all-fired hungry that they went out on the trail and tried to hold up a bull-train to get some corn. I would not have believed myself if I had not seen it. I tell you those chickens were getting desperate and you would have believed it if you had seen that Shanghai rooster strutting back and forth in front of those oxen and crowing. When the old man saw it himself he went down to John Conrads and traded his old fiddle and a cultivator for some Kaffir corn."

"Well," said I, "you filed on a claim, didn't you?"

"Not that any one knows of," said he. "I caught on to that game in time to save my fourteen dollars. It is nothing but a gambling game anyway, and I believe that the same law applies to poker and other games of chance, ought to reach Uncle Sam for trying to unload a lot of worthless land on a lot of poor suckers that can't help themselves. Why, he don't take any chance at all. He simply puts up one hundred and sixty acres of parched vacancy against your fourteen dollars that you can't remain on it for five years without starving, to comply with the contract he makes with you. I tell you he has a dead sure thing here in Kansas. He has made some good winnings. Some of those claims he has won back five or six times each and he still holds the land waiting for another sucker to come along."

Well, then, I said, you are not inclined to engage in agriculture, nor to remain in this part of the country, are you?

"Not if I know myself," he replied, "and I think it about time I was becoming wise. You told me the whole unvarnished truth about this country the first time I met you and if I had taken your advice I would not be in this disagreeable fix."

Here he took a side glance at his one-eyed mule, which seemed to raise his temperature to about 160 in the shade. He then raised his voice to correspond with the temperature, and striking his hands together said; "any gosh-durned country that gets so dad-burned dry that it will take an antelope—and he is the fastest animal there is—twenty four hours solid travelling to find a drink of water, is a little too dry for me. I am going back to Pennsylvania. That state will be good enough for me for all the time to come."

He hitched up his one-eyed mule and made ready to go. I bade him goodbye. He nodded, clucked to his mule and rode away.

CHAPTER 12
Indian Scares

In the autumn of the year of 1878, a gentleman by the name of John Joplin was sent out from Zanesville, Ohio, to select a suitable place in western Kansas for the purpose of locating a colony. The intention was to start a co-operative business in farming. After surveying the country at large, he came to the conclusion that the Crooked Creek valley, Meade County, where I was living at the time, was the most desirable for the purpose. He returned home and gave a glowing report of what he had done, and his efforts and report received the approval of the future colonists. They made their arrangements and moved westward in the following spring. When they had reached their destination, they learned that Chief Dull Knife, a leader of a band of northern Cheyenne Indians, had left the reservation at Ft. Reno where he and his followers were held as prisoners of war. Followed by a numerous retinue of tribesmen he started for the Black Hills and had passed through the Crooked Creek Valley, killing the settlers. They continued on their way, killing, burning, and destroying everything and everybody in sight until they were re-captured at Ft. Robinson, Nebraska. From there they were brought back and placed on the reservation once more. The particulars of the Dull Knife Raid will be given in another chapter.

Needless to say, these reports caused considerable excitement in the valley. Every few days rumours were circulated that the Indians were returning, or would return as soon as the grass had begun to sprout again. Hardly had one rumour died until another was put into circulation. Excitement reached such a degree that all deemed it necessary to organize for protection. A meeting was called which all the settlers were invited, or requested, to attend. The colonists assembled at the dug-out of a Mr. M. B. Wilson, one of the leading spirits of the movement, to devise ways and means for protection in case the Indians should return. After a general discussion of the prevailing conditions, it was unanimously agreed that we should appeal to the governor of Kansas for fire arms, as there were few of us that had any, many had none, and some had no money to purchase them, and some that did have them, had very little knowledge of their use. Our secretary was instructed to write to the governor, explain the conditions of affairs, and request him to send us the necessary guns and ammunition with which to protect ourselves against the Indians in case they should make another descent on the valley, which they would likely do as they were threatening to leave the reservation and go on the warpath a second time. After a good deal of correspondence and red tape we succeeded in getting the governor's attention, and he kindly informed us, after several week's delay, that if we wanted any assistance from the state, we should join the militia. He informed us that when we were duly sworn in, he would send the necessary arms for protection of our homes and families. To the disinterested reader this action on the part of the governor may seem magnanimous, but to the settler whose family was living in a dug-out with nothing to protect them but a fire shovel or a hatchet in case of an Indian raid, it looked very much like a case of criminal neglect. Another meeting was called, and it was well attended. There were many women present who seemed anxious to organize a company for the protection of their homes. After some discussion it was decided to organize and join the militia. Among those present was a veteran of the Civil war. He was elected captain on his war record—one of the home-made kind, as none of his comrades of the war recollected any time or place where he performed any deed of valour—as he would most likely know the best thing to do at the proper time. To hear the captain tell of his numerous exploits, the number of men took prisoners of war, how he had on several occasions leaped over the breastworks of some beleaguered fort in the midst of a shower of grape and canister, and tore down the Confederate flag, one would think that he, Capt. Milligan, bore a charmed life. It seemed strange to me that such a thoughtful man as Abe Lincoln did not send somebody down south to assist the captain as he seemed to be doing all the heavy fighting himself. Such was our captain, the last and the greatest of the Milligans up to that time, and it would require a remarkable scion to eclipse his record, if one hundredth part of what he said was true.

Returning to the thread of my story, and I hope you will pardon the digression but it would be impossible to pass over the merits of our worthy captain without bringing to the notice of the world at large his claims to the honour conferred upon him, we elected G. W. Brown First Lieutenant, Mr. Gantz, Second Lieutenant, and C. M. Rice, Sergeant. The above officers were veterans, or had been scouts, and the remainder required to complete the contingent had no military experience whatever. We instructed the secretary to notify the governor that we had organized and were ready to be sworn into the State Militia. We did not actually want to join the militia, but would rather join the Women's Relief Corps, or the Suffragette Movement, or the Populist party, anything to get the guns and ammunition. (The swearing part of the program did not play a very important part as there had been enough swearing done along the creek already over the governor's indolence and failure to send the relief requested, yes, enough to have sworn in seven regiments with some to spare.)

As the assemblage was about to disperse, some one called for a speech. Others called on Capt. Milligan to harangue the multitude. This was kept up until the captain, with all the dignity of a well trained parliamentarian, condescended to make a few remarks to show his appreciation of the favour conferred upon him, etc. He selected a small knoll from which to deliver himself of the sentiments that filled his manly breast. He assumed the pose of an orator of the old school and delivered a discourse in something like the following words:

"Fellow Citizens, Ladies and Gentlemen: We are now on the eve of a terrible conflict to decide whether the white man with tens of thousands of years of civilization, culture and refinement behind him, or the wily undomesticated, uncivilized, uncouth, uncultured, unrefined, undressed savage will rule the plains. Whether the untutored savage will continue to water the virgin soil of the rolling prairie with the blood of the best of our citizens, or whether the white man shall give to the unlimited area of the plains the advantage of a training developed by centuries of progress in the arts of peace and agriculture. (Cheers, and hurrah for Milligan). I am here to state my views and express my sentiments on the question that each and every one of us is debating in the depths of the individual heart." It was quite evident that the captain was labouring under difficulties, as he delivered the above in a very hesitating manner. What he lacked in fluency of speech, he made up by violence and frequency of gestures. He swung his arms and stamped his feet to emphasize the degree of his perturbation while contemplating in advance the horrors to which they were to be subjected. He became so wrapped up in his subject and was so earnest in his endeavours to move his hearers, that he did not realize that he was standing on a hill inhabited by a colony of red ants; nor was he aware that a regiment of them had set out to explore the depths of his unmentionables and were at that very moment making rapid progress through the recesses of his underwear. Suddenly he became aware of something peculiar about his feelings and to cover the difficulty under which he was labouring, and at the same time to prove to his hearers that his reputation was above reproach and his patriotism beyond question, he accentuated his remarks by more violent gestures than before, striking himself on the thighs and even reaching beyond the limits to which gestures were supposed to extend, realizing that farther speech with decorum was out of the question he was compelled by force of circumstances to desist from further efforts. He made an assault on his personal enemies as best he might under the circumstances in such a public place. He squeezed and pinched, slapped and crushed, but the greater the efforts he made, the more they seemed to be impelled to greater efforts of offense. He rolled up his trouser legs, as far as public decency would permit, but exposure only drove the enemy to seek more advantageous hiding places. He could not ask his friends to help him because it seemed such a personal affair, and besides, they were at that moment helpless in their efforts to stifle their laughter. In his desperation he started for the creek, which, fortunately for him, was close at hand. A clump of hackberry and plum bushes screened him from the multitude, and in the friendly cover offered him by nature herself, he began to put the enemy to rout. However, mindful of the position to which he had been elected, and the duty incumbent on him of stirring them up to the proper degree of patriotism, he sent word that he would return shortly to continue his harangue. More than half an hour elapsed before he returned, and to guard against more interruptions, we pulled an old wagon to the fore and fixed it up in proper shape for him to continue his remarks.

Upon his arrival he was assisted by Sergeant Rice and Lieutenant Brown to mount the newly made rostrum. After apologizing for his abrupt departure, he continued his address as follows; "Ladies and Gentlemen: I am ready for the worst if it must come. A brave man dies but once, whilst the coward dies every time danger approaches. There is no use of being timid nor chicken-hearted in the present cause. I do not encourage cruelty, but we must stand firmly together to defend our rights and protect our families and firesides. (Cheers). For my part I want to emphatically say that no invader can leave his *moccasin* track on my threshold, nor disturb the peace of my household until he has crossed over all that is mortal of Capt. Milligan. Do you think that I would sit silently and submissively by and see him shoot down the old family watch-dog, work him up into *bouillon*, and eat his repast in the shadow of my "sorghum stack." I say, No! a thousand times, No! I would prefer to meet their leader in single combat on the open prairie and when I had driven him from the field of battle, follow him to his *tepee*, destroy his totem pole, tear his *wampum* belt from his body and carry it away as a trophy of the expedition." (Tumultuous applause.)

As it was getting rather late, and many had long distances to travel before reaching home, the capt. closed his harangue, thanking them for their attention and assuring them that their interests were his interests, and that he was willing to go to extreme lengths to defend their rights, and homes.

In a few days we received word that the governor had instructed Adjutant General Noble to proceed to Dodge City and thence to Crooked Creek where he was to receive the oath of allegiance of the colonists, and deliver the guns and ammunition, and give us such instructions as he deemed necessary for us in our line of duty. On the following Thursday he arrived and went through the formality of enlisting us and delivering to us the weapons of war. Henceforth we were full-fledged members of the Kansas State Militia. After turning over to us the arms and ammunition, he delivered a short talk in which he instructed us in our duties to the State and to one another.

When the arms were distributed, it was found that there was a surplus left, which came in handy to shoot antelope with afterwards. These guns, in the meantime, were left in charge of Lieut. Brown. The Adjutant-General then bade us good-bye and departed for home.

We immediately set to work to provide for our defence. After some deliberation, we concluded to provide a fortification in which to place the women and children and all those who might happen to be in the neighbourhood in the time of danger. As funds were lacking, and rock, or timber was not to be had, we decided to build it of sod. The following Saturday was the day set aside to vote on the proper location of our future fortification. On the appointed day, all assembled. They expressed their willingness and eagerness to do anything to further the project. One thing each one was determined on was to have it built as near his claim as possible. It did not take long to arrive at a conclusion regarding the position in which the fort was to be built. As it was impossible to satisfy everybody, we abandoned the project entirely, and it was further decided that each one was to take his share of the guns and ammunition and take care of himself. Another subject that gave us much concern was the matter of drilling. The adjutant had told us to become familiar with the use of the arms, to meet at least once a week and drill to render ourselves fit for duty. When the time arrived for our first lesson in the "manual of arms," it was found that there was not a man present who knew anything about it. The old scouts who were present, knew all about how to ride a horse, and to lie down in a buffalo wallow and take a shot at an Indian if one came in sight, and they were, besides, first class hands at discovering watering places and the like, but in the matter of drill they were entirely unsophisticated. Even Capt. Milligan, if he ever knew anything about the matter, declared he had forgotten it entirely. He felt sure, however, that it would be impossible to perform the proper manoeuvres with those short-barrelled guns, and that if the governor would send some with long barrels that he would be right at home in the matter. As no one seemed capable of conducting the class, we settled the difficulty in the same manner as we did that of the fort, by abandoning it also. It was unanimously agreed that in case of trouble, each should go to the aid of his neighbour if assistance were needed. This was very satisfactory for me especially, as I was fortunate in the possession of splendid neighbours, Sergeant Rice living on one side of me, and First Lieut. Brown on the other. Both were possessed of abundant fighting material at all times, and knew how to use it in an emergency.

Things seemed to drag along in the usual way, everybody settling down to his own affairs and everything would have gone along tranquilly enough were it not for the numerous cowboys passing through the settlement, spreading reports as they went, that the Indians were mixing war medicine and would shortly make a descent upon the palefaces. It was a source of great delight to them to stampede the settlers by disquieting reports, and then have a good laugh about it. Their efforts at fun kept the settlers in a state of ferment.

It happened that Capt. Milligan's claim was located on the south side of the settlement and nearest to the Indian Territory. As he was rather nervous and always on the alert, he kept inquiring continuously of the cowboys, of the possibility of an Indian raid, and, of course, they filled his anxious ear with war news. Nearly every other day I noticed the captain calling on either Sergeant Rice or Lieutenant Brown, and as he had to make a ride of ten miles or so to make the visit, I concluded that there was some significance to these numerous calls. However, as they were my superior officers, I did not feel at liberty to make any inquiries about the captain's frequent visits. I did not have to curb my curiosity very long before acquiring the desired information. In a few days I saw the captain riding up in my direction on his old baldfaced horse and could see at a glance that his arrival was something of importance as he was riding straight up in his saddle with as much dignity as it was possible for one horse to carry. Upon his near approach I felt that I must do something to acknowledge the presence of my captain. Not being versed in military etiquette,

I doffed my Stetson hat. As I was leaning against the fence, with a spade in one hand and my hat in the other, I realized that my appearance lacked something of the military precision required in a subordinate, and I apologized for my lack of training in the case. He dismounted from his horse and condescended to shake hands with me and said that the salute was only a matter of form anyway; that he understood my position exactly; that he was a recruit once himself; that on such occasions as this he could overlook little technicalities of the kind, but on the field of glory he would have to be more exacting with his men. I then invited the captain to take a seat on a cottonwood log near at hand so that we could discuss matters pertaining to the company more at leisure I congratulated him on the choice of officers which he had made.

"Yes," said he, "they are all good men and true, but if I had it to do over again, I would try to have you act as First Lieutenant of the company. Brown is a good man and a good scout and has seen some service with the Indians, but he lacks aggressiveness. I want men who are aggressive and who will go into battle as if they are going to breakfast. By the way," he continued, "I dropped over to see you and to leave orders for you to go down into the Indian Territory and size up the situation. Find out if the Indians are in an ugly mood, and if they are likely to make a raid in the near future. Then report to me on your return and I will take some steps in the direction that will be best for all concerned. The cowboys have been circulating some reports concerning an intended raid, but I do not know whether any credence is to be placed in them or not. Consequently I decided to come over to see you and send you down to look the field over, and then I would feel more satisfied, and know just what action to take in the matter."

I asked the captain how he expected me to go down there, and who would bear the expense of my journey.

"Oh," said he, "you can take your own horse, and I suppose the State will be responsible for any bills you make whilst under my orders." I then asked him what I should do for food for myself as well as for my horse. A broad smile lit up his countenance and he replied, "Don't you know that the cowmen will be more than pleased to have a soldier stop at their ranches for the feeling of security his presence will engender? Your board and horse-feed will not have to be considered at all. You can go to the R-S ranch, the Doc Day ranch, the Y. L. ranch or the Driscoll ranch, and they will receive you with open arms. I can assure you that no charges will be even mentioned."

During this short interview I discovered a nigger in the captain's wood-pile. The fact was that the cowboys had him half scared to death by telling him all kinds of Indian war stories. The particular reason he had in calling on me, was to have me go down to the territory, and if I was not scalped while on my mission, and if I found that the Indians were really going on the warpath, I should report to him without delay so that he might be able to withdraw his precious(?) person from the zone of danger and escape to Fort Dodge. I told the captain that he was somewhat mistaken in the estimate a cowman places on a soldier as a means of defence where the Indians were concerned. I assured him that I had learned their personal views on the subject, and they had arrived at the conclusion that the soldier was a detriment and an encumbrance to them in case of trouble with the Indians, and, moreover, they felt quite capable of taking care of themselves in times of danger from such sources. I went on to tell him that if he were anxious to have an investigation of conditions made, he might come over to my place in a day or so and we would go down together and make the inquiries proper to the occasion, and that I would feel safer with him than if I were alone. I immediately saw that the captain was getting an attack of what the hunters call "buck-ague."

"Thunder and turf," he exclaimed, "I cannot go. I am subject to orders from the governor, and I should be in a queer fix if I were called to duty in some other part of the State while I was down in the territory. However, I can order Corporal Copeland to go with you."

I told him that the Corporal had no horse, and it would not be right to send him on foot. I also informed him that he would have to look around and make some other arrangements, as my horse was too old, and his knee was sprung from roping cattle, so that an Indian war horse could catch him without any trouble. Conditions being such, I told him I did not think I would go.

"What!" he shouted, "you do not mean to disobey orders!"

His eyes bulged out until they looked like old English watches, and his chest measurement seemed to increase perceptibly. He jumped up from his seat on the log and started for his horse, saying on his way, "If you persist in disobeying orders, I shall be forced to disarm you and court-martial you for insubordination."

"Well," said I, "you will raise the deuce court-martialling me, when there is only five or six members of the company who can read or write and they are all on my side."

I heard nothing more from the captain for several days. Finally I received a letter from him telling me that he had written to the governor regarding my disobedience. I replied to his message, saying that if the governor was as tardy in taking action on my case as he was in sending arms and ammunition, I should die of old age before the matter would be adjusted. I also informed him that I had received word that the Indians would be in our neighbourhood in a few days, and that he should see to it that means were taken for our defence. Next day I received another note from him in which he told me that he had changed his attitude toward me, and that I should call on Sergeant Rice and Lieutenant Brown and tell them to report to him for duty at once, and I was to accompany them. The message I received by special delivery. I made a visit up the creek to see my friends, Rice and Brown, and reported the change that had taken place in the captain's attitude, and also showed them his request and instructions, asking at the same time their opinions on the matter. Brown replied, "O pshaw, that does not amount to anything. Those cowboys over on Sand Creek have the old captain about frightened to death, and I think we had better remain where we are. There's not an Indian in the country, and I do not think there will be." We acted on Brown's suggestion and remained where we were.

At this time the cowmen were holding their Spring round-up on Sand Creek, to cut out and take back to their ranches the cattle that had drifted off during the winter, besides branding the calves before turning them loose again on the range. There were about one hundred cow-punchers at the round up, all well mounted and well armed. Each man had from three to five horses in his mount, all in good shape because they had been grain fed for the occasion. Their arms consisted of Winchesters and six-shooters. There had been so many rumours circulated about the possibility of an Indian raid that all went prepared for any emergency. One day while they were all lying around awaiting the arrival of the round-up herds from the southeast, a happy thought occurred to them to put to the test the bravery of Captain Milligan, of which they had heard much, thinking at the same time to have some sport at his expense. They formed a company of about thirty, dressed up like Indians, or near enough to the real thing to be mistaken for them at a distance. The leader was fitted with a red saddle blanket decorated with sage brush for a war bonnet, with a few cat tails for plumes. He looked more like a grizzly bear than an Indian, but his appearance was well calculated to strike terror into the heart of any civilized human being, especially when everyone was looking for trouble from such a source anyway. The rest of the crowd dressed up as each saw fit, carrying their hats inside their shirts so as to travel bareheaded after the Indian fashion. When all was ready they took a direct route for Captain Milligan's place. They all knew how to render the Cheyenne war whoop when the proper time arrived, and the leader rode along at a moderate pace chanting his war song. They came to a halt to decide whether they should burn him alive, or capture him and hold him for ransom. One man said it was useless to hold him for any ransom as he knew most of the company, and as for burning him alive, he did not think there was a cow-puncher in the crowd that would waste time necessary to gather chips for the sacrifice. In the meantime the chief kept ranging around and waving his hands, keeping his war bonnet as much in evidence as possible. They moved up to a position within about a quarter of a mile of the captain's house and then gave a war whoop. By this time the object of the joke became aware of their presence and felt his peril keenly. He made a dash for his corral where he kept a little, old, notch-eared, sore-backed pony that he always kept saddled for any emergency. To say that he went rapidly, is putting it mildly—he fairly flew. When he got started the Indians(?) made a rush to capture him, firing at him in the meanwhile. They remained a safe distance behind so as to be sure not to capture him, but kept up the shouting and whooping for about two miles. The captain took the shortest course to Fort Dodge, and the cowboys returned to camp laughing heartily at the brave man's flight.

When the captain had made about five miles of his hasty retreat, he happened upon one of his neighbours, Mike O'Shea, who had begun to dig a well. As he passed in his headlong flight he shouted to Mike, "Tell Rice and Brown they are here, and I am going to Fort Dodge for relief and succour." He was in too great a hurry to stop and explain the cause of his excitement, and as Mike explained it afterwards, he said he thought he was going for a "thafe and sucker" or something of the kind, or maybe it was "relafe and supper, or something like that." He also noticed that the captain's horse was almost out of breath, and the gentleman himself was very much excited.

Whilst Rice and Brown were interviewing Mike, another man came along and stated that he had seen the captain about ten miles north, and he reported having had an engagement with the Indians that day at his claim, and said that he had stood them off until they had retired. As he was about out of ammunition at the time of their departure, he took advantage of their retreat to make his way to Fort Dodge for relief and succour. He did not say how many he had killed, but maintained that he had a very narrow escape.

I suppose, if Captain Milligan is alive today, he does not fail to tell of the time he stood off five hundred Cheyenne Indians, single-handed and alone, and how, after driving them off, he beat them to Fort Dodge in quest of aid.

A few days after the encounter with the supposed Indians, Lieutenant Brown received the following note from the captain:

Fort Dodge, Kansas, April—, '79.
Lieutenant Brown:
Dear Comrade:—I am in receipt of a telegram from the governor, ordering me to go at once to Topeka, to take charge of the strike-breakers. The railroad employees have gone out on a strike, and it will take the strong arm of the militia to hold them in check. Sell my land and all my effects, and forward the proceeds to my address, which will be, State Capitol, Topeka.
Yours in command,
Captain Milligan
P. S. Regards to all the comrades.

Thus terminated the war of 1879.

CHAPTER 13
Hard Times

For three years, from 1879 to 1882, it seemed as if the very elements had conspired to render the attempt at settling western Kansas futile. The continuous drought, together with the hot winds, made any attempt at farming discouraging. As a consequence a great many settlers sold their holdings for what they could get for them, and returned to their former place of abode. The gathering of buffalo bones, which had been their chief source of subsistence during that trying time, was beginning to fail owing to the great number engaged in the business, and the distance they had to be hauled and the ever receding base of supply. Many abandoned the work entirely, and the few that remained actively engaged in that occupation found themselves daily meeting greater difficulties. The scarcity of the supply became so great that they would often be compelled to go a hundred miles or more to gather a load, haul them to the nearest trail, and then transfer them to some freighter on the way to Dodge City, the only market for them in the country. To make the exchange and have them taken to market usually required a division of the profits, and one can easily imagine what a small share was left for the original collector when the goods were sold. No matter how small the profit, on this the gatherer had to subsist as well as supply his family with necessaries during his absence. There was hardly sufficient remuneration in the work to obtain the plainest of provisions.

To the young people of America who may perhaps be reading this little story of the early settlement of the west, in the comfortable surroundings of their own cosy homes, I will say that they know little of the price paid to make such conditions possible. I have frequently seen, on the top of a wagon loaded with bones, a gunny sack containing the skeleton of a man, that had been picked up by some freighter or some cowman or some settler, and put in the sack to be taken to Dodge City for burial. That gunny sack contained a sermon as well as a skeleton. It told of the certainty of death as well as of the uncertainty of life. It told the reason why father, mother, Mary, Ellen and Julia never received a reply to their last letter, written to John, Jake or Jim, marked on the lower left-hand corner, "In haste, please," to be sure of prompt delivery. Quite likely, when the poor old mother would be grieving over the long disappointment, the girls would encourage her by saying, "Oh, that is one of his pranks. He is just waiting until we are all quite lonesome, and then he will come rushing in upon us to take us by surprise." He has never returned, but the family still keeps alive the glimmer of hope that flickers in the human breast, that they will all meet again, somewhere.

Confronted with such conditions as mentioned above, with no indications of any relaxation of the drought that was compelling even the big ranchmen to look around for water, we saw a very gloomy outlook for the future.

After weighing the matter carefully, I decided to make a change in my business affairs. I took into my confidence a cow-puncher named Bill Wagner, who is now living in Meade, Kans. Having fully discussed the situation from all points, we determined to embark together on a course that would at least promise us some profit from the undertaking. We made up our minds to go down into the territory and trade with the cattlemen who were coming north with their herds from Texas, on their way to Montana or Wyoming, either to sell or turn loose to graze on the northern range. We rounded up a few saddle horses, among which was my old favourite Jimmy, and set out for Dodge City to purchase the supplies necessary for the journey. I also wanted to deposit some money and dispose of some mules that I would not need, on my trip. On my arrival at Dodge City I formed the acquaintance of James Langton, who introduced me to a Mr. R. M. Wright, of the firm of Wright, Beverly & Co., who were engaged in a Wholesale Supply business. I found Mr. Wright one of the most genial men with whom I ever did business. Having previously sold my mules, I deposited my money with the firm I was introduced to. I told Mr. W. that I intended to go down into the territory on a trading expedition. I explained to him that the cattlemen would be on the trail, and as there were no stores to be found between the Red River on the north line of Texas and where we were then standing, there would be a good opportunity to trade provisions for some cattle that had become sore-footed on the way, with a good profit for me. He agreed with me that it was a golden opportunity, and added as an encouragement, "You will do well, if the Indians do not scalp you in the meantime." I replied that as conditions existed on Crooked Creek, a man would be no worse off dead in the territory than living where I had been. I saw very little difference.

I loaded my wagon with what goods I thought would be most in demand by the cattlemen. I selected a considerable quantity of tobacco, bacon, baking powder, canned goods of several kinds, a coil of rope, cartridges of different calibre, coffee, sugar, and some other things—all necessary on the trail. I also bought a tent and cooking outfit. The latter consisted of a coffee-pot, skillet, frying-pan, coffee-mill, six knives and forks, six tin plates, six cups and saucers, the latter of tin, in order to provide against the possibility of our having some company on the road. By the time I had my trading done, Wagner was ready and waiting. We hitched up and pulled across the river, where we encamped for the night. Part of the horses we hobbled, and two we kept picketed in order to guard against being left on foot the next morning if anything should stampede our stock during the night. When the stock had been cared for, we proceeded to make arrangements for ourselves, and while Wagner cooked the flapjacks I was looking around for sleeping accommodations, as it was difficult to find a place level enough to suit the purpose. The making of our beds did not cost much effort, but one had to guard against sand-burrs, cactus, tarantulas, rattlesnakes and centipedes.

The next morning found us up early after a good sound sleep, and hustling around to get ready for the first day of our new venture. When we had tended to the wants of the stock and ourselves, we hitched up and started off at a slow pace, as the team was not accustomed to the heavy work, and it would take some time for them to become inured to the hardship of the trail. Out across Five Mile Creek and up the divide along the old Camp Supply route until we reached the summit, we made our toilsome way. We reached the apex about noon time and halted for dinner. After giving the horses a good rest, we proceeded on our way, and as our route now lay down grade we made better time. Evening found us at Mulberry Creek, where Johnny Glenn and Dutch Pete kept a road ranch. This roadside caravansary served as a halting place for the stage coach, and furnished refreshments for passengers when needed. As there was a good camping ground there, we unhitched and turned the horses out to graze and made preparations for our own accommodation. When we had eaten supper, we brought the horses in for the night, and then after chatting and smoking for some time we turned in for a good night's rest. Early morning found us on our way again towards the south. We kept rumbling along until we reached the division point of the stage line, where horses were changed by the driver, P. G. Reynolds. This location, I believe, is not very far from where the present town of Ashland, county seat of Clark county, is situated. Here we stopped and had dinner at what was called the Widow Brown ranch. From this place we proceeded down the Bear Creek trail and reached the Cimarron River that same evening. The river being up, we could not cross, and we camped on the north bank not far from where an old German named Clem maintained a road ranch. The river as I said was full and this may seem strange, as it had not rained in this section for more than three months. The cause of the rise lay in the fact that there had been considerable rain in Colorado. This added to the snow melting on the mountains made the river rise to its full capacity. Here we had to remain for three days, waiting till the waters would subside enough to permit a crossing. We were not the only ones that met with an obstacle in our progress by the river's behaviour, but it proved a boon to us as well as adding to our store of knowledge. On the other bank of the river were cowpunchers with their herds waiting to cross also. It was amusing and instructive to us to watch them in their efforts to induce the leaders of the herds to take to the water. When a puncher succeeded in getting the leaders into the stream, he would ride or swim his pony alongside of them to keep them from milling, or drifting down the river. It was very exciting to watch those herds crossing the swollen stream with the cowboys yelling and whooping among them. It seemed as if pandemonium had taken a holiday. By the time the last of the herds had crossed, the river had subsided somewhat, and we pulled over to the opposite side without any great difficulty. It was with a sigh of relief we reached the solid footing on the other bank.

Then we were in the territory and bade farewell to civilization until we returned to the north bank of Cimarron River. We left the Camp Supply trail and went southward to the old Custer trail, which was being used by the cowmen at that time. We did not stop at noon time, but kept on our way, intending to make a short drive and camp where the grass had not been eaten off by the trail herds, and where there was a supply of water for our stock. About four o'clock in the afternoon we found a satisfactory location and went into camp. We turned the horses loose to graze. They needed it, as they had been living on rather short rations since we had started on our jaunt. For ourselves, we built a fire of cow-chips and made out a supper on bacon and flapjacks. This done, we looked over our outfit and made what repairs were necessary for the next day's drive. Everything being attended to, as security demanded, we turned in for the night, intending to make a permanent location the next day. As this was my first night in the territory, I must say that I felt very lonesome. It was a fine moonlight night, and the stars seemed to flicker and dance for my special benefit. I could see the handiwork of the Great Creator all over the firmament as far as the eye could reach, and my admiration for the beauty of the planetary system was unbounded. When I arose in the morning and threw the saddle on my old favourite pony, Jimmie, to get an idea of the lay of the land, things seemed to look different. When I had returned to camp after my survey of the neighbourhood, I had come to the conclusion from the general appearance of the country and the great contrast with what I had viewed from my bed at the wagon, that some Spirit of Evil had been brooding over things in general, and while in that mood had laid the country round about in waste, and Nature was doing her best to restore it to its primitive beauty. We travelled that day until we discovered what we considered an ideal spot to locate our store. It was not far from the trail, and there was plenty of good grass and water for our stock. We set to work to arrange things for our purpose, and it was not long before we had things in shape to do business. Our tent-store was, fortunately, placed about half a mile from where the cowmen used to halt and bed down their herds for the night. The presence of those men served the purpose of breaking the monotony of our surroundings, for it was a pleasure to hear them singing as they rode around their herds at night to render them quiet and keep them from drifting off during the night. Not only did they help to pass away the time for us, but it gave us an opportunity to do a little business also.

When we had located and arranged things to our satisfaction, we spent some time riding around looking over the situation and conjecturing the prospects. We found very few range cattle in our vicinity, which I afterwards learned was due to the fact that the ranchers kept their cattle away from the trail so that they would not become mixed with those on the drive, or become infected with the Texas or splenic fever. For the purpose of effecting this, they maintained men along the trail to turn back any range cattle that showed a tendency to wander in the direction of the through herds. During our ride we killed a brace of wild turkeys, and this gave us a welcome change from the monotony of rusty bacon.

Things did not look very prosperous as yet, and began to think that I had made my journey to no purpose, and would likely have to haul my load back to Kansas again. While in this frame of mind, and not being very cheerful over it, sitting in the shade of my tent, a man rode up to my emporium of commerce. We passed the usual salutations and had a chat. In the midst of our conversation he informed me that he had met a man who would likely purchase some of my wares. I could hardly realize the gist of his remark, as it was such a surprise, although I was there for the purpose of selling goods. I managed to recover from the shock with considerable alacrity, and invited him into my tent. He looked over my stock of goods, and before he left me he had purchased more than half of it, and gave in payment an order on Wright & Beverly. He said that his herd would be along in the evening, and he would have the grub wagon load up the purchases.

That evening the herd came along, and as the place was the bedding ground for the through herds, they made the necessary preparations for putting in the night. When the cowpunchers had eaten supper, they came over to our tent to purchase supplies of tobacco and cartridges. As there was nothing else to do, and as we had been getting rather lonesome in our retired place, we spent the evening agreeably, spinning yarns, relating experiences of the trail, etc. In the meantime the grub wagon arrived and was loaded with the goods purchased earlier in the day. Before bidding us goodnight, the boys invited us to take breakfast with them on the following morning. We accepted, and shortly after daybreak we heard the cook's cheerful announcement that "chuckaway" was ready. As the wagon was near our tent we did not have far to go, and before we reached it all hands were up and dressed and ready for the morning repast. We were somewhat surprised to find that the cook had fried salt bacon for the boys. In explanation of this he said that they were tired of fresh meat. We were weary of salt bacon, but good manners forbade our saying so, and we did our share with as much gusto as possible. A little fresh beef would have been much to our liking just then. By the time breakfast was over, the horse wrangler had arrived with the saddle stock. Ropes were stretched, one from the front wheel and one from the rear wheel of the wagon, and the horses driven in between them, where each man roped his mount for the day. The cook and the wrangler then attended to their own wants. After covering the camp-fires with soil to prevent the fire from spreading over the prairie, they were ready to set out on their long jaunt to Montana, or some other feeding ground. We bade the boys goodbye and returned to our store to await new arrivals.

As the business of the preceding day had been more than I expected from the general survey of things when I first arrived, I soon saw that if I had another customer of the same dimensions of the first one, I would have very little with which to do business. I determined to send Bill to Dodge City for another load of provisions. I made out a list of what I wanted, greased the wagon and started him off. Under favourable conditions, he should make the trip in about eight or ten days, but if the roads became bad, it would require a much longer time. Before he left I had him make a good store of biscuits for me, as I was not able to turn out an article of the kind that would coincide with the digestive powers of any human being. I gave him strict orders, among the other things, not to forget to bring something to read, as there was nothing at hand for that purpose except a Patent Medicine pamphlet, and I had read that so often and so thoroughly that I had some of the symptoms of seven different maladies that were therein pronounced fatal. If I had been in the neighbourhood of a drug store at the time I should have bought a supply of the cure-all regardless of results. Living as I was at the time, alone, I escaped the consequences of both the cure-all and the diseases mentioned in the pamphlet. When Bill was well on his way, I meandered around into the tent and out again, down to the creek and back again; in fact, I was just like a stray colt, did not know where to go, nor what to do. I soon discovered what my malady was. It was lonesomeness in its direst form. It settled on me like a fog settling over a marsh. It penetrated my very being. Everywhere I went I could feel it. Whatever I saw seemed tinged with it. I tried drinking strong coffee to drive it out, but that was no avail, so I saddled old Jimmie and took a ride over the prairie. On my way back to camp I killed a wild gobbler, thus providing myself with fresh meat. The cleaning and cooking of my prize relieved the monotony a trifle. I don't know whether I cooked him according to the recipe in the latest cook book published, but in any case he tasted fine. My pony seemed to realize how lonely I was, for whenever I went out of my tent he endeavoured to come to me, and strained at his rope to approach as near as possible. I went over to him and he put his head on my shoulder and seemed to say, "It's all right, Dennis, Bill will be back in a few days and then you will have company. In the meantime I shall try to keep you from becoming too lonesome." Needless to say, I put in considerable time with old Jimmie, currying him and fixing his water and feed in the best manner possible. I loved old Jimmie, for he was my friend. I knew not at what hour, nor what moment, my life would depend on his fidelity, and I knew that I could rely upon him to the last breath.

One day followed another without any perceptible difference between one and the other. In my surroundings I lost track of the time. I was longing for the return of my partner, and continued to picture the progress of his journey, where he was, what he was doing, etc. I felt like Robinson Crusoe, and in some respects his plight was more endurable than mine. He declared himself the monarch of all he surveyed, and his right there was none to dispute. Not so would he have issued his declaration if he were living in the territory at the time, as his right would likely be disputed by the first man that came along, and as for there being a monarchy at the time, it was not thinkable, at least under the conditions in which I was living.

That was a time when every man was supposed to remain silent about what he had heard, and have very little to say about what he saw. Horse stealing had become quite an industry at the time, and was carried on by bands of outlaws between Arkansas, Missouri and Colorado. As there was no telephone, telegraph or mail facilities, they were comparatively free from detection, especially as they travelled through the most unfrequented parts of the country. Their route brought them through the section where I was camped. One day I saw five of them coming in my direction, attracted by the sight of my tent. When they arrived where I was sitting, I invited them to dismount and come into my tent. They did so. They inquired if I had any tobacco, and I told them that was one of the commodities I was dealing in at the time. As that was all they wanted, they bought several pounds and then prepared to depart. I invited them to remain to dinner and they accepted the invitation. When they had consented to be my guests, I told them I had everything to make a first-class meal, but was short on biscuits, and could not make them as I did not know how, and I said I would be pleased if one of them would make them. One of them remarked, "Now, Jack, there is a job for you." I pulled out a sack of flour, a can of baking powder, gave one of them the coffee mill to grind some coffee, took a bucket and started for the creek for a pail of fresh water. The rest of them busied themselves building a fire of cowchips, and things began to take on the appearance of home. When Jack had his biscuits ready, I brought out my select assortment of tin-ware, passed around plates, knives, forks and whatever else was necessary, and we all set to work with a gusto. The gobbler, biscuits and other edibles did not last long, as each of us seemed to have a first-class appetite. While eating and joking at the same time, I told them of the reason of my asking them to remain for dinner, namely, that I was out of biscuits and that I was tired of living on crackers, and I knew there would be some one in the crowd who would be able to make them. I saw, besides, that their horses were jaded, and told them they might as well remain for a time to rest their stock. In all my joking and talking with them I took particular care not to ask them whence they came, nor whither they were going, nor what their business was in that part of the country, as that would be the height of impropriety. After we had chatted for a considerable time, they took the saddles off their horses, picketed one or two, and turned the others loose to graze. My loneliness was fast disappearing as the result of companionship of my fellowmen, even if they were a gang of horse thieves, and as a result I began to feel better and things began to wear a different aspect. I recalled a statement made by someone that it was not good for man to be alone, and I found it true, and made a resolution that I would never be left alone again in the future.

That night I saddled up old Jimmie, and taking one of my visitors, went out in search of some wild turkeys. I had previously seen a flock in the neighbourhood, and had a fairly good idea of where they were roosting. As soon as the moon had come up we began looking around among the trees that grew along the bank of the creek, and to our great delight discovered a few. We secured two of them and returned to camp. Next morning, Jack, who had been delegated to cook for us during his visit, was up and had the game dressed in the most approved fashion, and had also turned out a new supply of biscuits. When I rolled out of my blanket, I discovered that my company was made up of early and energetic risers, and I was delighted to know that the cook had done so well, and showed my appreciation later. The rest of the group had gone off in search of their stock, and were then returning. Breakfast was ready by that time, and we all set to without much preliminary apology for poor appetites, for we had good ones. The service was rather plain; a tomato can served the purpose of a sugar bowl, a sardine can for a salt cellar, and other utensils were provided in the same manner. During the meal one of the boys asked me which was the best way, through No Man's Land to Colorado. I divined immediately that they were horse thieves, for I had only a suspicion of it before. I gave him some kind of an answer, and I do not know whether it proved satisfactory to them or not. Breakfast being attended to and the dishes washed and put away, they made preparations for departure. They thanked me for my kindness and assured me that they would be glad to meet me at any time or place. When they had gone I began to feel the loss of company again, but I also began to realize the danger I had encountered owing to their brief stay, for if a posse of officers had happened along while they were my guests, it would have been hard for me to explain my compromising position. As it is usually the innocent bystander that gets hurt, I suppose I should have been the one to suffer, as there would have been some very warm work for a while. There was one thing impressed itself on my mind very much during the stay of my visitors, and that was the absence of vulgar or profane language. That went to prove that they had had good training by good parents who would have been proud of their personality, though they could not approve of their occupation.

When they had gone over the hill on their way, I thought I would improve my time by writing a few letters. I improvised a table for the purpose by bringing into service a cracker-box. The remainder of my office fixtures were in keeping with my desk. However, I was not ashamed of my surroundings, and sat down to write with all the dignity of an Indian chief sitting in council. It dawned upon me suddenly that it might be weeks before I would have an opportunity to post them, and as I was doing it to ward off another attack of lonesomeness, I decided that a good walk over the surrounding neighbourhood would serve the purpose as well. In my travels I discovered a cloud of dust rising on the horizon, and came to the conclusion that there was another herd coming along the trail, and it would only be a matter of a few hours before they would arrive at the regular halting place. I returned to camp and made out a lunch from the remnants of the breakfast, and then saddled old Jimmie and set out to meet the oncoming herd. I wanted to get acquainted with them as much as circumstances would permit, find out if they had any lame cattle they thought would be unable to make the journey to Dakota, Montana, or wherever they were going, and what would be the possibilities of a trade. If they would not ask too much I felt that I could make a little money by doctoring them myself and disposing of them afterward. When I came up to the cowmen they seemed to look at me with suspicion, as they did not expect to find a white man in that section of the country. When I explained to the foreman the nature of my business in that part of the territory, he seemed very much pleased to meet me, and to know that I was selling goods that he needed, as he had not had a chew of tobacco since he had left the Red River, nor lard enough to grease a skillet. I looked over the herd and made an estimate of the number of lame cattle they had. I rode back to my camp thinking over the situation, and when they arrived later I figured up what I was willing to pay for the lame and footsore cattle they had in the group. As soon as they arrived, the foreman rode over to my tent to look at the goods I had in stock. He purchased about what I had remaining after the previous sale. While talking on things in general he remarked that he would have to remain where he was for a day or so in order to let the stock rest, as he had driven them rather rapidly owing to the fact that the Comanches were troublesome to him while he was passing through their reservation, and he had to hasten along in order to get away from them. That determination to rest was as pleasing to me as it was to the cowpunchers, and the cattle showed it was agreeable to them, as they looked exhausted, which was inevitable after a long and furious drive. I sauntered over to where the cowboys were gathered around the grub wagon, and soon was on friendly terms with them as far as short acquaintance would permit. I heard the cook complaining about the dog, saying he would have to get rid of him as he was always nosing into everything, and had become a nuisance. I told him that I would gladly take him for the sake of his company, and he was handed over to me. I did not know that I was adding to my misfortunes or afflictions when I received him, though I might have suspected it from the ease with which the cook parted with him.

Next morning found me riding around the herd in company with the foreman, looking over the lame cattle, or drags, as they called them. I examined them very carefully, and made a dicker for about fifteen head. He agreed to have his men help me rope and brand them, to cross out the road brand, and also hobble them and help me doctor their sore feet. We built a fire to heat the branding irons, and soon everything was ready for the operation. I placed my brand upon them, a ladder on the left side and a crop off the left ear. While the irons were hot, I cauterized their sore feet, and applying tar and turpentine, wrapped them up in gunny sacks and turned them away from the herd to graze along the creek. Many hands make light work, and we were through with our task before noon. To complete the transaction, the foreman wrote out a bill of sale for me, giving a general description of the cattle and the road brands, signed it in the presence of witnesses, and turned it over to me to secure me against all claims for the stock I had purchased. This being done, I wrote out a check for him, and the sale was complete. I began to feel as though I were somewhat of a cowman myself when I looked down toward the creek to where my stock was grazing. I soon found out that I had much to learn.

A Bill of Sale was necessary in a cow country, and it was my only protection against the claim of some other cowman who might assert that the stock had broken away from his herd in a storm, and might say that I had caught and branded them. If the case were so, I might not only have the cattle taken away from me, but I would be lucky if they did not treat me as a cattle thief. But with the Bill of Sale safely tucked away in the safety deposit vault, which in this case was a cracker box, I felt easy about the matter.

Our business being completed, we sat around chatting and narrating experiences on the plains. Even this palled on us after a time, and one of the boys, in order to relieve the tedium of the delay, proposed a horse race. That suggestion seemed to please them generally. The proposal was greeted with enthusiasm, but it was a difficult matter to arrange the proper distance, or the amount of the wager. I was asked if I would care to take part in the race, and I replied that I could not say until I had seen who and what I was to compete with. That morning I had noticed on my trip around the herd that their horses seemed pretty well jaded from their long trip from San Antonio to the north side of the territory, and did not seem equal to a very long race. Just then one of the boys came up with a bunch of horses, and one of them was roped. They began to saddle him and one of the boys asked, "Are you going to run old Pinkeye? If you are, I am willing to bet a dollar on him if Slim Jim rides him." The boys continued to parley about what they would and would not do, and finally they asked me to match my horse against Pinkeye with Slim Jim for rider. I consented to make the match if we could arrange the preliminaries. I said I would ride a half mile or a quarter mile dash, whichever they preferred. They asked me who would ride my horse, and I remarked that I thought I would perform that duty myself. A knowing look and an incipient smile lighted up their countenances when I volunteered my information. One of the wise ones asked me where I came from, and I told him Maidstone Cross, Canada. Right there he set me down for a tenderfoot, and was out to have some sport with me. As far as they were concerned the race was as good as won, and all that remained was the shouting. Of course, we should have to go through the formality of a race, but that was of minor importance as far as the wager was concerned. If ignorance is bliss, they had a right to be supremely happy. They did not know that my pony, Old Jimmie, had not missed a feed of grain during the past six months, and likewise they were not aware of the fact that I had handled horses all my life and had spent the preceding four years on the plains. Yes, Jimmie was the dark horse of the race, as he was in prime condition, and had just enough exercise for the past few weeks to keep him in splendid shape. Of course the race looked bad for me, as I weighed two hundred pounds and Slim about one hundred and thirty. The odds seemed so much in favour of Slim, that I demanded twenty-five yards start for a quarter of a mile race, and I wagered a side of bacon against a three-year-old steer. We finally compromised the matter by my being allowed twenty yards start, and the bet to remain as it was. I saddled up Old Jimmie and we then made the necessary measurements, starting point, etc., in proper form. The signal for starting was to be a shot from the foreman's gun. The crowd would decide the winner, as they were to congregate at the winning post. We drew up to the mark and announced that all was ready. The gun flashed and we were off. When about half the distance was traversed, I looked back and discovered that Pinkeye was not making as good a run as I expected, so I slackened my pace a trifle and crossed the line a winner by about five yards, which would show that Jim and Pinkeye had gained about fifteen yards in the struggle. Then the air was rent with shouts and whoops for the victor. Roars of laughter followed one another at Jim's discomfiture, and he came in for some real joshing. "Oh, shucks! Jim, you can't ride and Pinkeye can't run fast enough to catch a *milch* cow. Next time you ought to race with a bull train."

After the first round of excitement and merriment had subsided, they proposed another race for the same wager. They wanted to make it an even start, but I would not agree to that, but they finally consented to give me ten yards start. Back we went to try it over again. By this time Old Jimmie began to do some fancy sidestepping and prancing, just to show that he had imbibed enough of the spirit of the race to make him feel good, and I was satisfied that he was in better fettle than at the opening of the first heat. The foreman called, "All ready," fired his gun and away we went again, Slim Jim pouring the rawhide into Pinkeye. This time I did not hold back, especially as I heard Jim urging his pony by words and quirt, but I had no fears about the outcome, as Old Jimmie would not permit anything to pass him as long as he was able to throw a hoof forward. When we reached the line, we were in about the same relative positions as when we started. He had not gained a yard on Jimmie. The usual whooping and yelling took place again. As it was getting late, I thought it best to get my two steers, brand and hobble them and put them with the rest of the little bunch I had bought earlier in the day. The boys good-humouredly branded them and the foreman wrote out another Bill of Sale which I tucked away with the other. As there was nothing else to do after the racing was over, I took a couple of the boys and we went out and brought in a few wild turkeys which the cook dressed and cooked for the evening meal. The rest of the evening we spent in chatting about life on the trail.

Next morning they set out on their long drive to Montana. I rode with them a few miles, bade them farewell, and returned to my duties at the camp. When I reached my tent, I found that the old dog, Nero, had declared himself dictator, and positively refused to let me enter. I could hardly blame him, as there had been so many around since I acquired possession of him that he could not figure out to whom he belonged. I went to my saddle and took down my lariat rope and gave him a liberal application of it, and established order once more on the premises. To rehabilitate myself in his affection I brought him out a good meal of bread and cold turkey. With nothing else at hand to require my attention at the tent, I rode down to where my herd was feeding to see if any of them had wandered off. They were all there and I felt satisfied.

On my arrival at the camp on my return, I found a man sitting on his horse awaiting my coming. He introduced himself as a line-rider of the Y. L. ranch. I invited him to come in and make himself at home. He gave me his name as Jack Jernigan, and said that he had been an employee of the ranch for some time. I asked him to remain for dinner and he accepted the invitation. I apologized for my inability to make bread. He assured me that I need not apologize as he would attend to that part of the matter if I would attend to the business of making a fire and getting the coffee prepared. His visit was a welcome one as it dispelled an idea that was forcing itself on me that I was likely to be alone for some time. His visit was short, but as he lived in the neighbourhood, he promised to come frequently to see me, and he lived up to his promise, frequently bringing turkey or venison with him as a proof of his marksmanship and thoughtfulness of me in my lonesome condition. In this way our friendship was cemented. When my visitor left me, I often experienced touches of lonesomeness that not even the presence of Nero could abate. Instead of being companion and comfort to me, he was just the reverse. He spent his days chasing rabbits, and made the nights hideous with the howls he emitted in answer to the call of the denizens of the wild. One night as I felt very tired from a long jaunt I had taken, I decided as there was no business to attend to, that I would have a good night's rest. I spread my blankets and settled down to slumber. I had turned the dog loose to take a run at leisure over the plain. I was just dozing off into slumberland when I heard a noise approaching. I could not distinguish what it was. It sounded like a cross between a fog-horn and a calliope. Before I could get dressed, in fact, before I got my hat on, Nero came tearing over the plain like a miniature cyclone. He rushed up to me and got between my legs for protection. I grabbed my six-shooter and went on a tour of investigation. I had hardly gone a hundred yards when I heard a coyote, and there never crossed the Atlantic a bagpiper who could emit such a variety of sounds as that coyote worked out of his system. He had been the cause of my dog's commotion. I returned to the tent for my Winchester, hoping to get a shot at him, but it was of no use, he had gone away. One thing I discovered in my midnight ramble was the fact that a mother skunk had moved into the neighbourhood with her whole family. There is one thing that a cowman dreads very much and that is the bite of a skunk. I knew personally two cases where men had died of hydrophobia after being bitten by the malodorous brutes. In my state of mind, sleep was out of the question until I had destroyed or driven away the newcomers. When I reached the neighbourhood of the late arrivals, I walked very cautiously, as a skunk is constructed very much on the principal of a "Queen Anne" musket, there was danger at either end, but it was hard to determine which end had the greater executionary power. As there was very little moonlight, I could not get a very good aim at them. When I thought I had located them properly I began to blaze away with my Winchester, and kept up the fusillade until the chamber of the gun was empty. Next morning I was delighted to find that I had killed four of my unsavoury visitors, and at the same time felt proud of my marksmanship in the dark. However, I had little rest during the night as I was not sure of my shots, and I did not like to take risks with them, so I spent the remainder of the night soliloquizing on things in general and nothing in particular. During my vigil I heard the wheels of a wagon rumbling along the trail and I knew it was Bill returning with more goods. I built a fire and made some coffee for him as I knew he must be tired after his long journey. After arranging matters in a sufficiently satisfactory manner for the rest of the night, we sat and talked over our experiences since we parted. We spent an hour or so in this manner and then turned in for a good solid sleep. Morning came and we put things in shape for business and awaited our next customer. We went down to the creek to take a look at the stock, and it was well we did so as some of them needed such medical attention as we could give them. As Bill had brought some books and papers, I felt much relieved. I discovered that, on consulting the almanac, we had done our horse racing and trading on Sunday. However, as I was in complete ignorance of the day, I hope it will not be held against me.

It may be of interest to the reader to know that the Comanche Indians and Texans had not been very friendly since Texas had gained her independence from Mexico. The Comanches claimed that the Texans had been stealing their horses, and also their cattle, and the Texans put in a counter claim of the same nature, and in addition to the stock the Indians were said to have taken, they kidnapped their children whenever an opportunity presented itself. As a proof that there was some truth in the statement of the Texans, I will say that Quanah Parker, the late chief of the Comanches was the son of a white mother who had been kidnapped when a child from a Texan family. He was a good chief and held in high repute by the whites as well as by the members of his own tribe. The result of the habit of carrying off the white children may be seen in the features of many of the tribesmen today. The unfriendly feeling caused by those savage incursions exists today, and will continue to do so for ages to come. It is true they do a little business with each other, but a close observer can readily see that it would take a very small spark to set the flames of hatred and vengeance aglow once more. The Texans in driving their cattle northwards were compelled to pass through the Comanche country, and the Comanche had advanced far enough in the white man's ways to levy tribute from them. It was not long after a herd had passed the Red River until an Indian, or perhaps several of them, made a visit to the cowmen and demanded *wohaw*, or in other words, beef. That meant the delivering over of one or more steers. The Texan understood the situation well enough to make no refusal to demand. If he failed to comply with the demand, that night, the same Indian would likely appear among the herd in the guise of a gray wolf, or a cougar, and stampede the herd. Such a movement, would cost more than the price of a brace of steers, as it would take days to collect the cattle once they scattered, and some of the stock they might never see again. Without much parley they turned over the stock to them and the Indian went on his way rejoicing. The first demand did not always settle the difficulty, as they were likely to appear again in a day or so and demand more. Such a course of proceedings was very expensive and aggravating to the cowmen, and as a consequence they pushed on as rapidly as possible to get away from the dark shadow of the trail, and get over into Chickasaw, or Caddo country to avoid further trouble. By the time they arrived at the Cherokee Strip, where I was located, they had several lame, or sorefooted cattle which they were willing to dispose of at a very reduced price.

As I was the only man on the ground who would take them off their hands, I came into possession of several head of cattle. After a few weeks rest and some surgical attention, they would again be in good condition and ready to forward to the market. Usually I sent them to my ranch in Kansas where I kept them until I could dispose of them to good advantage.

A few days after Bill's return, another herd happened along and I did considerable business with them, selling what goods they needed, and buying several head of injured cattle which I tended to in the customary manner. It happened that they had an extra man with them and I hired him. I put him on the wagon and sent him after more supplies. I kept Bill with me as I was determined not to remain alone in that locality. When the herd had gone forward on the drive, we went out to look after our own stock, and found them as well as could be expected. Shortly after our return to camp, we saw a horseman coming towards us, and I concluded we were going to have some more company. When he rode up, I invited him to dismount, as that was the custom of the country. He thanked me, but declined, saying that he was in a hurry, that he had had some trouble with the Comanche Indians, in which there was some shooting done, that he would like to get a fresh horse to push on his way. I saw that he was pretty well upholstered in the matter of armament, as he had two six-shooters in his belt and a Winchester in his scabbard and looked, as though he would be able to protect himself. I asked him no questions as the condition of his horse told the story as plainly as any words he might use. The spur marks on the pony's sides showed that his vitality was about expended and that he would not be able to go much farther. When he asked if I could supply him with a new mount, I told him I could furnish one. I asked Bill to change his saddle for him, and gave him some directions to guide him towards a cow ranch. He proposed leaving his horse with me as a guaranty that he would return mine to me. I told him that was out of the question, that if the Comanches came along and found his horse with me they would conclude that I had hidden him somewhere, which would mean trouble for me, a thing I did not want just then, especially with the Indians. I told him to take his pony along with him and if he could not keep up with the fresh one, to turn him loose upon the prairie and some cow-puncher would take him in and care for him until called for. He put a *hackamaw* on his jaded steed, mounted his fresh pony and made ready to start. I told him not to spare the quirt, as the horse could stand a good dash, and that he would be at the ranch in a little over an hour if he rode steadily. He was off in the direction I gave him, and Bill and I set in to make a checker board to while away our idle hours. Something shortly afterward attracted our attention, and on looking up we beheld three Comanche Indians riding towards our tent, with their rifles across their saddles, which meant business. I spoke to Bill and he stepped into the tent and buckled on a pair of six-shooters. I happened to have my Winchester near at hand. When they rode up close enough for us to see plainly what they were doing, they stopped and began to make signs. I could not understand the Comanche sign language, so they had to resort to some other means of communication. They drew closer and one of them said 'How,' the second one grunted something and the third remained silent. Bill and I went on making our checker board apparently oblivious of their presence, but all the while I kept my eye on the rifle with an occasional glance out of the corner of my eye at the Indians. Finally one of them spoke in broken English and asked if a white man had been there. I told them a white man had stopped for a short time, but went north, and I pointed out the trail. After they had sat in silence for some time, they wheeled their ponies around and galloped off. It would not take much of a genius to see that their visit was not a friendly one, and that they were looking for trouble, and particularly wanted to see a certain white man that had passed that way shortly before. If they could not find the object of their desires, they would likely make some trouble for some innocent party. As they saw that Bill and I were pretty well furnished with fire arms, they thought it better to pursue the object of the search. I knew that, by this time, the pursued was beyond the reach of the pursuers and was likely safe among the cowboys of some neighbouring ranch, where the Indian would not follow him. The Indian had a wholesome respect for cow-ranches and did not care to go prowling around that locality, for at that particular time the cowman had lost all respect for the Indian's feelings. As we did not know at what time they would return, if they ever did, nor did we know what humour they would be in, though we could give a shrewd guess, Bill and I thought it better to make what efforts were necessary to protect ourselves and our stock in the event of their returning with designs, upon us, or our cattle. We took our blankets and guns and spent the night on the prairie near our horses. During the vigil we were keeping we heard some horsemen passing and concluded the Indians were returning from their white-man hunt.

Next forenoon a line rider came over to see us, bringing with him the horse we had loaned the visitor who was in such a hurry. He said that he had seen nothing of the Indians at the ranch. He said that the fugitive horseman had received a new mount at his ranch and had gone on his way, but did not fail to send back his compliments saying that he was grateful for the kindness we had shown him and hoped some day to be able to repay it.

That afternoon, the herd, from which the fugitive above mentioned had taken his departure, arrived in our neighbourhood, and from the boys of the outfit I learned the particulars of the whole occurrence. The foreman gave me all the information in the case, and I shall detail it here. He said that the Indians had met them over in the Comanche country and had made their usual demand for *wohaw*. As he had given one steer already down in the Red River district, he did not feel obliged to yield to their demands for a second contribution. In order to get rid of them, and at the same time to make a peace-offering he said he would let them have another. That did not satisfy the Indians and they started for the herd to cut out what they wanted. That was the thing that brought matters to a focus. They might have known that their presence in the herd would cause a stampede. When they persisted in doing so in spite of the warning to desist, then came the signal for the disturbance which followed.

The first steer they cut out from the herd was met and driven back by a young fellow by the name of McRay. An Indian tried to prevent his driving the steer back to the herd. That spelled disaster for the Indian, for the young fellow drew his forty-five and shot the Indian off his pony. All was confusion for a brief space, but no more shooting took place. The Indians picked up their wounded comrade and bore him away as fast as they could, and then the herd moved on. McRay, acting on the advice of the foreman, sought safety in flight towards the north. That was the fugitive that came to my tent in search of a fresh pony. If he had remained with the herd, serious trouble would have resulted, and if they had caught him in his flight, he would likely have been scalped, if not subjected to other barbarities.

I am not going to say anything about the merits of the case as it stood, but will say that if the same conditions existed today, the same would occur again.

As on the arrival of the former herds, we made another bargain for some of the foot-sore cattle, and after doctoring them to the best of our ability, we turned them in with the rest of our stock.

We did considerable business with the foreman of the outfit. After getting what goods he wanted, he moved onward with his herd.

When they had gone, I saddled Old Jimmie and took a ride down to where our stock was feeding along the creek, to look them over and see if they needed any attention. They seemed in good condition, so I rode on, more for pastime than with any object in view. When I had passed a mile or so beyond where our herd was grazing peacefully, I saw something that I could not account for, and proceeded to make an investigation. As I drew nearer to the object of my curiosity I found an Indian sitting on the bank of the creek. I was rather surprised to see that he had no pony in sight, nor were there any other Indians in view. I approached him with the purpose of making a closer scrutiny of this lone denizen of the plains. His wardrobe consisted of a breechclout, a pair of moccasins, and three feathers in his hair. I rode up to him and saluted him with the customary Indian "How." He made no reply, did not give even a grunt of recognition. I studied him carefully for awhile. I noted that his hair was well braided and hung down his back, and was tipped with strips of Beaver fur. I rode on a short distance, and returned again to take another look at him. I addressed him as before, with the same result. He set me thinking very seriously as he had no fire-arms and no pony. I thought that, perhaps, he might be one of the three that had visited me the day they chased the cowboy.

When I returned to camp I found a visitor, a line-rider. I explained to him and Bill what I had seen, and the line-rider volunteered the explanation that the Indian was a runner, or what one would call a mail-carrier and was likely carrying some message to the Caddos, perhaps, an invitation to a green corn dance, or some other festivity. His appearance there had no further significance, so I let the matter drop. In the meantime, Bill was busying himself cooking some venison the cowboy had killed, getting ready for our next repast, which was about due. While waiting for Bill to put the finishing touches on his work of art, we amused ourselves with a game of checkers. When luncheon was ready we abandoned the checker board with alacrity and threw ourselves very earnestly into the work of demolishing what Bill had taken so much care to prepare.

A strong friendship had sprung up between Bill and Nero. It was very much like the story of Mary and her little lamb, wherever Bill went, there was Nero at his heels. Such devotion was very touching, but in Bill's case it was almost too touching for it nearly cost him his life. As my partner was not much given to riding horseback, any more than he could help, he used to divert himself by taking a stroll over the prairie, and of course, the dog was at his heels. It amused Bill to see the dog chasing jack rabbits, or diving at prairie dogs, but both species seemed to have an uncanny way of avoiding his onslaughts. He never caught any of them. One day as he was tearing around after a rabbit, a herd of wild cattle came over the brow of the hill. The dog was heading for them straight as an arrow; barking and cavorting in a fashion wonderful to see. Any man who has had any experience with wild cattle will know what danger my friend and partner encountered at that point. Wild cattle are curious, and when they see a man afoot, they begin to investigate immediately, and therein lies the danger. If anything were to excite them at the moment they would trample him to death. That was just about what was due to happen to Bill as the dog had excited them and they were coming toward the man afoot. The idea of self-preservation struck Nero about the same time as the cattle began to move toward Bill, and he rushed to his master to save him. The cowboys added to the pandemonium already turned loose, by trying to shoot Nero. I always kept a horse saddled at the camp for an emergency, and when I heard the commotion, I mounted and set out at full gallop to the scene of action. I was just in time, for there was Bill hitting only the high places in his flight for safety. I met him and he needed no invitation to mount behind me, but caught the horn of the saddle and swung himself up with alacrity and away we went at top speed. The danger was not entirely passed, for there right behind us was Nero, the cause of a great part of the trouble. Bill pulled his gun and shot the dog. That itself seemed to check the herd, but we had a narrow escape. One stumble of the horse, and we would both have been trampled into such small pieces that there would be left only a damp spot on the ground where we had fallen. However, we were safe and that was the chief thing for us. We saddled our ponies and went to help the cowboys round up the herd that had become scattered through the playful antics of Nero. As it was time to eat when we had got the cattle back on the trail and quieted down, we joined the cowmen in their meal. There was considerable joking and laughing over our predicament, but they said not one word about the danger we encountered in our flight before the stampede.

As this was an opportunity for us to do business again, we took advantage of it. Bill bought some of the footsore stock, and I sold them provisions to last them until they could find a more convenient market.

When the outfit had gone northwards, things began to assume the monotonous routine of dull times. We did the best we could to entertain ourselves with checkers and talking over prospects, but it was not very exciting at best. From a business point of view it seemed a success, and we thought it advisable to establish ourselves in a dugout and make a lengthy stay of it. The prospects were good, the success of the past argued well for the future, but *"The best laid plans of mice and men gang aft aglee."*

Next morning I rode down to take a look at our growing herd and had not gone very far when I found that one of my cattle had been killed. I dismounted to examine the carcass more closely and found evidence that the cow had been killed by some wild animal. I could not say what animal had killed her as the manner of attack was entirely different from any I have ever seen. It was not a gray wolf, as I was familiar with their mode of destruction. I examined the ground and found the foot-prints of two animals, one large and one small. I followed their trail for some distance and found where they had been rolling in the sand after their feast. I endeavoured to follow it farther, but it was soon lost in the long buffalo grass, and I had to give up the task.

I returned to camp and reported the matter to my partner, and he said that he would fix things for them. He concluded that if he put strychnine in the carcass they had already killed, they would come again, and in that way he would rid us of the intruders. We applied the strychnine in the most approved fashion laid down by old hunters and trappers, but it was in vain. Next night they returned and killed another steer, but did not go near the one they had killed before. As we were looking over the result of the night's work, a line-rider came by, and we explained the situation to him. He said the mischief had been wrought by a cougar, or Mexican lion, and that it was useless to try to poison him as he would not eat anything in the nature of flesh except what had been freshly killed by himself. Furthermore, he said, they had been attracted by our cattle because, being footsore, they could not put up a fight to defend themselves, and thus fell an easy prey to the marauders. We saw at once that there was only one way out of the difficulty and that was to shoot the lions, as they seemed to wary to be taken by poison. If we did not take that course, we would soon be out of cattle. With that end in view we moved them up in the neighbourhood of our tent. We made a temporary corral for them, and awaited an opportunity to send a bullet into the expected visitor. He came as usual, but we did not get a shot at him, as he did not give us a chance. I wish to say that in all my experience I have never met, in Canada or in the west, another animal so cowardly and treacherous as the Mexican lion. I have known them to kill an animal not more than four rods from where I was sitting, and before I could reach the corral, he would be out of sight. I could not shoot towards the corral for fear of killing or crippling some of the stock. I have known them to kill a two-year-old steer, and by the time I could get there the cougar was gone, but the attack was so swift and sure that the poor beast would be still standing with his entrails hanging on the ground. That gives some idea of how short a time it takes a cougar to kill a cow. In spite of all his great strength, he is a great coward, as he will not face a man. I tried to rid myself of the pest that was thinning out my herd, and devoted a good deal of time in trying to find his den, to get a shot at him, but my efforts were to no purpose. I had to do the best I could, watch and wait, in the hope of success.

While engaged in the hunt for the cougar one afternoon, I saw, at some distance, a horse grazing along the creek. He had a saddle and bridle on him, but no rider. I thought he had run away from some outfit, and went down to where he was to secure him and bring him to my tent, so that the owner could call for him when he had time. Upon reaching the place where the pony was grazing, I saw a strange sight. There sat an Indian on a knoll, wearing a Navajo blanket, ear-rings that hung down like small sleigh bells, his hair plaited and hanging down his back, his head decorated with eagle feathers, all of which made me think I had met a very distinguished gentleman. As a neighbour I greeted him with the customary, "How." To my greeting he made no sign of recognition, did not even move a muscle. I rode past him for some distance and then returned on the opposite side of him, and then I discovered the cause of his sullen dignity. He had fastened to his blanket a small-sized pewter plate polished as bright as a new dollar fresh from the mint, and around the rim of it was inscribed the letters of the alphabet. I saw that he had left his rifle in the scabbard of his saddle, and if he made any move of a warlike nature, I could do a lot of business before he could get organized for battle. This condition made me bolder and encouraged me to make a more critical inspection of his wardrobe than I would have done if he had his Winchester near at hand. He wore a pair of moccasins highly ornamented with beads of all colours. Whether he had any under garments I was not in position to know, but he looked to be clothed in the highest degree of cool, calm, unruffled dignity. As I had seen no cartridge belt on the saddle, I was satisfied that he wore one around his waist, with the customary pair of six shooters for ornaments and use. As he remained stolid in his attitude towards me, I gave up any hope of finding out anything about him, and rode home. I related my experience to Bill, laughing over the dignity displayed by the Indian, based on the possession of a pewter breast-plate that once belonged to some white child, and which he had found on his meanderings over the plains.

After a quarter of a century has elapsed, and taking a retrospective view of the situation at that time, I can see what a trifle it would have taken to send one of us, if not both, over the Great Divide to the Happy Hunting Grounds.

Bill had been out in another direction in search of the cougar, but met with as little success as I had. It became a question of sitting up nights guarding the herd, with the hope of being able to get a shot at the cause of our misfortunes, but it was in vain. Every morning brought us evidence of further devastation wrought by the bloodthirsty brute. Things came to such a pass that we had to choose between losing the whole herd, or moving to Kansas, and we chose the latter.

Chapter 14

Returning to Kansas

Reluctantly we folded our tent and started off in the direction of the Sun-flower State, where our ranch was located. Business had been good and we were loath to leave such a good opportunity for increasing our profits, but the unseen enemy made further delay impossible. Our outfit on the trail did not present a very inviting appearance, but there was something substantial about it that cheered us considerable. We had increased our holdings during our sojourn in the territory, and were now returning with the fruits of our venture. Personally we were not much to look at, as we had not had a shave in several months, but that fact did not interfere with the happiness we felt at the prospect of seeing the old homestead once more. On the first night of our advance we camped in the brakes of the Cimarron River. We were fortunate in killing a deer, which provided us with a change of meat. It was the last wild game we expected to obtain, as the antelope and other wild game had been shot at so much that they had become gun-shy, and it was impossible to get within any close proximity to them to obtain a shot at one of them. The antelope in particular we did not expect to see, as that animal does not frequent the low lands, and the only time he is found there is when he is on the way to get water. Even then they seem to have on one guard at all times, so that at the sight of a man they are off like a shot and soon out of sight. Antelopes and wild horses are very much alike in their habits, as neither will enter a creek or a canyon except for water or shelter.

Next morning found us up and away. As the travelling was

down grade, we got along nicely. We were very much pleased on reaching the river to find that the sand was packed down owing to the numbers of cattle that had forded the stream during the preceding weeks, and we were able to cross without much difficulty. Having crossed the stream we pulled our outfit into Clem's ranch, where we sold the greater part of our supplies for a fair price. With a lighter burden, we set out on our way again, leaving the supply trail, and moved in a north-westerly direction toward Meade Co., Kansas. Frequently we were compelled to cross what is called a sand-draw, but we managed to do this without much trouble, as by fastening our lariat ropes to the end of the wagon tongue and fixing the other end to the horn of the saddle we could assist the team in pulling through the canyon and reach the firm footing on the other side. Our route lay through the section about midway the Beverly cow-ranch on the South Sand Creek, and the place where Ashland, the county seat of Clarke County now stands. We crossed several small trails, but as they were running in another direction they could not be of any assistance to us. That evening we made a dry camp, but expected early next day to reach the head waters of Little Sand creek, or as it was afterwards called, Johns Creek, in time to water our stock. We went through the usual procedure of picketing the horses we were using, and hobbling the loose ones, and getting the cattle in shape for the night.

On my tour around the herd I found that there was a dug-out in the neighbourhood. I went on a visit of inspection to see if there was any one there, for there seemed to be some signs of improvement around it. I was agreeably surprised to find a solitary man walking around the dug-out, with his hands behind his back and his head bent as though deep in meditation. I decided to call on him and find out something about the topography of the country, also the distance to Crooked Creek, Kansas. I introduced myself and told him the purpose of my visit. Once the ice was broken, the conversation took several turns. From his remarks I gleaned that he had not been there very long, and was likewise anxious to sell out, in fact, he even seemed to insist that I should buy him out. I told him I was sorry that I could not take his offer, as I had some property of my own in Meade County and felt that was all the Kansas real estate I cared to handle just then.

During my interview I cast my eyes around the place to get a general view of my surroundings. I noted that he had placed four forks in the ground and roofed them over with hay and brush, the whole forming a sort of arbour to protect him from the sun and rain. About three feet from the ground he had fixed a scaffold for a bed. I was nonplussed at what I saw, and ventured to inquire the reason of the arbour-like structure. He replied that he was unable to sleep in the dug-out, for he had tried to do so, but found that it was impossible, owing to the number of tarantulas and centipedes that infested the place. The arbour was a partial solution of the difficulty, but did not quite meet all the demands of the situation. The fleas he could not escape, they were in his bedding, and he was unable to discover a means of putting them to flight. What he could not avoid, he had to endure. I could see at a glance that his opinion of farming in western Kansas was not very elevated. He was determined to sell out at the first opportunity that presented itself. As I had to return to camp to make arrangements for standing night guard over the herd to prevent their wandering off, I bade my new-found acquaintance farewell, wishing him all manner of good fortune in his new home. When I reached our outfit, I found that supper was ready, and we were ready for it. We attended to the duty of providing for the wants of the inner man with considerable alacrity, though our manner of doing so might have lacked some of the etiquette required by the rules and regulations of refined society. After a chat over things in general and prospects in particular, the boys rolled up in their blankets for the night, and I went on my solitary errand of looking after the herd. The stillness of the night was unbroken save by the hooting of an owl in the neighbouring canyon, or the barking of a coyote on a side hill. Even they would cease their clamour for a time and then the stillness of the night was appalling. I sat on my pony in meditation evolving thoughts and considerations induced by the calm of the surroundings in which I found myself. My reflections were interrupted by the musical notes of the lone settler, borne over the prairie on the wings of the night. He had a voice that was rich and melodious, though art had never tried to improve the natural gift. The first sweet tones that fell upon my ear were the strains of an old familiar strain I used to hear back home in Canada, and they never seemed sweeter than they did then. I listened entranced. A flood of memories came rushing from some long forgotten corner of my mind, and I sat entranced. I was in hopes that he would repeat the song again, but my hopes were not realized. Instead, he changed off into some old-time granger rhyme that had more philosophy than music in it. It might well be entitled *The Lament of a Kansas Granger*. I was glad when he was through it. Then he came back with one old and ever new, ever welcome and ever sweet, the song called *Home Sweet Home*. I do not believe that the effect produced by Jenny Lind, when she first rendered it could have been as great as that produced in my heart at that moment. The days of boyhood were returned again. I saw the old log house where I was born, and the surrounding forest. I saw my playmates on the green and took part once more in their merry games. Memories came rushing so fast that I could not analyze them in their kaleidoscopic passage through my brain. Half consciously I wiped away a tear that began to trickle down my cheek. The music ceased and I sat as one dazed; only to be rudely awakened by the resumption of the barking of the coyote near at hand. I looked across to where the settler had his home. The embers of his fire were burning low. He must have retired to his arbour for a rest. I could not then imagine why he had chosen that hour of the night to give vent to his feelings in the manner mentioned. It may have been out of the bitterness of a discouraged heart that he poured forth his soul in such harmony, but whatever it was, I must say that he had a very attentive listener in one lone horseman standing guard over a herd of weary cattle.

The hours of the night passed slowly. The silence of the tomb seemed to enfold everything in its mantel. I made my rounds to see that things were in proper condition, and then returned to camp to arouse my partner, Bill, to take up the burden of guarding the herd while I obtained some much needed sleep. It seemed to me that I had hardly lain down when I heard the cook calling to all hands, "Chuckaway," which, in the language of the civilized nations, means breakfast is ready. I awoke with the call, and found the sun streaming into my face. In the meantime Bill had come in from his tour of inspection, leaving the cattle grazing quietly. It did not take me long to arrange my toilet, a ceremony that the cowpuncher does not usually give much attention to, and I was soon in the midst of the bustle of getting my share of provender for the morning meal. We simply took the first articles of tableware that we happened to find convenient, seized upon the proper allowance of food, and then we sat down on the prairie and gave our undivided attention to the work at hand. As it was agreeable work, we devoted a lot of energy to it, and accomplished the task in a very brief time. This done, we made arrangements to set out again. We rounded up the stock that had wandered off while grazing, got the ponies together, loaded the wagon and were on our way once more.

Having given the boys the direction to follow, I set out to pay a farewell visit to the singer of the night, saying that I would overtake them before they had proceeded very far.

I reached his dug-out and found him up and around. After the usual salutations, I offered my thanks for the pleasure he had afforded me during the preceding night. He thanked me for the compliment, and said that the pleasure was mutual. He said it was a boon to him to have some one call on him, as his nearest neighbour was seven miles distant. Not only that, but there were difficulties about his neighbour coming to visit him as he had only a team of oxen to travel with, and they were not very well broken yet, and travel under such conditions was not very inviting. I saw from the tone of his remarks that he was disconsolate, or rather discouraged by his present condition in life, and I ventured to repeat the advice given by Horace Greeley to young men, namely, "to go west and grow up with the country." "Oh," said he, "that is all bosh. That man, Horace Greeley did not know the first 'jump in the road' of what he was talking about. When he came through this country, he was riding in a Pullman car, with lackeys and servants to wait upon him. He knew absolutely nothing of the real condition of this country and I am willing to bet that he would not take a thousand dollars and sleep one night in that dug-out of mine. He was a very smart man, well versed in politics, living in New York where he could sit in his parlour and look into his neighbour's house and see what the family had to eat. Such advice is sound enough in theory when delivered through the columns of the New York Tribune, or in the heat of some political campaign, to an audience composed of tenderfeet, but the same idea promulgated whilst leaning on a hoe handle, between two rows of sorghum, in western Kansas, would have a different effect. Horace Greeley was a very good citizen, but knew comparatively nothing of the trials and tribulations, privations and hardships, to say nothing of the lives it cost to move the boundary line of civilization one step farther west." Such were the sentiments of my philosophical friend, and they contained more truth than poetry. By this time the herd was almost out of sight, and I was forced to bid him good-bye, requesting him, at the same time, that if he were ever over in Meade County, to call on me, for there would be a welcome for him at all times and that he would always find the latch on the outside, that meant for him to walk right in and make himself at home. I left him, and as I was topping the crest of the hill I looked back and saw him sitting on the top of his dugout, waving farewell.

We did not delay for dinner, as we wanted to reach Little Sand Creek, where there was plenty of water. As this was to be our last night out, I can assure you that we did not lose any time along the way. We reached our camping ground about three in the afternoon. As we were only about eight miles from the home ranch, we turned everything loose, and laid ourselves out to have a general good time. The cook had been advertising his ability to make custard pie, and we thought this a convenient opportunity to put his ability to the test. Of course, he had to have milk, for there is no substitute for that article in a first-class custard pie. Being that Bill and I fairly doted on custard pie, it was our duty to provide the milk for the occasion. For the benefit of my readers, let me say that if you have a longing for custard pie, try to throttle it in infancy, or train it so as to render it subject to proper environment, but do not, at any cost, let that hankering exercise its influence on you when you have to invade the rights and privileges of a wild Texas cow,—unless you are prepared to fight to a finish. Bill and I felt equal to the occasion and set out to produce the required article. We chose a cow that seemed to have more milk than her calf required. Bill roped her, threw her down,— which was a cruel thing to do to a young mother—and hog-tied her. I was on hand with a can. I held her down while he was

Goodbye

endeavouring to separate her from her milk. With much labour and some verbal protests against her restlessness, he succeeded in extracting about a pint. I took the fruit of our labours and rope up to the camp and proudly gave it to the cook. He informed me that there was not enough for a first-class pie, and I had to enlist the services of Bill once more, to procure the required quantity. It took considerable wrangling with two more of those restless creatures to persuade them to favour us with some of their milk, but in the end we succeeded and returned to camp again. In the meantime the cook had uncovered some turkey eggs that he had found a day or so before, and set to work on his masterpiece—a custard pie. Needless to say, his production was up to the advertisement, and, also, to our expectations.

Our cook was a genius in his line of endeavour. It was a rare thing to meet a cowpuncher who could not turn out biscuits of some degree of edibility, but we had a master hand. When he turned over to the inspection of an outfit such an article of food they were light and fluffy, and when dipped in antelope gravy, one would have to have a case of indigestion in an alarming condition if he could not eat them with an appetite like a section hand. His manner of preparing the dinner table was simplicity itself. He used to spread out the wagon sheet for a table cloth, and use mother earth for the table. When everything was ready he called out "Chuckaway," and found us ready and willing to pay a compliment to his endeavours.

When we had demolished the supper, and particularly the custard pie, Bill went down to the creek to wash out a few shirts as he did not wish to return to the ranch with his clothing in an unpresentable condition. While he was gone the cook and I played checkers to see who would wash the dishes. I lost.

When the usual routine of camp life with the herd had been completed, we turned in to have one good rest to be ready for the final drive next day. As a reward to Old Jimmie for his fidelity I gave him an extra measure of grain and a few caresses to show that I remembered what he had done for me. Next morning found us about ready to start, when we met with an unavoidable delay, Bill's shirts were not dry and we could not go without him. We filled in our time picking up wood and filling the water bucket for future use. In due time Bill's lingerie was in a proper condition for use, and we were on our way once more.

We set out in a north-westerly direction. When we had gone about two miles we crossed the trail of the wood-haulers coming over from Meade county, for fire wood and fence posts, which they were compelled to collect from the vicinity of Sand Creek, or its tributaries. As the trail was nearly parallel to the direction we were going, we followed it slowly homewards. We halted our herd for the purpose of getting dinner, and to permit the cattle to graze or rest as they wished. We remained a couple of hours, knowing that we could make the home ranch by sundown. We set out for the final drive, moved along slowly, taking things easy as there was no need to hurry. About four o'clock, much to our surprise, it clouded up and a drizzle set in. It was the first rain we had seen in months, and we fairly enjoyed it. However, we put on our slickers to avoid too much of a good thing. It lasted only a short time and then the sun shone again. When the sun broke through the overhanging clouds a peculiar phenomenon presented itself to our view. Not more than two hundred yards in advance of the lead cattle was formed, as if by flash light, a small rainbow directly across the trail. It did not seem to be more than one hundred and fifty yards from side to side, and not more than half that distance in height to the arch overhead. I have seen cyclones, blizzards, and mirages, but I was totally unprepared for such a phenomenon as I then witnessed. I confess, if I had been alone, I would have ridden around it rather than pass through the archway. I could not give a scientific explanation of the affair, and luckily for me Bill did not ask for one, as he was one of those impulsive, unimaginative men who take things as they see them and inquire not into the causes that lead to their existence. Not so with the teamster, he was from Arkansaw, and was very superstitious. When he saw the wondrous arch stretched from side to side before him, he stopped the team until Bill shouted at him to go on and not be a fool. He got in motion with fear and trembling. The cattle seemed to realize that there was something strange about the affair and crowded through as though going through a gateway. When we had passed on for some distance I looked back, and the phenomenon was gone. I asked the teamster why he had stopped the team, and he gave me a characteristic reply, "Gosh, I was afraid it would fall on me. I heard a Sunday School teacher say once that the Lord was going to put up one of those things every once in a while to show that he was not going to destroy the earth by flood any more." "That's all right for western Kansas," said Bill, "but it does not apply to Arkansaw where they are drowned out every spring."

We reached our ranch by sundown, and turned the cattle loose to graze. We unsaddled our horses with a sigh of relief that the long trip into the territory was over. By the time we washed ourselves and combed the sand out of our whiskers, supper was ready and we sat down and placed our feet under a table for the first time in months.

CHAPTER 15

The Race for Land

In the spring of the year 1889, the president of the United States issued a proclamation that Oklahoma was opened for homestead settlement, the few Indians that had already settled there to be allowed to remain in undisturbed possession of their holdings. As the proclamation included but a small portion of the present state, the other little nations were left for future consideration.

The manner in which the homesteader secured his claim is unique in the annals of history. I do not believe that any other people under the sun ever acquired the right and title to a homestead in quite the same fashion as that employed to dole out to homeseekers the claims which they had acquired a right to by registering at the land office. I am under the impression that it is an institution peculiarly American. Whatever the merits of the system maybe, it produced results more or less beneficial, according as you look at it from the point of view of the homeseeker, or the grafter. For the benefit of posterity I shall set it down that they may see, at least, how it was done, and be able to judge of the merit of the means employed to insure the results intended.

On the day set aside for the opening of the new territory to homeseekers, all those who had filed on an allotment, were to take their position on a line marked for the purpose, just as the foot-racer toes the scratch awaiting the signal for the dash. Some had been there for some time, others came at the last moment. No one was permitted to invade the new territory until a signal was given and then they were to rush pell-mell to secure the claim they found to be the most in accordance with their wishes. It was a strange sight to behold them drawn up in every conceivable kind of vehicle, and those who had no vehicle were on horse back, mule back, or on foot. Anxiety was pictured on every countenance. Those who had waited longest had their patience tried to the limit. In order to insure every man a chance for an equal opportunity, a company of soldiers was drawn up to prevent any one taking any undue advantage of his neighbour. At least, they were supposed to do so, but under the cover of darkness during the night before, hundreds of persons known afterwards as "Sooners," crept through the line and hid themselves in some convenient ravine and remained there under cover until the signal was given next day. These men, as soon as the word was given to go, rushed out and staked a claim, and when the lawful owners appeared, they were ordered to move on, and the order was enforced at the end of a gun. The Sooner was not only in possession, but stood ready to defend his claim against all comers as he had witnesses to prove his statements about the pre-emption of the property and his prior right to the land in question.

On the day appointed for the start of the race, every one was in a fever of expectancy. The starter was eyed keenly in his every move to detect some indication of the signal about to be given. Horses heads were pushing over the line, the driver standing in his wagon ready to ply the whip to produce the required speed for the occasion, old ramshackle buggies were there whose very appearance signified that this was likely to be their last run. Even oxen with their necks bent beneath the weight of their bows, felt the fever of the excitement and were anxious to be off. Horsemen stood in the stirrups with a quirt ready, to make a dash across the rolling plains. As the hands of the watch crept toward twelve, one could notice a tightening of the jaws and a look of grim resolve come over the countenances of those participating in the race. Eagerly they looked for the signal, slowly the hands of the watch in the timekeepers hand moved on. The starter was seen to move hand to the pistol scabbard and draw his weapon. Up it rose slowly in the air and absolute silence prevailed. For one moment he held the gun aloft and then, "Bang" went the forty-five and the race was on. Yelling, whooping, swearing, off they dashed in their mad flight. Wagons rumbled and bounded over the uneven ground, whips were wielded with pitiless abandon; horses dashed in mad affright to gain the front of the wild careening mob; oxen tossing their wide-spreading horns, with lumbering gait, dragged their burden of a rattling wagon in their mad dash. All was confusion in the first mad plunge. Then slowly but surely the better mounted and better bred gradually drew away from their slower-footed competitors, and disappeared on the horizon. Naturally those in advance secured the better locations, excepting where the sooners had stealthily pre-empted some desirable location. With the slower ones, it was a case of take that was left and make the best of it. In case a man found himself dispossessed by a Sooner, there was only one recourse remaining and that was to buy him out at once, or go to court about the matter, and that was as hazardous as trying to drive him out, as the courts were largely operated on the kangaroo plan. The judge of today might be the criminal of tomorrow, and the criminal of today might be tomorrow seated on the judge's bench administering justice? in a very summary manner.

This transpired a quarter of a century ago, and some of those who went into court to contest for their rights are still pleading their cases with little likelihood of their ever attaining a solution of the difficulty as long as there are fees to be collected.

I noticed in my experience during the opening of the territory to homeseekers, that Cash, Clemency, and Justice travelled on parallel lines, and when the Cash failed to put an appearance, Clemency and Justice disappeared also, as the dew dissolves before the morning sun. There were some Sooners sent to the penitentiary for perjury, but they were likely to be pardoned in time to vote at the next election. In view of the number of felons who have been set at liberty, one is forced to conclude that there have been some very tender-hearted governors in the state.

When the first homeseekers were drawing up in line for the mad race across the plain, I joined them. I was very curtly told that I had not any right to take part in the free-for-all scramble for property, as I had 640 acres of land in the Panhandle of Texas. Being that they felt that way about it, I did not press my right, but gracefully withdrew, and took only an observer's interest in the headlong gallop that occurred. When the excitement had somewhat subsided, I returned to my holdings in the Panhandle and took up the burden of making what improvements I thought necessary to make it a desirable homestead. I had in view the completion of an irrigation ditch that I had begun before I left to see the opening in Oklahoma. On my return I hired a few labourers to help with the work. It took considerable labour and money to complete the task, and when I had it done, I found that all my labour and money had been in vain. When I did not need water, there was too much of it, and when I did need it, the creek that was to furnish me the supply, was as dry as a bone. I became disgusted with that place and sold out for about fifty per-cent of what the improvements cost me. Times were hard just then. There was but little money in the country, a long hard winter had killed off multitudes of the range cattle, and the long dry summer had killed off all hopes of relief to be found in successful farming. To make our condition more lonely, the mail facilities were not what they should have been for some time. Sometimes a week would elapse, and very frequently several weeks would pass by without our hearing anything from the outside world. Our postmaster was not entirely to blame as he did the best he could in fulfilling his duties. As he could read or write very little, it placed him at a great disadvantage, but he struggled along against the disadvantage of his lack of training to try to satisfy his patrons. When the mail arrived, he opened the sack and dumped the contents out on a barrel head and permitted each patron to help himself. If Big Jim, or Little Ike happened to be in from some ranch or other, they would look over the pile and take the number of letters they thought belonged to their respective ranches, put them in the pocket of their slicker, mount their ponies and ride away. Perhaps, in a week or so, some of the letters would be returned to the office marked, "opened by mistake," and others were never returned at all. I will say that there were more letters opened by mistake in that office than in any office in the whole United States, taking into consideration the numbers of letters received. As many years have passed since that time, I have often wondered what became of the efficient postmaster of Wolf Creek. As he was a good, loyal Democrat of the Andrew Jackson type, I thought I might see him some time in the Oklahoma Senate, but have looked in vain. He may have received an appointment to an Ambassadorship in Mexico, but I have not heard of it. However, wherever he is, if he be living, I wish him well.

About the time of which I am writing, it was currently reported and generally believed that a millionaire named George R. Timms was building a city at the head of Kiowa Creek, and that there were churches, schools, and all the improvements that go to make a prosperous town. One could get all the advantages of such a place by buying a lot or two on the instalment plan. I decided to take advantage of such a brilliant opportunity of getting into closer touch with civilization. I rounded up my horses and cattle and set out toward the land of so much promise. Imagine my surprise and even astonishment when I reached the place, to find it almost totally abandoned. I rode around through the deserted streets without seeing a single person. I was about to pronounce the thing a complete failure, from the point of view of population, when I discovered a bench-legged, bullet-eyed individual approaching me. Where he came from I do not know. In questioning him about the place I was informed that he had been one of the original inhabitants, that the rest had left, but he couldn't get away for lack of means. In his desire to take advantage of opportunity, he offered to sell me a town lot. I replied that I did not think there was any great demand for town lots just then, and that there was little likelihood of a boom there for some time if present conditions were any indication of the business prospects of the town. I inquired where I could find a house to move into, and he told me to take my choice of the whole place. I looked the town over and finally decided that the hotel was about the best building for my purposes just then. There I remained during my stay in Timms City. I made some further inquiries of my fellow townsman as soon as I had taken up my abode in the Timms House, and he told me that all the population had gone away to Oklahoma to take up land; that there were only two persons left behind. I remained in the forsaken city for some time, and spent my leisure moments in hunting antelope. I did not meet with much success in this line of endeavour, as there were very few left in the locality.

One day, while sitting in front of my new abode, I was called upon by some ranchmen in the neighbourhood. They asked me if I would take charge of the post-office. They explained that it was very difficult for them to get their mail, and if that office was closed up, it would leave them in a very serious predicament. I replied that it was impossible for me to take charge of the office as I was about to take a trip east, and hence would not be able to attend to the official duties of the place. I told them that I appreciated the confidence they had in me, a stranger, thanked them for the offer, but declined firmly to undertake the duties of the position. I made mention of the fact that my wife had had some experience in the work, and if she would be willing to undertake the running of the place, it would be agreeable to me. She undertook the task and after three months of trouble and worry incident to the business, the returns showed that she had received *one dollar and thirty-nine cents*, a handsome sum for the time and energy spent upon the thankless task. After that matter was disposed of, they requested me to accept the office of "Justice of the Peace," an offer that I declined, as I never had any hankering for political preferment. They told me they had to find some one to fill the office until the next election took place. They gave me to understand that the man who had filled that important position knew nothing of the Texas laws. To give me an example of his mental acumen and his judicial integrity, they said that, on one occasion he tried a man for stealing a cow. The theft was proven beyond the shadow of a doubt. When the evidence was all in, he took the case under advisement for ten days, and then he sent the man who owned the cow to jail for ninety days and turned the thief loose. When asked why he had taken such a course in his administration of justice, he replied that, in his judgment, they were both thieves, and he had sent the man to jail who could best endure the confinement.

CHAPTER 16

An Arkansaw Traveller

A short time prior to the period of which I am writing, there had been taught and promulgated by some half-breed, a religion which afterwards became known as the "Messiah Craze." It had spread all over the northwest territories and finally reached Oklahoma. The principal tenet of this strange religion was that the Great Spirit was going to remove all the white folks and restore the buffalo to his native plains, which were to become a sort of "Happy Hunting Grounds" for the Indians, or a heaven on earth where everything was to be peace, joy, and chuckaway without end.

I had heard something about it, but had paid little or no attention to it. The current of events lent an aspect of truth to the prophecy, as, about that time the cowmen were being removed from the Cherokee Strip, their fences and ranches torn down and moved away. All this seemed to say to the half-crazed Indians that the white man's race was about run. All they had to do was to wait a while and their earthly paradise would be opened for Indian occupation. I could not see things in the same light as the Indian enthusiast. It looked to me as if the government intended to throw the Cherokee country open to homestead settlement. The truth of this conjecture was proven shortly afterwards, and showed that I had the correct solution of the movement.

I made up my mind to make a journey down through that section to learn something of the topography of the place and also to find a good location in which to make a settlement when it was opened for the purpose. I fitted out my wagon with the necessary supplies for the jaunt, took five head of horses, and took my little boy, Emmet, then about twelve years of age, for company. When all preparations were properly made, we started out on what was to be a perilous journey.

On our first night out, we stayed with Judge Gard, on Mammoth Creek. He was County Judge, one of those whole-souled men who never knew what it was to pull in the latch-string-that hung on his door. We spent the evening very pleasantly exchanging experiences of former days. Next morning we set out before dawn, and sunrise found us on Wolf Creek trail. We followed this along the creek until we reached its mouth, where it joins the Beaver, and forms the head-waters of the North Canadian River, about a mile and a half from Ft. Supply. From there we took the trail leading to the little town of Woodward, only a station erected alongside the railroad which had been recently built through that country. Here I had the pleasure of meeting Thomas Bugbee, an old-time cowmen who was shipping his cattle preparatory to leaving the Cherokee Strip. I had a friendly chat with him, and then pulled out and proceeded on my way along the Canadian River. We had not gone very far on our way when we met an old frontiersman and prince of scouts, Amos Chapman, taking a band of Cheyenne Indians to Camp Supply to draw their rations. As it was now past noon, we stopped to let the horses graze while we prepared something for our wants. Whilst there we inquired of Amos how things were running down the river. He told us something about the excitement that had been stirred up. While we were eating the Indians filed by, and their appearance was not any too encouraging. Before parting with us, he advised us to keep a close watch on them as they were all affected with the Messiah Craze; that they had been making medicine, and were liable to break out at any time, but that up to the present they had done nothing more than was customary with them. As he had several bullet marks as souvenirs of former encounters with them, and had also lost one leg in an Indian fight, I knew that I was talking to a man of no small experience, and felt that his advice was worth taking. He noticed that I had some good horses with me, and warned me to keep them picketed close to me while I slept, as a good horse was a very great temptation to an Indian, especially a bad one, but generally speaking my stock was safe enough. I thanked him for his counsel, and as the afternoon was fast slipping away, I moved on.

As the cowmen had nearly all left that part of the country, and as the Indians had all gone to Camp Supply for their rations, we did not meet many travellers on the trail that afternoon. We went into camp early, and pursuant to the advice given us, we picketed our horses near at hand. There was no curfew rung that night, but there was a good substitute, for, about a mile away there was camped a company of soldiers, sent out from the fort ostensibly for the purpose of exercise, but in reality to watch the movements of the Indians. At the passing of every hour we could hear the sentry call out that all was well. As this was my first night to camp out in some time I did not sleep very well, and, consequently, was up at daybreak ready to start. The usual formalities of breakfast for ourselves and attention to our outfit had been attended to, and we took up our journey once more. We had not gone more than a mile when I discovered a lone man standing beside the trail with a gun in his hands. What he was doing there was a mystery to me. I could not see any horse near him, nor was there anything else in sight to give a clue to his presence there. In the meantime I kept moving on, with one eye on the man and the other on the trail. When I was within a few hundred yards of him, he raised his gun and fired. I could see the smoke and hear the report, but could not discover the object he was trying to shoot. As I approached him, I discovered that the man before me was an Indian, bare-headed with his hair plaited down his back, and wearing a good suit of Uncle Sam's clothes. His foot-gear consisted of a nicely beaded pair of moccasins. His was a majestic figure as he stood there straight as an arrow and measuring about six feet, four inches in height. He saluted me with the customary Indian, "How," and I returned his salutation. I enquired of him what the difficulty was, as it was an unusual thing to meet a lone Indian on the prairie. I knew there was something out of the ordinary, or he would not be there. Then my difficulty began. He knew comparatively nothing of the English language and I knew less of his sign mode of communication. He seemed rather eager to communicate with me, and I was anxious to know the cause of his rather unusual predicament. It seemed a hopeless task to try to make anything out of what he was trying to tell me.

However, by battling with his broken English, and mixing in a few Cheyenne words that I knew, I arrived at some solution of the difficulty. The fact was that he had been over on the South Canadian on some mission from the sub-agency, and his horse had thrown him and left him afoot on the prairie. As there were no Indians in the neighbourhood from whom he could borrow a horse, (they were all away attending the Messiah dance), he was trying to make his way back on foot. As he had had nothing to eat since the day before he had been trying to shoot a prairie dog, but he had met with no success. Then I knew that he was hungry.

The government has succeeded in moving the Indians around from one agency to another, and in some instances the agents have plundered the wards of the government of their provisions and clothing, but they have never succeeded in removing a live Indian's appetite.

That Indian's condition aroused my sympathy, and I felt that something should be done to relieve his immediate wants. I reached behind the seat to the grub-box, and brought forth some cold biscuits that remained from the meal of the day before. When he saw what I had in my hand, a broad smile of satisfaction spread over his face. When I saw that he relished the biscuits so much, I cut open a can of tomatoes and handed it to him. This seemed to delight him even more than did the biscuits, and it was a pleasure to see him drink the liquid first and then with a broad grin eat the tomatoes one after another with all evidence of deep content. There I was doing as the Good Samaritan had done, to the man that I thought was standing beside the trail to shoot me. During my interview with the Indian, one of the horses had strayed away some distance, and Emmet had ridden after him to bring him back to the buck-board. When the Indian saw him, he said admiringly, "Heap good *papoose*." He seemed to take a great interest in the boy, but I was wondering whether it was the boy or the rifle he was carrying on his saddle. As I had learned the direction of his *teepee* I invited him to take a seat beside me so that we might be moving onward. When he settled himself into the seat, he gave a loud grunt of satisfaction. We rode along for several miles to where the river make a bend, and came close to the trail. There I decided to camp as it was convenient for wood and water. I turned in there, and I had no sooner stopped than the Indian was out gathering wood and kindling to start a fire. I unhitched and Emmet drove the horses down to the river to get a drink, and let them graze until they were needed again. At this time I needed no interpreter. I handed the Indian a knife and a side of bacon, pointed to the skillet, and he understood the signs perfectly. He immediately set to work to attend to the frying and I undertook the work of getting the dishes ready for our meal. As I had a guest, I took out an extra quantity of coffee, and an extra plate, etc. The Indian showed himself no novice in the line of cooking, and we soon had a repast ready that would satisfy the craving of any hungry man, prince, potentate, or plebeian. Some folks might think it intolerable to dine in the manner employed on such occasions. We bade defiance to all the germ theories that were being advanced at that time, and adapted ourselves to the conditions of time and place. After the horses had grazed for some time we hooked up again, and set forth without any further ceremony. My guest seemed to wish to communicate some idea to me and kept his hands and fingers as busy as a Drogheda weaver, but all to no purpose as I could not understand him. I drove along on my mission, the Indian all the time making his signs. At times he looked disgusted because he could not break through my ignorance. Probably, if I had made more of an effort, I might have understood enough to avoid some unpleasant complications which followed soon afterwards. In the meantime, Emmet, boylike, had been keeping his eye open for anything in the shape of game and held his gun in readiness to bring it into immediate play. We were jaunting along rapidly enough, and the rattling of the buckboard disturbed the repose of a coyote that was lying in the sage brush along the trail. When he jumped up to take a survey of the situation, Emmet fired at him and, whether through accident or good marksmanship, I cannot say, brought down the beast on the spot. At the crack of the gun, the Indian turned his head just in time to see the coyote fall, then turned loose some more sign language and closed his efforts by saying, "heap good *papoose*." We proceeded along our way until we were in the neighbourhood of Cantonment. Then my fellow-traveller made a sign that he wanted me to stop, which I did. He left the buckboard and started off through the brush, I suppose, to where his *teepee* was located, some place along the river.

I learned afterwards through an interpreter that my companion was not a bad Indian, but one of the numerous Red Men appointed by Uncle Sam to look after the movements of the different tribes who at that time were taking part in the Messiah craze, and report to the fort or agency the condition in which he found them.

In the distance I could see the timber which skirts a small creek running into the river, where I concluded there would be a good place to camp as there would be plenty of wood and water there, and likewise good pasture for the horses. It was now past the middle of the afternoon, and I decided to go into camp early so as to have a good night's rest, and give the horses an opportunity for a good graze to freshen up after the long drive.

It did not take me long to reach the creek, and when I drove over the hill and down into the bottom lands, what was my surprise and consternation to find that I had driven into the storm centre of the Messiah Dance then being held on the bank of the river. There were between five hundred and a thousand Cheyennes and Arapahos in the assemblage. Just at the moment they were holding what the cowmen call a *powow*. I was evidently in a very ticklish situation. What to do I did not know. One thing I decided on in a very hasty manner, and that was that there was no use in showing the white feather just then. I drove up within about twenty rods of their headquarters. I got out and began to unhitch. I was certainly taking the dilemma by the horns and determined to make the most of the situation. While trying to make myself feel comfortable, which I was far from doing, I told Emmet to hobble the rest of the ponies to prevent their wandering away. Then I set to work to make flap-jacks and coffee, and I do not believe that flap-jacks were ever turned out under such circumstances before or since. I had been doing a lot of thinking over the situation, but found that, no matter what angle I viewed it from, I was in difficulties. I did not dare to tell Emmet what was passing through my mind for fear he would lose his courage, and I must say that my own was fast ebbing. I did not like to acknowledge to my boy that I was afraid. They say that God hates a liar, and I must say that I am no greater admirer of such a man myself, but when Emmet ask me what the disturbance was all about, I had to evade his question and put him off by saying that there was nothing wrong, that the Indians were out on one of their picnics, which they were accustomed to hold frequently. I knew I was deceiving him, but felt that it was the best I could do under the circumstances. I knew that the Indians claimed to be in touch with Messiah and Messiah had promised to remove the white man and restore the buffalo to his native plains, and I began to think seriously that I might be the first pale-face on which that order might take effect.

While making my flap-jacks for supper, I had a visit from some eight or ten bucks dressed up in white sheets. They came and stood around me in a half circle. They did not speak a word, nor even utter a grunt. I continued to give my undivided attention to the work at hand, apparently unaware of their presence. They remained there motionless as statues for fifteen or twenty minutes. If one of them moved a muscle, I did not know it. Their presence was rather disconcerting, to say the least, but what could I do about it? Why they were wearing those white sheets, I could not understand. It might, probably, have been a part of their regalia for the ceremony. Whatever it was, it did not add anything to my feelings of comfort. At a signal from headquarters they left me as unceremoniously as they had come. I had a Winchester leaning against the front wheel of the wagon, and a six-shooter lying on the top of the grub-box, and Emmet had a rifle close at hand, which went to show that we were pretty well able to look after ourselves in case of emergency. Just then my attention was attracted by the rumbling of wheels and on looking around I saw a man driving a small team of ponies in my direction. I was rather glad of his arrival, whoever he might be. Someone has said that "misery loves company," and I have yet to learn which was the greater nuisance, my misery or my new-found arrival. I was anxious for a relief from the present embarrassing conditions, and invited him to stop and have something to eat. He complied with my request, or rather invitation. He unhitched his ponies, not a very difficult task as he employed a simplified harness of the chain variety, with corn-husk collars, and no throat-latch to the bridles. When he went towards the wagon the old ponies seemed to know what was coming, and shook their heads and the bridles fell off, and they went to grazing. While Emmet was making more coffee and frying an extra quantity of meat, I went over to inspect his outfit. It was certainly a strange make-up for a man on a journey. There was no bedding in sight, and no kind of cooking outfit. There was an old gun that had once been a flint-lock, and might have seen service in the battle of Waterloo. The breach had been cut off and it had been restocked. The barrel was about four feet long, and for a front sight it had something that very much resembled a brass collar button. The butt of the stock was wrapped in a gunny sack and tied up carefully with binder twine, which I learned afterwards was for the purpose of lessening the concussion on his shoulder when firing it.

My guest sat down to eat, and while he was thus occupied, I made bold to question him as to whence he came and whither he was going. He informed me that he was from Arkansaw and was on his way to No-Man's Land where he had relations. I then ask him to mention some of the folks he was going to bless with his presence. From the reply he gave me I knew that I was face to face with an artistic liar, as I knew all the settlers up in that part of the country. Having in earlier years made a study of phrenology, I thought this the proper time to put some of the principals I had learned to the test. I began to make a sort of mental examination of the formation of his cranium and came to the conclusion that he would violate at least seven of the commandments without a second thought, and the remaining three would have to depend upon circumstances for their observation. One thing I found in his favour and that was that he would not commit murder as the bump of combativeness was almost entirely lacking a view which in a very short time proved to be correct, for almost immediately, without any preliminaries or forewarning, as if by magic the Messiah Dance was opened, and the man from Arkansaw almost melted away through fear.

As it was now dark, I could see plainly the movements of the Indians by the glare of the camp fires around their *teepees*. Their leader commenced intoning a weird *Hi-Yi-Hi-Oh-Yip-Yip-Hi-Oh*, and maintained the monotonous chant as an accompaniment to the tom-tom. This was kept up without intermission until the first set of dancers became exhausted. Then everything became quiet once more. The silence remained unbroken until the next performance was ready. When the recess had lasted about half an hour, the signal was given a second time, and all the dancers, bucks and squaws, fell into line and began a performance which resembled very much a continuation of the old-time hop-step. They leaped and chanted at the same time. The melody of their song was very much in keeping with the music of the tom-tom, but entirely unlike anything I had ever heard, before or since. Most of the bucks were decorated with the insignia of the rank they held in their respective tribes, while the remainder were clothed in the regulation blanket, moccasins, and breach clouts. The squaws, like their white sisters, endeavoured to outdo each other in the matter of fantastic habiliments. They wore no head dress, and their hair was done up in the latest style. They wore some splendid blankets which I judged were of Navajo make, and were highly ornamented. Besides this they wore moccasins beaded in many colours, and leggings.

Still the dance went on with the same *powow*, with no variation in the music. It was left for the third and final dance to make the grand display of the evening. When they had enjoyed the second recess in sullen silence, they broke forth in one grand effort to make the finale the piece-de-resistance of the evenings entertainment. They seemed to have restrained themselves for this special production of their hideous and welkin-splitting pandemonium. Everything they had done in the way of cavorting in the complex measures of their former dance, seemed to be nothing to what was expected of them in the last grand splurge. From my own observation of the performance I should best describe it by saying that it seemed as if the infernal regions had been turned loose for a holiday. The readers imagination will have to picture what really took place in that final orgy of riot and disorder. Words cannot adequately describe it, and I would be unwise to attempt to do so. But just to give a faint idea of what really took place I will say that at a given signal they all fell into line again as in the previous performance. In addition to their former efforts, they included the call or cry of every bird or beast known to them, from the guttural growl of the wild bear to the call of the peewee. It was all there in one jumble of discordant sound, the neighing of the horse, the roaring of the bull, the call of the bobwhite, the barking of dogs, the howl of the coyote, the call of the peacock, the familiar gobbling of the wild turkey, etc. This was continued until they dropped from sheer exhaustion. The revel and riot was at length completed and silence reigned again.

In all my experience I have never heard or seen anything like it. Anything that I had ever seen before was like a children's picnic when compared with the Messiah Dance. I had read of Tam O'Shanter peeping through the crannies of the Auld Kirk of Alloway, feasting his eyes upon the dance of the witches, but it was not to be compared with the Messiah Dance, for here there were real, live mortals enacting a dance that was incomparable in its weird peculiarities.

When the festivities had ceased, I asked my Arkansaw guest what he thought of it. He replied that he had just about concluded to leave at once. "If," said he, "they do such things in play, what would they do to us if they took the notion to put into practice some of the barbarities for which the Indian is famed." I told him to get that notion out of his head immediately, for, if he did, the Indians would likely follow him and take his scalp for a prelude to what they would do afterwards to him. I assured him that there was some security in remaining where we were, but that there would be none in leaving, as they would think he was afraid and then would follow him with results not to be desired. After a good deal of persuasion, I induced him to share my blankets with me and my boy, which was a great trial for him.

The bucks and squaws had, by this time, retired to their tents, and everything, was quiet. The camp fires were still burning and lit up the trees and shrubbery so plainly that one could see each separate branch and twig. The reflection of the blaze lit up the little valley in such a way that we seemed to be walled in by a cordon of liquid fire.

As I was fatigued after the day's journey, I turned in like a trooper's horse, with my shoes on, to be ready to meet any emergency that might arise. As innocence knows neither crime, nor danger, Emmet was curled up in sleep like a babe in its mother's arms. But such was not the case of the Arkansaw Traveller. He was lying on the opposite side of the "bed," next to Emmet, but in spite of the fact that he was removed from me in that manner, I could hear his heart beating so distinctly that it seemed like the fluttering of a bird trying to break from its cage. For myself, I just trusted in a kind Providence, and slept the sleep of the weary.

At daybreak we were up and thankful that we were still alive. We went about the preparation of breakfast as though nothing unusual was taking place around us. As the weather looked as though we would have rain very soon, I set about the task of building a *teepee*, as I had no shelter. I intended to cover it with a wagon sheet, as that was the most serviceable for the purpose of keeping us dry. In the meantime Emmet had strayed off through the trees and brush to see what he could find in the way of game. I had just cut some willows to make the framework of my *teepee*, when the boy came running excitedly back to camp and exclaimed, "papa, papa come down to the river and see what those Indians are doing!" As I saw he was excited about something, I dropped everything and followed him to the river which was not far from our camp. There I saw something that was novel to me. There were about five hundred bucks and squaws in the water taking their morning bath. They were not in one group, but were separated about seventy-five yards, bucks in one group and squaws in another. Between them was an imaginary dead line over which, by tribal custom, no young buck or brave had the temerity to cross. They were splashing around in the water like nymphs, disporting themselves after their own fashion. I did not notice that indispensable attaché of refined society, the chaperon domineering over those simple, stainless daughters of the plains to keep them from drifting from the path of moral rectitude. A native sense of modesty, as well as tribal traditions dispensed with such a guardian. There was no need of one. There were no ladies of high-degree lolling on benches on the bank, with a broad brimmed hat, and all the other follies that go to make up what is called "style," neither were there any little, black nosed, red eyed, fluffy-haired dogs with expensive collars around their necks, nor pugs with tails curled up so tightly that it would be almost impossible for their hind legs to touch the ground. No, they were not there, neither were many other devises that go to improve the figure to make it Juno-like, nor were bathing suits in evidence, but in spite of all that they seemed to be enjoying the frolic in the water.

As I had left the kettle of beans simmering on the fire, I had to return and look after them as the mind of the man from Arkansaw was too much perturbed to be in condition to mind anything so commonplace as beans. When I reached my outfit, I was surprised to find a half dozen Indian police awaiting me. They bore a message from the Indian agent stating that he wished to see me. As I was rather anxious to depart from that locality, I was not long in making the necessary arrangements to do so. When I arrived at the agency, I made inquiries of those who were there as to the whereabouts of the agent. I was directed to the office. I entered and introduced myself and inquired what was wanted of me. The agent, who introduced himself as Boak, a very nice gentleman, told me that the Indians were holding their Messiah Dance and did not care for the presence of white folks, as witnesses. As they had seen me begin to build a *teepee* they came to the conclusion that I was going to become a permanent fixture there, and they requested the agent to invite me to choose another locality for my habitation. Of course, he informed me that I was welcome to such hospitality as the agency could furnish. I believed him and thanked him for his generosity. I assured him that it had not been my intention to disturb the Indians in their religious proceedings. I did not say anything about my being afraid that I would be disturbed by them. It chanced that our feelings in regard to the matter were mutual. The more we discussed the matter, the more he seemed to insist upon my partaking of his hospitality, which led me to believe that he was rather uneasy on account of the Messiah Dance and wanted not only my company, but whatever assistance I could give in case the Indians became threatening. I did not find any fault with him for having that feeling, and it would take a man better versed in Indian lore to tell what was likely to happen next.

As it was getting along in the forenoon, and I saw there was no further use in prolonging the interview, I left the agency, went and got my belongings and set out on my journey up along the river. I took the bottom trail that wound a zigzag course through the timber. My progress seemed to be made through a leafy tunnel. The trees on each side of the trail were heavily leaved, and the branches above reached across the trail, forming a beautiful corridor-like passage. When I had gone on my way for a mile or more,

I happened to glance behind and saw an Indian on a pony, with a Winchester across his saddle, who seemed to be following me. I did not like the looks of things just then. I concluded that if the Indian had any trouble he wanted to settle, the best thing was to have the matter attended to without delay. I drove on until I came to a rather lengthy passage, free from windings, and then stopped the team. I motioned for him to come up to where I was. He did so. When he arrived, I asked him in an uncertain tone of voice what he wanted? He uttered but one word, "tobac." I had about half a sack of Duke's Mixture which I handed to him. He took it hastily, turned his horse around and plunged into the brush at the side of the trail, and that was the last that I saw of him. I found it hard to reconcile myself to the belief that it was tobacco alone that he was wanting.

The rain had begun falling in the meantime, and to say that it was merely raining will not convey the proper idea to the mind. It poured in torrents, and continued to do so all day long. About noon we stopped and tried to make some coffee for dinner, but it was no use. We set out again and plodded along in the deluge until late in the afternoon. I was continually on the look-out for some sort of shelter, and my sight was at last gratified by observing at some distance from the river, a stockade building. I set off in the direction of the expected shelter, and when I reached it, found that it had a good dirt-roof, but no windows nor doors. It was what is called a wind-break and I determined to pre-empt it for the night. I knew it belonged to some Indian, but as he was likely off to the Messiah Dance, he would not return just then, and even if he did, I would try to make him as comfortable as circumstances would permit, divide my chuckaway with him, even go so far as to share my blanket with him, but as for deserting that shelter just then, it was not to be thought of. If he were to become hostile and wanted to fight, I would accommodate his longing as there would be little or no chance to seek safety in flight. I made preparations to cook some supper, and Emmet attended to the horses, hobbled them and turned them loose to graze. In the meanwhile, I must not forget to say that Arkansaw had been following me like a shadow ever since I left the agency. To see him as he was then in his bedraggled condition, with his ramshackle outfit, one would think that the genius of famine and desolation had descended upon the land. I carried the chuck-box, bedding, guns, and utensils into the shelter preparatory to getting things ready for supper and bed. I enlisted the services of Arkansaw to gather some wood to build a fire, and I must say as a hauler of wood he was a dismal failure. However, we finally managed to get a fire started and set in to dry our clothes, bedding, etc., along with getting something to eat. We were all ravenously hungry, and the flap-jacks disappeared with wonderful alacrity. When our appetites had been satisfied, things did not look so bad to us. It was not the most comfortable place to spend the night, but it was far better than the rain soaked ground. To add to our discomfort, it began to turn cold. We crawled under the partially dried blankets in the hope that wearied nature would provide a good sound sleep. As we were not distracted by such howling and yelling as we had endured the night before, things would have been favourable for a good night's rest. But I cannot say there was much prospect for a refreshing sleep as it is one thing to find repose under dry blankets, and another to seek the same balm for a wearied body under bedding that has been exposed to a downpour of rain for hours. No, it was not going to rest, it was just lying down for want of something else to do. I noticed that the heart of the Arkansaw Traveller did not beat as loudly as on the preceding night, and it was not long until he began to snore with all the variations of a steam calliope. I was glad to know that he at least could find sleep under such conditions, but for me, there was not much comfort. I thought that by this time my fellow traveller was over his scare, but in the midst of his dreams he let a yell out of him and exclaimed, "Let up on that, you can't scalp me, I'm from Arkansaw." I reached over and gave him a poke in the side and told him that it made no difference whether he was from Arkansaw or New Jersey, that he would be scalped unless he was ready to put up a pretty stiff fight. When we rolled out shivering in the morning, we found that it had frozen during the night. We welcomed the coming of the dawn, as the night had been one continual toss from one side to the other, and no comfort was found. I arose and shook myself to see if I were all there, and found myself intact. The others followed my example with the same results. I stepped outside to see how the horses were faring and found they had wandered off. I left word for Arkansaw to prepare something to eat and went off in search of the ponies. I had a rather good idea of where they had gone, and after walking about a mile I found them. They were huddled together for warmth. Their hobbles were frozen stiff. I removed the frozen hobble from one of them, mounted him, and drove the others back to camp. When I returned to the shelter, breakfast was ready and soon attended to. I gathered up my belongings once more and we set out again. It was a beautiful morning and the sun seemed to be trying to compensate us for the hardship we had endured during the night. The horses seemed anxious to go, and their speed shortened the time of our journey considerably. We rode on for about ten or twelve miles, when we came to a beautiful grazing ground sheltered by a sand hill. With such a fine location I decided that this was a good opportunity to spread out the bedding to dry, and attend to our other wants. It seemed as if we were always hungry, and when a fine opportunity presented itself for preparing a repast, we simply had to yield to the occasion. I set Emmet and Arkansaw to cooking, while I attended to the horses. I then took a ramble around for I had seen where there was evidence of a flock of wild turkeys in the neighbourhood. It was no great difficulty to follow their trail in the soft earth, and I soon happened upon a flock of forty or fifty feeding on the heads of wild rye that was growing in a sort of pocket formed by the hill. I took in my surroundings at a glance, and to my agreeable surprise I saw a deer about two hundred yards away nibbling at the leaves of a shin oak. I determined to take a chance with the deer first. I took careful aim and fired. My shot was not true, but I succeeded in breaking his hind leg. He did not seem to realize where the shot came from, and turned and came straight for me. I will admit that his advance upon me was disconcerting as it was so unusual. I waited until he had come within about twenty yards from me, and fired again. The bullet struck within about six inches of where I was aiming, which showed that I was influenced by what is called "buck fever." While all this was taking place, the turkeys had flown off over the hill. I followed them, knowing that they would not be far away. I came upon them.

They were all huddled together in one dense mass. I sent a bullet into the midst of them and succeeded in killing two of them. The others flew away, and I knew by their flight that more of them had been hit. I gathered up the two that I had brought down and took them back to where the deer was lying. I found that I had carried them about as far as I cared to, and went off to get some dinner, intending to have Emmet saddle up his pony and bring them in later. I accompanied him as he was too young to attend to the matter alone. I hung the turkeys on the saddle horn, and the pony seemed to object as he bucked considerably. He did not take kindly to dragging the deer after him and showed his displeasure by performing such gyrations as only a Texas cow pony can accomplish. However, we succeeded in persuading him to perform the task and set out for camp. When we had returned to our outfit, and I had begun to dress the deer, Arkansaw came to me in an apparent state of trepidation and told me that, during my absence, a band of Indians, seven in number had called at the camp and left word for me to leave the reservation. To be sure that I understood him aright, I asked, 'how many?' "Seven" said he. I asked him if they were all on horseback and he said that they were, that one of them wore a war-bonnet. I made no reply to this, but when I had completed the task of dressing the deer and turkeys, I made a circle around the camp, about fifty yards out, and found no traces of any Indians being there. When I returned to the camp, I felt satisfied that Arkansaw was about the most artistic and monumental liar west of the Mississippi. I then knew that he was still frightened and wanted to get as far away from there as he could and that as soon as possible. He was afraid to go alone and originated the tale to induce me to set out at once. I did not tell him what I thought of the originality of design he manifested, but if he had an ounce of judgment he would have seen that I would easily detect his falsehood as my horses were all shod, and I could easily detect the marks of the unshod Indian ponies in the soft earth if they had been in the neighbourhood. I did not make any preparations to depart immediately, but left Emmet and Arkansaw to look after the things about the camp, and set out again to secure more game if possible. It was with reluctance that my brave? friend consented to do such a little thing as greasing the buckboard, as he felt there was grave danger in delaying there any longer. Before leaving I informed him that I was thinking of departing next morning, but if any more Indians appeared on the scene while I was gone, to inform them that I was not in a hurry to leave those parts, and, furthermore, if they were looking for trouble, I was there to accommodate them.

The absence of danger is sometimes a great stimulus to a man's courage, and I felt that there was no peril in store for us as it was most likely that there was not an Indian within fifteen miles of us, and, besides I wanted to scare the Arkansaw Traveller properly.

I took my gun and sauntered off over the hill, enjoying the walk after being cramped up in the buckboard. I could have killed several turkeys, but preferred to get another deer if possible. In my meanderings I came upon an Indian grave. He had been laid to rest upon a platform, rolled in his blanket and wrapped in an outer covering of bark. I must confess that I had an uncanny feeling as I approached the last resting place of that noble red man, but it was a sensation entirely different to the ones I had experienced in meeting some of them in the flesh. However, since he was there and I was close by, I thought it a good opportunity to satisfy my curiosity about their customs of burial. I approached him with about as much alacrity as one would expect under the circumstances. I found the blanket in which he was rolled, incrusted with sand that had blown upon it from the neighbourhood. It was rotten from long exposure to the elements and had about the same consistency as paper. I turned back one corner to get a view of the condition of the remains. The flesh had disappeared, the long braided hair was there, but from its appearance I could not tell whether he had been there thirty days, or three years. It had a gloss to it that seemed to indicate that his burial took place recently. I turned back the blanket and left him as I found him. I retraced my steps towards camp, as I was beginning to have another attack of what usually ailed me, hunger. On my way, I discovered another deer near the place where I had killed the first one, and was able to bring him down at the first shot. I left him where he fell and went back to where Emmet and Arkansaw were whiling away the time making ready for the next lap of our journey. I sent the boy back with the pony to bring in the game.

While we were alone, Arkansaw, while watching me get supper, grew confidential. He told me about leaving his native state, and how he had traded coonskins for the gun with the remarkable action. I asked him why he did not use it when an occasion presented itself for bagging a few turkeys. He replied that he was rather afraid to shoot the weapon, as, just before leaving his home, he was short of ammunition and had no opportunity of procuring any. Besides that, one of his neighbours told him that he would be likely to meet some bad men on the way to the territory, and advised him to put a plough bolt down the barrel to keep the load that was in it from getting damp. He said that he was afraid the bolt had rusted in the barrel and consequently he had not the courage to fire the gun. Just to add to his pleasurable feelings at that moment, I thought I would give him some of his own coin and told him that I had seen an Indian on my travels, who was dressed differently from those we had seen at the Messiah Dance, and that there were likely more in the neighbourhood. I warned him to prepare for an emergency by getting that gun into working shape. I advised him to pour bacon grease into the lock and try to get it into working order, for if those Indians he saw would return, there would be some moments of activity around that neck of the woods. As Emmet had by this time arrived with the deer, I set to work to dress it and put things in shape for our departure in the morning. To have some more sport with Arkansaw I tried to get him to stand guard during the night. I told him that now that his gun was in good shape he would be in a position to protect himself, and at the same time warn us of the approach of Indians. He tried for a while, but I could see that he was suffering agony untold on account of his fear of an attack. The rustling of a leaf caused him to tremble, and any louder noise made him jump. It is a wonder that in his excitement he did not turn loose with the old gun, but I suppose he forgot all about it. I took pity on him and told him to lie down, that there was little or no danger. He gladly sought the shelter of the blanket and was soon giving me selections on the calliope. Next morning we still found ourselves in possession of our scalps, and felt much refreshed after the good night's rest. We gave the usual attention to breakfast, which did not take long. We were about ready to start, except for one thing. I did not like the idea of Arkansaw carrying that old gun around with him, especially since I learned that it was loaded with a plough bolt. I tried to get him to fire it off as the jarring of his old wagon or some other concussion might explode it and kill some person, or injure some of the horses. To rid myself of the danger, I agreed to fire it for him, to which he readily consented. I took the gun and tied it to a tree, fastened a rope to the trigger and when all preparations for our farewell salute were made, I pulled the trigger. The old gun went off in two different directions. The barrel went forward, and the recoil kicked the old stock backwards about five feet and it stuck fast in the sand. Right there my worry about the old gun terminated.

With our game packed on the buckboard and covered with the wagon sheet to keep off the sand which was blowing plentifully at the time, we started for Timms City. The horses were fresh and the trails in good condition, and we advanced rapidly. My only trouble was to keep Arkansaw and his festive steeds out of the way, as he was determined to put as much distance between him and the scene of his fright as possible. At times he had his poor old nags on the gallop. Such a pace they could not maintain, and about noon time they gave out. We stopped for refreshments. When we were ready to set out again, I pointed out the way to Sod Town in No-Man's Land and left him. When I parted company with him I felt that I had met one of the strangest characters I had ever encountered in all my days. I reached home the same night. In conclusion of this article I wish to say that I have never had another hankering to attend a Messiah Dance.

CHAPTER 17

Savages on the Warpath

Before setting down the narrative of the Dull Knife Raid, or any other, it is not amiss to relate something of the conditions that prevailed prior to those events.

In 1878, and for ten years prior to that time, the most of the plain Indians had been on the war-path for some reason or another. To give an idea of the size of the country which was the scene of their endeavours, it is well to outline the frontier as it existed then. Civilization was supposed to have terminated its advance at the Saline, Solomon and Cottonwood Rivers, though a few straggling settlers had established themselves on the Little Walnut, and White Rivers, with a colony at Council Grove. Beyond that line the domination of the white man was supposed to cease, and it was not the Indian's fault that it did not. He did his best to have it do so, but the result was far from successful from his point of view. Beyond the line above mentioned there existed only the Indian, the buffalo and a few venturesome spirits who formed the trains that forced their way overland to Colorado and the Black Hills, or endured the more hazardous undertaking of making the long march to California in 1849. They were, indeed, venturesome, for to undertake such a trip, one took his life in his hands, and the result was that many of them paid the penalty for their daring. Not only were they harassed by the Indian tribes they encountered on their way, but privations beset them on all sides and starvation often travelled with them to their sorrow. At any moment such a wagon train as they conducted was liable to attack from savage bands, and there then occurred a fight for life. Nor were all those attacks engineered by the Indian alone. The Mormons did their share of the dastardly work under the guise of the Indian. This statement may appear a trifle strong, but it is proved beyond all doubt that John D. Lee with a gang of cut-throats perpetrated the Mountain Meadow massacre, with all the ferocity and butchery of the most savage of tribesmen. He did his work too well, and endeavoured to cover up his tracks by making it appear that it was the work of the Indian. He not only murdered the members of the train, but mutilated the dead bodies of the slain after the fashion of the Indian. He and his accomplices then looted the train, and what they could not carry away, they destroyed. The world was well rid of such a man when he was shot off his own coffin lid to pay the penalty of his crimes, though in his death he did not make compensation for one per-cent of all the butcheries he had committed. To return to the thread of the narrative, all that scope of country lying between the western boundary of settlement and the foot hills of the Rocky Mountains, was estimated by competent judges to contain about fifteen hundred square miles of territory. It was the grazing ground in 1870 for about three million buffalo. The fighting forces of the Indians roaming that huge tract of country at the time was approximately six thousand, five hundred men of different tribes, not to say anything about the number of squaws who followed in their wake dealing death to the cripples and mutilating the dead. At that time, each lodge had on an average of about 125 or 150 ponies for use in their raids. Taking all these things into consideration, one must come to the conclusion that there was a formidable force to contend with, especially as the Indian mode of fighting was not governed by the laws of civilized warfare. To protect the settlers from the destructive raids of these tribes, the government had erected a line of forts manned with an insufficient force for the work at hand. The list of such forts comprised, Ft. Hays, Ft. Wallace, Ft. Harker, Ft. Larned, Ft. Dodge, Camp Supply, and Ft. Elliot. As I said, they were poorly garrisoned, as the best men they had, had been called away to fill vacancies in the regiments used in the Civil war, and their places were supplied by raw recruits, or old soldiers who had re-enlisted for want of something else to do. To add to their inefficiency in Indian warfare, they knew nothing of the topography of the country in which they were expected to serve. One can imagine what a predicament they would be in on the first occasion of their engagement with the natives of the plains, and an example will be shown presently. I do not wish my reader to think for a moment that I want to say anything derogatory of the valour of the American soldier. His reputation for bravery established on scores of battle fields, is too well founded to be shaken by anything I might say to the contrary. But this I will venture to state, namely, that when he came face to face with the Indian mode of warfare in a country of which he knew practically nothing, he was confronted by a set of circumstances over which he had no control, and all the military training of former years was of little value to him. This is true both of officers and privates. Bitter experience has proved that both officials and men in the ranks were in the same predicament as regards the best mode of meeting the wily Indian on his own ground. To give the proof of this assertion I shall mention two cases, one briefly and the other at greater length, to bring into full view what these men had to contend against.

In the first case, the disaster to Gen. Custer proves the correctness of my contention. Gen. Custer was a man with a national reputation for valour and military experience, yet he allowed that wily old Indian chief, Sitting Bull, to inveigle him into following him and his band into the valley of the Little Big Horn where he turned upon him with all the savagery of which the Indian nature is capable, and not only defeated, but totally annihilated his command. No, not a living man was left to tell the tale of the disaster.

In the second case which I will present to the reader, I shall show not only the inefficiency of a man trained in any other school than that of the "plains," to fight the Red Man on his native heath, but will bring out some of the characteristics of the Indian's mode of procedure.

Gen. G. A. Forsythe was the man whose military reputation as a commander was second to none in the service of Uncle Sam, a man in whom Gen. Phil. Sheridan placed the greatest confidence, a man with whom the same Gen. Sheridan took counsel in any matter requiring military strategy. To show the general's esteem of this man's skill, and at the same time show his appreciation of his worth,

Sheridan took him with him, to Germany to view the manoeuvres of the Franco-Prussian war. The above will give the reader an indication of the character of the man who met with so much ill success when fighting the Indians.

In 1868 Gen G. A. Forsythe was located temporarily at Ft. Wallace, having gone to that point for supplies. While there, daily reports were brought to him of the numerous depredations committed by the Indians along the railroads. The last report to reach him brought the unpleasant announcement that two freighters had been murdered and their stock driven off. This was too much. The Indian seemed to be committing all manner of misdeeds with seeming impunity, and he decided that he must put an end to such a state of things and at the same time punish the guilty ones for past misconduct. With this purpose in view, he gained permission from Gen. Sheridan to organize an expedition against them. The license was granted and with forty-seven scouts, among whom was Surgeon Moore and Lieut. Beecher, he set out about the tenth of the month of—, in a north-westerly direction to overtake the savages. In the inception of this expedition he made one grave mistake for which he paid dearly in the near future. He took along provisions for only ten days, on pack mules. He had no ambulances, nor wagons. In the case of an engagement he did not have men enough, nor sufficient quantity of supplies, to meet the requirements of a cattle round-up, much less an undertaking of the kind he had in view. He set forth in high spirits, for he did not realize the magnitude of the undertaking he had mapped out for himself, nor the danger into which he was rushing. The weather was favourable and the country rather level, so there was nothing to impede his rapid progress. On the fifth day out, some of the scouts discovered a few Indians. Their trail was picked up and as they progressed it became plainer, which showed that they were nearing the vicinity of the foe. On the fifth evening out, they went into camp in a small valley in the northwest corner of the state of Kansas, and not far from the eastern line of Colorado, just where a small stream called the Arickaree flows into the Republican River. In that little stream was a small island covered with scrubby timber. It could not be exactly called an island, as the water flowed on one side of it only, and at a depth of only about a foot, while the other channel was absolutely dry and filled with coarse grass and brush. As they were all weary with the long march already made, they lay down in their blankets to secure a good rest, little thinking what the next day had in store for them. About daylight, the next morning, some of the scouts heard a commotion among the horses and jumped up to see what was wrong. They discovered the Indians in the act of endeavouring to stampede the horses, and they gave the alarm. As soon as the scouts saw the situation, they opened fire upon the redskins and drove them away. The shooting was a signal for all to rise. They realized that danger was near, and they did not have long to wait until it was present. In less than an hour's time, between five and six hundred Cheyenne warriors appeared on the hill side, painted and decked out in all the paraphernalia of a full-fledged war party under the leadership of Roman Nose who at that time was the Bonaparte of the Cheyenne tribe.

It seems that the Indians had been keeping close watch on the movements of the little parties of scouts, and as they were now about eighty or a hundred miles from their base of supplies, thought that if they could stampede the horses, they would be able to secure the band as an easy prey. When they failed to make way with the horses and mules, their next move was to open fire upon the men, which they did without delay. This turn of affairs was so sudden and unexpected that the general seemed to lose his head, and stood there in profound amazement. While the general was in this state of uncertainty as to what to do, with his men exposed to the Indian fire, Jack Stillwell, a boy of nineteen, without any regard for formality of ceremony, yelled out, "Why in blazes don't you go over on that island?" The general took the advice so freely and informally given by his subordinate, and all broke on the run for the shelter of the pseudo-island. They arrived there, but not before several of them were wounded in the dash in which several of the horses were killed, or crippled. The scouts utilized the dead horses as breastworks and poured such a hot fire into the Indians that they withdrew to the shelter of the hills. The scouts employed their time in digging rifle pits, as they were sure that the Indians were not going to give up the fray without another effort to wipe out the little band. It was only a very short time until the Indians were seen coming down the hillside with intensified ferocity due to their first repulse, howling warwhoops from six hundred lusty, savage throats, and adding to the din by beating *tomtoms*. It was a sight to send a chill to the stoutest heart to see them wildly flinging their arms in the air to the accompaniment of their thunderous yells, the rumbling of the flying horses as they descended upon the little band, in their mad career. At their head rode Roman Nose encouraging his followers and urging them on to deeds of valour with shout and gesture. One may imagine the chill that crept over many a heart at such a terrifying spectacle, but it was not time to show the white feather, as they could expect no quarter from the blood-thirsty band coming upon them with all the intensity of a whirlwind of fury. When the Indians were within rifle shot, the scouts opened upon them with a fusillade of bullets, with deadly effect. Many a horse was tumbled to the earth and many an Indian bit the dust, either entirely killed, or mortally wounded. The savages returned the fire with but little effect as the scouts were entrenched behind the dead horses, or in their rifle pits. On they came undaunted by the first shock of battle. They advanced almost to the bank of the little stream that flowed between the half-island and the main land. There Roman Nose was seen to reel and fall from his saddle, shot through his body. Another chieftain, I shall not say more daring than the others, but more favoured by good luck, succeeded in fording the little stream and advanced to the very bank of the sand bar, or island, before he fell riddled by the bullets of the desperate little band. The continuous fusillade of bullets poured into the serried ranks of the Indians at such close range, together with the loss of their leaders impelled the savages to retreat to the hills once more. This they did accompanied by a shower of bullets that emptied many a saddle before the retreating savages were out of danger. They disappeared behind the hills, but not with the intention of giving up the fight, as they considered their plans for massacring the little band to be too well laid to be set aside on account of the two repulses they had already received. They waited till afternoon to make a third and final assault upon the island. On they came again, but with the same result as before. They were driven back before the galling fire of the besieged. Determined to continue the fight at all hazards, they kept themselves out of range of the rifles of the islanders, but maintained a desultory fire which had no effect upon the men entrenched in the rifle pits. They then spread themselves out and rode around the island in a circle, but out of range of the guns of the entrapped soldiers. It was plainly their intention to starve the scouts to death or into submission, which was all the same to them.

In the meantime the situation on the island was far from pleasant. Though they had defended themselves with desperate valour, the members of that heroic little band did not escape from all injury. The dead numbered a score, among whom was Lieut. Beecher, a nephew of the renowned Henry Ward Beecher. Among those seriously wounded was Surgeon Moore, who was lying at the point of death, and General Forsythe, with a bullet through his leg and his scalp creased with another leaden missile.

The situation was critical in the extreme. Their food was gone, and the only substitute they had was the flesh of the dead horses that lay around them. From these they cut pieces of flesh which they ate raw, as there was no opportunity for cooking it. This stayed their hunger for a time, but it was a poor substitute at best. They lacked, also, for want of water, for, although the stream lay within a few feet of them, to reach it was impossible, for, if a man showed his head but for a moment he was greeted with a shower of bullets that made him seek cover without delay. The exigency of the situation made them inventive, and as they were almost desperate from want of water, they had recourse to a very slow method of digging down to the water level in order to secure even a scant supply. They cut open a canteen in such a way that it would serve the purpose of a shovel, and with this crude implement went to work to scoop up the sand to such a depth as would bring them to the object of their search. Their patience and persistence was rewarded better than they expected. Not only did they obtain sufficient to meet their immediate needs, but also plenty to bathe the general's wounds. As far as the dead were concerned, to bury them could not be thought of, as even the movement of a branch would be a signal for a dozen or more bullets which would drive them back to the shelter of their defences. Though the Indians seemed to realize the predicament of the besieged, they did not have the temerity to make a final dash to complete the work of butchery they had originally planned. Their first, second, and third attempts had cost them too dearly, and they were content to hover near with the intention of cutting their foe to pieces if they should make an attempt to escape. They waited patiently, apparently secure in their conviction that the besieged would eventually make a dash for liberty, and if such were to occur they would descend upon the stricken little band and with one fell swoop annihilate them completely. Their long desired wish was never accomplished. Intent upon the final destruction of the whites, they neglected to bury their own dead, not only because they were too busily engaged, in watching the besieged, but principally because they did not care to risk the danger of adding to the already too long list of their fellow tribesmen who had recently gone to the Happy Hunting Grounds. Moreover, the approaching night would give them a better opportunity to secure the bodies of their slain without incurring any risk of being sent to join them in the land of their forefathers.

Night fell, and with it came a cessation of hostilities. It must not be concluded that the Indians had abandoned the fight, for they did not, but kept a wary eye upon that little island, knowing that delay would surely put the palefaces in their possession. Nor did they make any venture to attack the stronghold of the enemy under cover of darkness. That was not the Indian's way of conducting his warfare. The hour favourable for the Indian raid is just about dawn, when they expect to find the enemy asleep, when they fall upon their unsuspecting victims and butcher them unmercifully. As for the little band on the island, they put in a most miserable night. An enemy could not wish them more discomfort than what they experienced. Tired, hungry, surrounded by their dead companions, they were not in a condition to find comfort in a situation where they were surrounded by their mortal enemies who, they thought, would take advantage of the darkness to crawl up to the very edge of their retreat and do them to death without mercy. However, in spite of such unpleasant conditions, the besieged kept up some show of cheerfulness. Morning found them far from depressed though the situation had not changed for the better. One wag, in spite of the fact that death might be lurking in his path, cheerfully remarked, "Well, boys, I guess I shall have to rustle some mule meat for the general's breakfast. I suppose he will like a change of diet as

Starving Elk

he had only horse meat yesterday." It was this spirit of mirth amid trying surroundings that kept the little band alive and ready during the long days of imprisonment that followed.

The next evening did not bring any change in their environments. The day had been spent very much like the preceding one, except there were no direct assaults upon the island. In the meantime the general's leg had become badly swollen, and inflammation had set in. Whilst bathing it, one of the boys discovered the bullet close to the surface, and with the general's permission performed a surgical operation with a pocket knife and removed the shapeless mass of lead. In order to keep the inflammation down as much as possible, the embryo surgeon continued the application of cold water to the affected part, which was somewhat efficacious. With the condition of the camp in such a demoralized condition, the outlook did not appear very promising. Even though the Indians should leave, which was not very likely, the situation would not be relieved to any great extent, as the general could not travel without the aid of a horse, and just then all the horses were dead, or had been stampeded. Things were beginning to assume a desperate aspect. Their food supply was about reduced to nothingness as the horse flesh on which they had been subsisting was no longer available as it was fast becoming tainted. This told them only too plainly that their stay upon the island was to be of short duration, and the prospect of relief from the outside world was very slight. Their only hope, and that a forlorn one, was to cut their way out through the ranks of the hostile Indians, and even the prospects of success in such a venture were not very alluring. Though they might succeed in breaking through the red cordon that held them prisoners on the island, the hope of reaching Fort Wallace could hardly be thought of in their enfeebled condition. It would amount to this, that they would have to fight their whole way back to the fort without so much as a cracker or a drink of water to sustain them on the way. It is hardly possible to imagine a body of men in such straitened circumstances keeping up, and even fighting against hope for delivery. After reviewing the situation from all its different angles, and with the desperation that urges a drowning man to grasp at a straw, the general saw but one way, and that one indicated very meagre chances of success, namely, to call for volunteers who would endeavour to make their way to the fort and bring assistance. Immediately, upon the proposal being made, S. E. Stillwell, better known by the name of Jack, and another scout named Pierre Truedell, expressed their willingness to make the attempt. It was sad enough to have to admit the failure of the expedition and report the news of the disaster, especially when they had started out with high hopes of success, but it was a measure that had to be taken if any relief was to be expected.

It was a perilous undertaking fraught with all manner of hardships. Danger lay all around them, and whether they would reach the end of their journey, or be taken prisoner and tortured by the Indians, they did not know, but brave at heart, they feared not, but set out to do their best or perish in the attempt to bring succour to their beleaguered companions. That same evening they stole forth from the camp and crossed the little stream, taking with them the best wishes and prayers of their fellow scouts for success. If ever men prayed fervently and expressed sincere wishes, it was on that occasion. No sooner had they crossed the stream than their difficulties began. As soon as they had crossed the water, they found their shoes filled with sand and water, and they were compelled to stop and empty them as well as they could. Then they started on their perilous undertaking in earnest. They did not know at what moment they would encounter some of the lurking foe and be compelled to fight for their lives. They did not dare to walk upright, but got down on all fours and crawled along over the sloping hillsides like dry land terrapins. Slowly, carefully, they wound their way among the dead Indians that littered the plain. Painfully they picked their way with tedium through the sullen foe, at times making haste as best they could in their stooping position, at times lying flat upon the ground while some restless Indian kept guard and patrolled his beat upon the hillside. During one of those unavoidable delays, Stillwell took time to change his shoes from which he had not been able to entirely remove the sand, and which were hurting his feet on that account, for a pair of moccasins which he removed from the feet of a dead Indian he encountered in his slow progress. After creeping like an infant on all fours or worming themselves along on their stomachs for over a mile they decided to risk standing up and in this manner increasing their speed, as they felt certain they were outside of the circle of Indians who were keeping watch on the little band of their comrades on the island. Their conclusion about their position relative to the savages proved correct. When they had gone far enough to permit them to risk whispering to each other, Truedell complained that his feet were hurting him on account of the quantity of sand in his shoes. As there was no dead Indian near who had no further use for moccasins, he adapted himself to the necessity of the case and removed his shirt. This he tore into bandages in which he wrapped his feet. They were well aware of the fact that there was no time to be lost in their mission, as every moment of unnecessary delay meant hardship, suffering and danger to their companions recently left behind. They strode on at a greater speed than before, but did not feel safe in talking in their natural tone of voice until they had put several miles between themselves and their starting point. Daylight found they still trudging hastily on, but the light compelled them to seek shelter in a friendly canyon, as the Indians would be sure to find their trail sometime during the hours of light and likely set out to overtake and kill them. Into the canyon they crawled and sought the shelter of the most secluded nook they could find. They then sat down to take a much needed rest. Fortunately for them, they had taken the precaution to bring with them some of the horse meat. They had matches but did not dare risk lighting a fire as the smoke would attract the attention of the Indians and bring them down upon them post-haste. They contented themselves with making the best of a bad situation and ate the horse meat raw. Then they turned over and went to sleep. Nightfall found them on their way again with renewed energy and determination. They felt that the loss of a whole day on their journey meant added sufferings to their companions, but such delay was unavoidable if they wished to reach the fort alive. On through the darkness they went, now running, now stumbling over the uneven ground, but doggedly moving forward with unceasing ardour. Daylight found them far from the canyon where they had spent the preceding hours of sleep. The only shelter that presented itself to their view was a dry buffalo wallow. Into this they crawled and spent the remaining hours of the day in sleep if possible, or reflecting on their trying difficulties. They had neither food nor water. It had been hours since they had taken the last sup of water, and they suffered acutely. Their lips were beginning to swell and they found talking difficult. Hunger, too, added to their discomfort, but there was no relief at hand. They had to make the best of a bad situation and hope for the best. They were willing to suffer the pangs of hunger and thirst, if they could only bring relief to their beleaguered friends. Night came at last, and they dragged themselves out of the wallow to make the last desperate effort to complete their journey. Hungry and thirsty they plunged into the darkness. Their progress was impeded owing to their weakened condition, but on and on they went, staggering and stumbling along, half mad with thirst, and tormented by hunger. Morning found them in a pitiable condition. Weary and wan they seemed as the morning sun showed them that they were not yet within sight of the fort they sought. Half maddened with suffering they were ready for anything. Truedell shot a rabbit, more by accident than design, and this they fairly tore to pieces and ate raw. They were too ravenous to wait until they could build a fire to cook it. On they went again, until they came to a buffalo hunter trail leading to the fort. Footsore and weary they dragged themselves along till almost exhausted they found their way into Fort Wallace. They sought Colonel Bankhead's quarters where they delivered to him the news of the disaster that had befallen the ill-fated expedition. This first and most important duty done, they then sought the canteen where they found everything that was necessary to satisfy their pressing wants. Relieved of the excitement of the journey, tired and worn in every member, conscious of the fact that they had done their share in forwarding relief to their friends still in distress, they sought convenient bunks and were soon dead to the world in deep repose.

 The next night after Stillwell and Truedell had left the island, the general deemed it a prudent move to send two more scouts on the same mission. He feared that, perhaps, some misfortune had overtaken the first emissaries, and if such were the case, the report of the disaster would never reach the fort, nor would succour come to him and his command. He called for two more volunteers who would be willing to try to elude the hundreds of savage eyes that were glinting with hate on the courageous little band, and watching every movement that took place in their primitive defence. No sooner had he issued the call than two volunteers offered themselves for the perilous undertaking. They realized the danger they would dare, but as they then stood, there would hardly be more peril in their efforts to break through the encircling foe, than there would be if they remained inert upon the island with starvation staring them in the face, and a band of bloodthirsty Indians ready to pounce upon them at the very moment they showed signs of distress.

If they did not go, total annihilation awaited them; if they did go, there was some slight chance of being liberated from their present predicament. With the odds against them, they were willing to do their best. The two courageous volunteers for the second effort were A. J. Pliley and Jack Donovan. They set out in about the same manner as their two companions did on the night before, and were very successful in eluding the foe. Things went well with them until the second day. Perhaps their first success in eluding the Indians made them over-bold, but the fact remains that they were followed by a band of Redskins who discovered their trail. On the second day out on their mission they experienced a great scare. They were lying in a dry buffalo wallow when Pliley heard a noise. He peered carefully over the edge of the wallow and discovered in the distance, about half a mile away, a band of about thirty warriors coming directly towards the spot where they were lying concealed. He turned to his companion and said, "Jack, I guess it is all up with you and me. There are about thirty Indians coming straight for this wallow."

"Well," replied Jack, "if that is the case, I am not going to trade even; I want two for one."

They were certainly in a dreadful predicament. Surrounded as they knew they would be by those relentless warriors, they determined to sell their lives as dearly as possible. They knew the process only too well. They could see already that band of warriors riding around the wallow in a circle, shooting at them on the run, or perhaps, even making a rush of it to overpower them by weight of numbers, and murder them heartlessly. Perhaps, they might make them prisoners, to be reserved for future torture.

Carefully keeping an eye upon the oncoming band, Pliley kept his friend informed of their movements. It would not do to expose themselves too soon, as there might be some hope that the Indians had not discovered their actual whereabouts. On they came, and the two men spontaneously reached for their weapons to defend themselves. Nearer and nearer they came, and the besieged made ready to give them an opening salutation of welcome. A little nearer they approached and then they halted. They cast a scanning glance over the surrounding country, and apparently they were satisfied that their intended victims had eluded them. Then they turned their ponies and rode away in the direction whence they came. With a sigh of relief, the two men put back their guns, and felt that they were safe for the present. That night when they set out again, they hastened their steps as rapidly as possible, knowing that the foe was on their trail. Stumbling along in much the same condition of hunger and thirst as the two former scouts had done, they reeled into the fort the same evening as Stillwell and Truedell. It was needless to say that there were heartfelt congratulations expressed when those four scouts met at Fort Wallace.

The band of Indians seen by Pliley and Donovan, were undoubtedly a part of the Roman Nose contingent. They had discovered the trail of the men shortly after their escape from the island and pursued them with the determination to overtake them and put them to death, but all to no purpose. They little knew how close they came to being successful in their efforts, especially as at one time they were within about forty rods of them as they lay in the dry buffalo wallow. Apparently they became discouraged in their efforts and gave up the chase.

Having received the message delivered by the four men, it did not take Colonel Bankhead long to call out every available man and horse, to fit out ambulances, and wagons laden with provisions, and make whatever preparations were necessary to relieve the wants of the distressed.

When the Indians knew that the messengers had eluded them and had likely reached the fort in spite of all the measures they took to forestall such an event, they thought prudence the better part of valour and withdrew their forces from the neighbourhood of the island. They foresaw that relief would come to the brave defenders of the little sand bar in a very short time, and as they had such small success with a small band, they felt that they would hardly be able to contend with a greater force which would be certainly sent out for their relief.

Once the relief corps got in motion, it did not let the grass grow under its feet. Their progress was necessarily slower than that of the expedition on account of the baggage they were carrying, and, also, because they had to exercise the greatest care in marching for they knew not at what time they would encounter a band of hostile Indians. The journey to the locality of the disaster occupied several days. They were rather surprised to find the nearer they approached their destination the less the presence of Indians was noted. When they drew up in sight of the island, not a savage was to be seen or heard of.

In the interim of the departure of the scouts for relief, the prisoners' on the island suffered acutely. Around them lay the dead bodies of some of their companions whom they did not dare to venture out to bury. They were rapidly decomposing and the atmosphere was laden with the nauseating smell that accompanies such a condition either of animal, or man. Added to this was the number of dead horses, which added to the intensity of the malodorous smell. The wounded suffered more and more as inflammation set in or increased. Their condition was pitiable as very little could be done to relieve their sufferings. Above all this, they had to endure the pangs of hunger, which every day grew more and more irksome. It was a sad spectacle that the eyes of the relief corps beheld when they came upon them first. Hardly able to raise their weakened bodies from a recumbent position, the wounded endeavoured to give a cheer at the sight of their deliverers, but it was such a mockery of cheer that it was enough to bring tears to the eyes of many a veteran. Those who had not been wounded, and they were few, lent a willing hand to the administration of medical assistance to their stricken companions. They felt so overcome with joy themselves that they could hardly express themselves in the intensity of their happiness. But their newly-arrived fellow scouts and soldiers knew by their looks the depth and sincerity of their feelings of gratitude, and felt happy to be able to reach them before death had overtaken the whole band.

The first duty to be attended to by the relief party, was the burial of the dead. Delay would have been dangerous and, perhaps, fatal, as they were, as mentioned above, badly decomposed. They performed the sad duty over the remains of their former companions with all the reverence that their circumstances would permit. Next, they had to look after the wants of their general. He had been suffering intensely from the wound in the scalp and in the leg. They administered such remedies as they had, which produced some relief. The rest of the wounded were attended to in much the same fashion, each one receiving what attention could be given them. When all this had been done, they made ready to set out for the fort. It was a slow journey, but in time they reached their destination where proper remedies soon restored them to fighting condition again.

The expedition of Gen. Forsythe, which he insisted on making against Roman Nose and his band, terminated in dismal failure. It had cost the lives of several valuable and experienced men, and marred to some degree the reputation for success which he had hitherto gained. Nevertheless, the lesson bore fruit. It taught the American people at large, and General Forsythe in particular that all the knowledge of Indian warfare is not taught at the military academy at West Point. In fact, it was impressed upon the minds of several who were in a position to profit by the lesson, that the "University of the Plains" was far better adapted to produce men who would be successful in that mode of fighting than any of the academies established for the purpose of instructing the neophyte in the art of conducting warlike manoeuvres.

The writer is indebted to S. E. Stillwell, better known to his friends as "Jack," for the information regarding the battle of Arickaree, in which he played so prominent a part. His feat, alone, of bearing the message from Gen. Forsythe to Fort Wallace was sufficient to win him undying fame. In such high esteem was he held by those to whom he lent his services, that Gen. Phil. Sheridan characterized him as being the bravest and most daring young man he ever knew, and he knew a multitude of them. He was, later on, the trusted and boon companion of Buffalo Bill, "Col. W. Cody," in fighting the Indians on the plains. At one time, later on, he was Police Judge of the City of El Reno. This position he retained until he was appointed United States commissioner at Anadarko, Okla. This position he resigned and went to the North Plate, Neb., where he died and was buried within a day's ride of the battle ground of the Arickaree. While he was filling the office of commissioner at Anadarko, the writer frequently spent hours with him chatting over the events of former days upon the plains. During one of those visits, he ventured to inquire of the commissioner if he thought he himself had killed Roman Nose. He replied that he did not know, but after taking a few puffs of his cigarette, he naively remarked that if he did not, it was attributable to his aim and not to his intention as he gave him his undivided attention from the time he came within range of his rifle until he fell from his horse. He paused then and took a few more puffs, and closed the subject by remarking, "perhaps, some of the other boys did it."

CHAPTER 18

The Whirlwind Raid

For several years succeeding to terminations of the Civil War, the whole plains country, as I have said in the previous chapter, from the frontier settlements westward including a great portion of the Rocky Mountains, and from the British line on the north to the Red River of the north line of Texas, was claimed by the Indian by virtue of his title begotten of prior possession, and was used by him as a hunting ground, and also as the theatre in which to stage the settlement of tribal difficulties. As a variation from those internal battles, or wars, as you may wish to call them, they frequently made raids upon the white settlers, killing and scalping the men, kidnapping the women and children, and running off their stock as spoils of war. They roamed that vast expanse of territory at will, seeking their sustenance from the abundance of wild game with which the plains were teeming. Buffalo and deer were there in innumerable quantities and were easily slaughtered. Smaller game abounded everywhere. When the bucks returned from the chase with a buffalo or a deer to show for his efforts, the squaws took possession of the carcass, cutting off huge chunks of meat for provisions, and then tanning the hides at which they were experts. In times of peace they worked faithfully at the task of converting the green hide into something serviceable, but when the war alarm was sounded, they readily threw aside the work at hand to follow their lord and master on the warpath, not as an idle onlooker, but armed with a scalping knife and tomahawk, they followed up the work of slaughter by assisting in the scalping, or mutilating the bodies of the dead. In this last feature of the raid, they seemed to be carried away by a sort of frenzy, and the manner in which they treated the corpses of those slain, was brutal and inhuman in the extreme. In my own experience I have known squaws who were so fascinated by this kind of brutality or rather ghoulishness, that at the first notes of the war song they deserted their white husbands to follow in the wake of the war, although at the time they were drawing rations from the government and were in possession of comfortable homes.

In this connection, it may not be amiss to say something of the Medicine Man, and the part he played in the Indian raids. I might say that he was the most important factor in such undertakings, as well as in the inter-tribal disputes. He seemed to have such an influence over the destinies of the tribe in which he was operating, that the chiefs and their followers placed implicit confidence in his decisions. On him alone, rather than the chiefs in council, depended the undertaking of any raid, or struggle. Whenever there was any prospect of trouble arising, he called the chiefs and warriors and held a séance in which he made inquiries of them as to their opinions and views regarding the matter under discussion. This done, he set about a series of orgies and incantations to discover from some secret agency the advisability of making the venture, or abandoning it. A consultation of this kind often took several days, but when he arrived at some conclusion, it was announced to the chiefs and their followers, and his decision in the matter was final and devoid of any appeal. As soon as the result of his incantation was promulgated, the warriors buckled on their armour, if I may use the expression, though there were few buckles and oftentimes no more armour than a breach-clout and a blanket with some instrument of warfare, and made ready for the raid on some white settler's cabin and stock, or to engage in a death struggle with some other tribe. The success or failure of his prediction did not affect the medicine man in any great degree as regards his position in the tribe. If the raid was a success, he became the lion of the hour and the tribe looked upon him as something of a supernatural being, but if, on the contrary, things resulted adversely, he had little to lose except his reputation, and that would be so badly shattered that no other member of the tribe would care to wear his mantel of prophesy. To illustrate the case in point, I shall mention what befell chief Black Kettle's Medicine Man. After holding a séance for several days, he arrived at the very pleasing conclusion that the white man's gun was no good; that the bullets would fall to the ground close to the muzzle of the gun and consequently would not injure an Indian. When Gen. Custer fell upon him, one winter's morning, on the Washita and killed more than one hundred of his warriors with Black Kettle himself, and took the remainder of the band prisoners and brought them to Camp Supply, the estimate on that Medicine Man's ability as a prognosticator was diminished to a vanishing point. We are inclined to smile at the credulity of the Indian in the matter of consulting the Medicine Man, but, in this curiosity to secure a knowledge of future events, especially where they refer to his welfare, they were not much different from the rank and file of white folks who consult some street fakir or clairvoyant, turning over half a dollar to find out whether a business man is dealing fairly or otherwise, or to discover if the partner of one's joys and sorrows, is travelling the path of rectitude or not, or to discover some secret source of wealth that will place the inquirer beyond the reach of want. Such foolish curiosity is not confined to any race or tribe, as I find in my varied reading that the practice of clairvoyance, soothsaying, etc., has been in practice and fashion from the days when Moses led the Children of Israel out of Egypt down through the ages to the present day, and you will find on investigation that the clients of the *fakir* are not limited to the unlettered class, but embrace members from every grade of society from the proletariat to the Four Hundred. However, to return to the thread of my story, I must say that since the day when the long range gun has been put in the hands of man, the calling of the Medicine Man has become almost obsolete.

In regard to the manner of conducting campaigns, there was no fixed rule, but every chief conducted his fight as circumstances dictated, and some of the later day chieftains manifested an ability in their campaigns that would stamp them as Napoleons of their tribes and times. Precision and alacrity were seldom wanting in the raids. If they came in contact with the soldier, they outclassed him to some degree, as, after the first few volleys, they scattered and disappeared from view with a readiness that was astonishing. Nor could the trained soldier of the line follow up his foe to any advantage as they seldom left a trail behind that would guide him to their hiding place. The untrained eye of the military man militated against any success he might otherwise have had, and it required the scout of the plains to ferret out the marks and signs that would give any opportunity for pursuit. In the meantime the Indian on his fleet-footed ponies would likely be fifty or one hundred miles away from the point of encounter.

The Indian did not always confine his raiding propensities to the white man, but as frequently gave his attention to some of the neighbouring tribes with whom they had some matter to adjust. Needless to say, when two tribes met in conflict, the fighting bore a character of savagery that was in keeping with the untamed nature of the participants. Naturally, the Indian was compelled to confine himself to the use of such weapons as his limited ingenuity could provide, but in the use of what he had he was an adept. Before the introduction of fire-arms his chief weapons consisted of the bow and arrow, the tomahawk, and the scalping knife, but if an opportunity presented itself for him to make use of the more up-to-date weapons of warfare, he took advantage of it, as is instanced in the case of the raid made upon the Sack and Fox Indians by their more southerly neighbours.

The Sack and Fox Indians were located in Kansas, and by reason of their close proximity to the settlements of white men, and also on account of carrying on trade with them, they came into possession of fire-arms which they used with considerable success in hunting the buffalo. They found it to their advantage to use the weapon for laying up supplies of meat and hides. This opened up an avenue of trade for them as they found a ready market for the buffalo skins they procured, but in their prosperity they nearly were overcome by disaster. The plain Indians learning of the success of the Sack and Fox Indians, became jealous of them and resolved to exterminate them. A conference was called and invitations issued to the different tribes to take part in the general *pow-wow*. The assemblage was to take place on the Arkansas River, where they were to decide on what measures to take, or, in other words, lay out a plan of campaign. The Kiowas, Comanches, Arapahos, Apaches, and Cheyennes presented themselves on the day appointed, and initiated the proceedings with a Medicine Dance. Then a council of war was called and they came to the unanimous conclusion to go north to the Smoky Hill River and wage relentless war upon the Sack and Fox Indians and thus terminate the slaughter of the buffalo on the plains. The leadership of this expedition was by common consent bestowed upon Chief Whirlwind. They then indulged in their customary war-dance and set forth upon their mission of destruction.

It was Robert Burns who wrote that,

The best laid plans of mice and men
Gang aft aglee,
And lea' us naught but grief and pain
For promised joy.

This quotation applies definitely to the Whirlwind raid. He started forth like a "plumed knight" chanting his war song and whooping along the way to instil courage into his braves, each of whom carried a back-load of arrows and a couple of well-strung bows as his weapons of war, and expected to share in the glory of a great victory. Nor did the chanting and roaring of their chieftain fail of its purpose. By the time they reached their destination they were all strung up to the highest tension, in fact they were all but counting the scalps they were about to carry away in triumph, etc. They reached the canyon in the Smoky Hill country where the Sack and Fox Indians had secreted themselves, prepared to give the invaders of their hunting ranges a warm reception. Whirlwind and his band advanced in confidence, knowing they outnumbered their intended victims, but they were not acquainted with the new ally of their foe. They knew absolutely nothing of the use of fire-arms, their efficiency, and death dealing powers. They had not become acquainted with the sound of the carbine, nor of the shot-gun. This was a power they did not to reckon with, nor knew how to estimate its value. The only thing that concerned them just then was to make a sudden whirlwind dash upon their foe, butcher them, and carry off the spoils. They were led up to the mouth of the canyon chanting and shouting, when the muzzles of a hundred guns belched forth thunder and lightning, and a hail of leaden bullets flew around them in death dealing myriads. They turned and fled, stampeded like a herd of antelope toward their starting point. They reached the Arkansas, but oh! how their bright expectations had been rudely shattered. One conclusion they arrived at as the result of their unprofitable venture, and that was that bows and arrows was no weapon to offset the effect of a musket or a carbine. It was a sad return for all their brilliant hopes. Behind them lay the corpses of fifty of their bravest warriors, whilst twice that number came limping back home, crippled by the unthought-of ally of their foes. Nor could the loss be estimated at the death of their fellow braves, nor in the wounds borne by the cripples, nor in the number of horses that had been shot from under them, but in the blow to their tribal pride. There they suffered most, for it was inconceivable to think that one-hundred and twenty-five Sack and Fox Indians should in any manner possible overcome the flower of the various tribes that participated in the raid. It is estimated by those who know, that there were between twelve and fifteen hundred warriors of the southern tribes under the command of the mighty Whirlwind. As a battle, there was little or nothing to it. The chief with all his experience could not get his men to face that leaden hail that smote the ranks so mercilessly. There was nothing to do but turn tail and flee, which he did.

When they returned to the Arkansas, they mutually agreed that the expedition from the view-point of results obtained was a failure. From there they made their way south until they reached the North Canadian River and there disbanded, each tribe seeking its own reservation, or hunting grounds as it saw fit. They never again returned to molest the Sack and Fox tribes in their peaceful occupation.

It was currently reported and believed by many that Whirlwind on his return to the hunting grounds on the North Canadian, said that every feather had been shot from his war bonnet during the engagement, in the Smoky Hill canyon. I never had the pleasure of being intimately acquainted with that doughty warrior, but I have seen him on several occasions and have also seen his war bonnet, and I know something of the amount of feathers required to decorate it. Since he has passed to the Happy Hunting Grounds, I shall take this opportunity of denying that he ever made such a statement, for I do not believe that he ever said it, as the evidence would plainly indicate that he would not be telling the truth, which would be plain to all. Knowing how much the wily old warrior prized the emblem of his former prowess in the field of battle, I feel certain that he would never submit to have it disfigured by the bullets of his foes, particularly, whilst his head was beneath it. So I shall repeat what I said before, "He did not say it."

The reader may be pleased to have a little insight into the general character of Whirlwind, the leader of the expedition that failed. Like all leaders whether white, black, or bronze, he always made it his motto to win. Kill, conquer and destroy were the methods he employed in his campaigns. In the heat of battle, he was relentless and uncompromising, but when the battle was over and he had returned to his own hunting grounds, he showed a spirit of forgiveness and generosity, as well as many other redeeming qualities, for which he should receive due credit.

CHAPTER 19

The Sun Dance

It may not be amiss to insert here a description of what was known to the various Indian tribes as the Sun Dance. Each nation, people, or tribe in past history has had some ceremony, symbolic in its nature, by which honours and dignities were conferred upon those who sough honour and preferment. Nor has this custom been confined to any particular class, for all have, at different times, indulged in the practice, nor was it without its influence and effect upon those who sought advancement. The Knights of the Middle Ages, when in the act of receiving the symbols of their office and vocation, were compelled to submit themselves to some kind of ordeal by which they manifested their fitness to wear the honours they sought. So, too, it was with the denizens of the plains, as the following narrative from unimpeachable authority will illustrate. Just as in the days of old, the ceremony was partly religious in its development, so, too, the children of the plains invested the conferring of honours and rights to preferment with religious ceremony and physical tests.

The Sun Dance, as practiced by the Cheyenne tribe of Indians, dates back to time immemorial. In the performance of it, the Indian makes a profession of faith in the Supreme Being, and at the same time subjects those who engage in it, to a physical test that is sufficient to try the heart and soul of even the most valiant. The first step in the proceedings of this semi-religious festival, is to select the proper location for the celebration of it. Weeks, and perhaps months in advance, some *pow-wow* is held at which they make the selection of the place in which they wish to hold their festival.

Usually some well-known camping ground is chosen on account of the abundance of fuel and water, both of which were necessary for the proper conduct of the ceremony, for it was essential that there should be means at hand for preparing the final feast, as well as an abundant supply of water for the multitudes assembled from the different districts for the purpose of watering their stock, as well as, affording bathing facilities to such a vast number.

For several days prior to the actual enactment of the ceremony, Indians would begin to assemble, straggling in from long distances, bringing with them the greater part a their household belongings. North, south, east, and west sent their contingents. Whole families with their *teepees*, ponies, and dogs, assembled from all parts of the reservations or the plains to participate in the festivities or to be merely on-lookers hoping in their mere presence to receive some benediction from the Great Spirit whom they assembled to worship. Long before the arrival of these scattered bands, the Medicine Man was on the scene to give his attention to whatever preparations were required for the occasion. He usually selected some central point wherein to erect his place of worship. In this chosen spot he was to enact the two-fold role of High Priest and Medicine Man, to minister to their spiritual and corporal necessities.

Many days elapsed before the arrival of the final contingent, and the intervening time had to be employed as best they could. This gave those who had already arrived on the scene, an opportunity of visiting their relations and friends, whom they had not met, perhaps since the preceding Sun Dance. The older folks were content to while away the passing hours in social converse, whilst the young engaged in feats of skill, contesting in games peculiar to the tribe. It was quite evident that they were supremely happy in their childish amusements, and enjoyed them as thoroughly as their white contemporaries found pleasure and enjoyment in their more up-to-date and scientific play toys. One thing particularly noticeable in all their endeavours was the spirit of prompt obedience to parental authority. The control that the Indian parent exercises over his child is marvellous, and in all my intercourse with the children of the plains, I have never known of a parent chastising his child in a cruel or harsh manner. It is a thing unheard of, that a child ever raised a hand or uttered an unfilial expression of contempt towards his parents. I believe that if an Indian child were to emulate the example of many white children, whom I have known not only to treat their parents with contempt, but even go so far as to treat them contumeliously, the Indian father would be so staggered by such an outbreak and disregard for the proprieties of his position, that it would require a council of chiefs to decide upon the proper mode of dealing with the case, as it would lack all precedent. The little redskin is attentive to the wants of his parents, and at all times exercises a continual watchfulness over their wants to forestall any command to fulfil some duty. Nor do the parents fill the childish mind with tales of goblins and hobgoblins to excite terror in his little heart. Even the customary punishment of locking the little child up in some dark corner, is lacking, for there is no need of it. Obedience to authority is part of the nature of the Indian child and it comes so easy for him to render it that it never becomes irksome.

When the last stragglers have arrived, and the interchange of social courtesies is fulfilled, the large central *teepee*, or amphitheatre is erected and ready for occupancy. In the centre of this *teepee* is placed a large pole much the same as the old-time May pole used by the people of the Middle Ages on the occasion of their annual celebrations, but in this case the purpose was very much different, as will be seen later on in this narrative.

During the time the rank and file of the Indians were enjoying their intercourse, the young men who were candidates for honours in the trials of endurance, were busying themselves plaiting their hair and painting their bodies. They decorated their faces and other portions of the body with every conceivable kind of animal and reptile that human ingenuity could invent, as taste or custom suggested. Some of the productions were very artistic, and some were rather grotesque, but the tout-ensemble served the purpose for which the work was intended. They were no novices in the art of extracting colours from the plants and shrubs that grew in abundance on the plains, and at the same time had developed the art of applying them to the human body for decorative purposes. The paints were not indelible, consequently they could be easily removed and another application made as circumstances required. At times, the renewal of the decoration took place as many as four or five times a day.

The ceremony lasted four days without any intermission. During that time the candidates for honours were obliged to such a strict fast and abstinence, that not a morsel of food, nor a drop of water passed their lips during the time. One favour was conceded to them; they were allowed to smoke. One might be inclined to think that, at times, the regulation was not faithfully observed, but there he would be mistaken. There were too many eyes upon the candidates to permit of his stealing off to the commissary department of the assemblage, nor could he by any means carry off beneath the folds of his garments a morsel of food as the extent of his habiliments would not permit such a thing as his outfit consisted of a breach-clout around his waist and a few feathers in his hair.

At the hour appointed for the opening of the ceremony, a chief mounted his horse and rode through the assembled throng crying out that the ordeal was about to begin. It was his duty also to set down the rules and regulations governing the performance. When he had explained the ordinances sufficiently to be understood by all the candidates, he withdrew and the Medicine Man appeared on the scene. He was decked out in his most gorgeous array of feathers and finery, with his hair plaited down his back and ornamented with more feathers and quills. Truly, he was an imposing spectacle to the simple minded tribesman and they looked upon him with a species of awe. In his hand he bore the wing of an eagle. He took up his position in a very conspicuous place and struck an attitude very much like some of the Indians we see pictured standing on some eminence with his hand shading his eyes and looking far away over the plains in search of something of interest. The Medicine Man assumed about the same attitude, using the eagle wing to protect his eyes from the sun. He stood motionless for a period lasting about half an hour, gazing in the direction of the blazing sun. I never came to learn the true meaning of this action on the part of the Medicine Man, but I presume he expected to discover some supernatural visitor coming from the direction in which he was gazing. I can readily imagine what his consternation would be if one of our modern aeroplanes passed close over his head while he was making observations of the heavens. There is no doubt he would drop his eagle wing and make a dash for his *teepee* labouring under the impression that the devil was out making morning calls. Such an apparition would most likely interfere with the completion of the programme, and the tribesmen would probably seek shelter or protection from the whirring, roaring monster, in the depths of the nearby timber. However, as no such occurrence took place, the Medicine Man continued his vigil until such time as he thought proper to terminate it. Upon his return to camp, the *tomtom* sounded and the dance was on. All the braves fell into line, and the *pow-wow* started with each brave keeping step to the beatings of the primitive instrument. No squaws were permitted to engage in the ceremony as it was to be a strict, test of physical endurance. Much less, are white men permitted to participate in the Sun Dance, as this is an institution particularly appropriated to the Indian tribes. The squaws had their share of the work to do, and while the ceremony was going on, they spent their time in making preparations for the feast that was to follow upon the completion of the dance. The young men who were not otherwise engaged and who did not care to undergo the terrible ordeal about to follow, mounted their ponies and scoured the plains for game. This was a necessary undertaking, as the amount required to supply the throng present with food, was very great. True, each tribesman brought some provisions, but that supply would be inadequate to the demands of such an occasion.

If any white man had an opportunity to witness the proceedings of the Sun Dance, he would most likely arrive at a very erroneous idea of the intent and purpose of the occasion, nor would he understand the significance of what he might see. The wild, weird scene before him, the fantastic movements of the participants in the drama would probably create in his mind a false impression of the nature and character of the ceremony. However, to arrive at the true meaning of what was being done, it is sufficient to say that the heads of numerous families were present on the occasion I speak of, to do homage and worship the Great Spirit, and offer thanks for favours received in the past. This goes to show that the Indian was not unmindful of his obligation to the Great Spirit, but brings out to our view a side of the Indian character that is very seldom mentioned by those who appear or seem to know all about him. They were grateful for the gifts received from the hand of their Creator and on occasions of this kind strove to show it. They probably had some friend or relative who escaped from some calamity. If so, this was the occasion on which they showed their gratitude to the Father of all. Perhaps, some of them had wives and children who had recently recovered from some ailment. If so, they were grateful. Sundry were the purposes for which they assembled on this occasion to offer up their mead of praise and thanksgiving to the Great Spirit. Their devotion was as sincere and deep-seated as the pilgrims who made long pilgrimages to the Holy Land to visit the sepulchre of Him, who died for us all. The scoffer may not be able to see it, but there is One who sees and judges, and who will render to each and all the just reward on the day of the final reckoning, and the Indian may not be as bad as painted when seen in the light of the Kingdom of Heaven, where he will be judged according to his lights.

When the hunters have returned from the chase, each deposits in the commissary department the trophies of the hunt, antelope, deer, badgers, coons, rabbits. All is grist that is brought to that mill. Even the dogs contribute their share to make the supply equal to the grand display of culinary art that is to be staged at the close of the ceremony. It may appear strange to the reader that the turkey had no place on the menu card of the feast. The reason of this lay in the fact that the Indian considered him too cowardly and timid to be food fit for the brave and warlike members of the tribe, as it would have a tendency to diminish, if not destroy their spirit of bravery and fortitude.

In the meantime, all had been a scene of activity in the ranks of those who were contending for honours, as I have mentioned in a former paragraph. The tom-tom had sounded the call to the test. The old warriors and the young bucks who were out for preferment, had formed a procession and were marching toward the amphitheatre. The old bucks who had won their honours on the war-path were dressed in their fanciest blankets, while those who were to undergo the ordeal wore nothing save the breach-clout, and a few feathers. When the excitement of the preliminary movements had taken possession of the young men, one of the most reckless of the young bucks broke from the ranks and began to dance around the pole. There he gave himself up to a frenzy of movement, gyrating and gesticulating in a manner marvellous to behold. Swinging his hands, kicking up his heels, twisting, twirling, performing antics of all kinds supposed to be of the nature of warlike movements, he all the time gave vent to a series of yells, whoops, and screams of the most unimaginable kind. At the proper moment, a new feature of the ceremony took place. A man selected for the purpose came forth bearing a knife in his hand. His duty it was to make incisions in the back of the aspirant for honours. Two incisions were made on each side of the back, about half an inch apart. When the knife had done its work, the flesh was raised between the gashes and a skewer of wood, much resembling the old-fashioned husking peg, was forced through the flesh beneath the skin. Around the projecting ends of this was tied a buckskin thong to which was tied a lasso. This operation was performed on both the incisions. A buffalo skull was then tied to the lasso at its further extremity. The operation is then complete, unless the young brave should request an additional skull which would be provided if convenience, or opportunity, permitted. If it were not possible to provide a buffalo head for the occasion, the skeleton of a deer, or a bear would answer the purpose as well. In fact, the skeleton of any beast of prey was considered to suffice, as it was supposed to engender a warlike spirit in the candidate. This feature of attaching the skeleton of a beast of prey was not always performed in the same way, as some of the tribes preferred to have it attached to their breasts.

When properly equipped with this new attachment, whether buffalo skull or skeleton of a deer or other animal, the young buck was then turned loose. He joined in the chanting and kept step with the other dancers, but did not mingle in the ranks, as the appendage attached to him and dragging along might interfere with the rhythmical movements of the dancers. He did not, fail to keep step with his fellows, nor neglect his part of the singing, but confined the field of his operations, separate from the others, where he could conduct himself with what freedom the impediment he was dragging, would permit. There he discovered himself confronted with difficulties at several points, as the buffalo skull might become entangled in a tuft of grass and intensify the pain he was already suffering so heroically. In case of difficulty of the kind, he received no assistance from outside sources, but was compelled to wiggle and twist until he succeeded in loosing it from its hold or tore the flesh and skin from his back. It might happen that the first obstacle that he met would break the fleshy bonds that hold the skewers in place, and free him from his burden, or he might drag his burden around for days. Oftentimes, in a spirit of playfulness, some young redskin, prompted by the genius of mischief, would jump on the skull and tear it loose from its moorings, but lacking this fortuitous event, and weary of the burden, he would frequently in desperation wilfully become entangled in something or other and break it of his own volition. When he became detached from the buffalo skull in the manner described, there necessarily was left a gaping wound with ragged edges. Then he received attention from the Medicine Man who was close at hand for such an emergency. With his knife he trimmed off the rough edges and expectorated the juice of some herb which he had been chewing, into the wound. This remedy was supposed to be sufficiently potent to eradicate any infection that might be lurking there, and produce beneficial results owing to the healing qualities of the plant he masticated. That was the total of the medical treatment the candidate received during the whole term of his torture. Frequently there were as many as a dozen candidates on, trial at the same time, and all were compelled to endure the same torture. It frequently happened that some of them weakened by hunger and exhausted from the pain they were suffering, fell in a swoon. If such were the case, he was left where he fell, and no attempt was made to render him any other assistance than throwing a buffalo robe or blanket over him where he lay. There they permitted him to lie, to recover or die as the case might be. It made no difference to the other dancers what his condition might be, they continued their gyrations apparently indifferent to the condition of the victim of hunger and torture beneath the blanket. If he revived, he began again his dancing and chanting as though there had been no interruption, which he continued until freed from his burden. The test is the same for all, and the attention and medical assistance rendered is identical in every case.

As I said before, other tribes prefer to have the incisions made upon their breasts, but in such a case do not bear the burden of a buffalo skull, but are attached by the lariat rope to the limb of a tree, or to the centre pole of the amphitheatre round which they dance until they succeed in breaking loose by tearing the skewer through the flesh that holds it. As for the medical treatment, it is the same in all cases.

The ceremony is continued until the supply of volunteers for honours is exhausted. Those who have passed through the ordeal successfully are in line for promotion to the higher offices of their respective tribes providing a vacancy occurs through death or accident. They are considered the proper material to fill the offices of chief. They have been put through a test sufficiently harsh to try the heart and soul to its utmost capacity for suffering. Their courage and constancy was beyond question, and henceforth were looked upon as men having a prior right to fill the place of any old chief who might go to the Happy Hunting Grounds. They were not only proud that they had borne the test successfully, but also were more pleased that they had lived up to the traditions of the family. They were firm believers in heredity, and were proud of the distinction of being descended from some former warrior of prominence as the present day white man is jealous of his descent from the first colonists who came over in the *Mayflower*. I have met Indians who gloried in their descent from Roman Nose, Black Kettle and other noted leaders who have long since passed away, and I have found others who traced their lineage back to Tecumseh, and Black Hawk.

The system of dancing just described was suppressed by Col. Woodson whilst he was in charge of the Darlington Agency, as he considered it too cruel and barbarous to be permitted on the Reservation because he thought it would have a tendency to retard any progress the younger Indians might be making towards a more civilized manner of life. I understand, however, that Col. Woodson's order was rescinded by another commissioner of Indian affairs at a later date, and they are now permitted to practice it in a modified form.

It has been my lot to witness nearly every form of dance from the Irish Jig to the latest form of Tango, or Bunny Hug, Scotch Reels, the French Four, the Dutch Waltzes, the old American Cotillion, and the Virginia Reel, but all these combined and set in motion at the same time to the wildest and weirdest music known to the white race, would fail to produce the soul thrilling, hair-rising emotions created by the Cheyenne Sun Dance when in full swing. The sound of Patrick Gilmore's band, in its palmiest days, would be as the twittering of the snow bird in comparison with the roar of the Rocky Mountain lion, when the festivities were at their height.

When the time limit of the Sun Dance expired, everything was placed away for future use. The buffalo skulls, sacred utensils of the feast, were carefully secreted, and the amphitheatre removed. Nothing remained but the trampled grass to show that anything beyond the ordinary had taken place.

The dance having been completed, the feasting begins. During all the time the braves have been engaged in their soul thrilling, hair-raising performance, the squaws have been busy. They were running back and forth, making preparations for the banquet. Some spent their time skinning a coyote or other animal, others dressing and cooking the food already prepared, others looking around for choice morsels to tempt the appetite of some lord and master, as they felt he might be in need of something delicate to meet the wants of a stomach sensitive from long fasting. Whatever the occupation, they were all busy, as the number to be waited upon might number thousands. It was no easy task, but they were equal to the occasion. At the signal given as before, the feast is on. To see them plunging with reckless abandon into the midst of the feast, one would be forced to conclude that the long fast had little effect upon their appetites except to render them sharper. All thought of the stomach being in a delicate condition was forgotten, and the chief work at hand was to give undivided attention to devouring as much of the viands within reach as the capacity of the stomach would permit, and that was some capacity. Nicety of choice was not manifested to any great degree, for their hunger was usually at such a pitch that they could devour anything that the teeth could masticate to some degree. Here you might see a lordly old chief manipulating the hurricane deck of a gray wolf, or a skunk with wonderful dexterity; there another warrior bold making a savage attack upon a handful of raccoon claws, and so it went from one end of the multitude to the other, each earnestly intent upon demolishing the pile of viands set before him and wondering if there was any more left for a second assault. The time generally allotted for the repast was sunrise. Then each and all squatted upon the ground anxious for the welcome ordeal to begin. Sitting on their haunches, facing the rising sun, not a word was spoken. It might have been that they were too worn out from the long fast, or perhaps they were so pre-occupied with the thought, of the great spread before them that they had no inclination to talk, but the more probable reason is that it was one of the regulations set down to govern the termination of the festival. No matter what the motive was that governed the conduct of the throng in the matter of maintaining silence and avoiding undue noise, the fact was that they set to the work of supplying the wants of the inner man without delay, either in beginning, or continuing the work of demolition. All the rules of etiquette, as prescribed for the four-hundred, were suspended. It was a case of "Reach what you can, and while making way with it keep the eye on the lookout for more. Anything you do not see is not good for you." They did not merely eat their food, they seemed to absorb it. The execution was rapid and effective, and the final result might have been summed up in a huge pile of bones from which the meat had been thoroughly removed.

The breakfast, as one might call the repast just ended, did not terminate their stay in the locality, but each and all felt it a bounded duty to remain as long as there was any of the huge pile of provisions remaining. They were all jubilant over the happy termination of the ordeal, and the young men who had endured the test successfully strutted about with a pardonable pride in their bearing. Feasting took the place of fasting and all were merry as far as their method of life would permit the expression of that feeling. When the last vestiges of the immense store of game disappeared, they all gathered up their possessions and made ready to set out to their respective camping grounds. Prior to their departure they held a sort of conclave in which they decided when and where to hold the next meeting, and also outlined the nature of the dance to be performed on the occasion. It might be a Medicine Dance, or a Green Corn Dance, or some other festivity peculiar to the notions of the tribes and the exigencies of the occasion. Whatever the decision was, it was abided by faithfully on the time appointed. This settled, they returned home with the satisfaction of having done what they considered a duty, and felt that they had fulfilled their obligations to the Great Spirit.

I feel very much indebted for the above description of the Sun Dance, to a lady who spent many of her younger years among the tribe who conducted it. She is familiar with the customs of the tribe, knows their traditions, and, in fact, may be considered an authority on things relating to the history of that nation. Her name, at the time of which I write, was Mina E. Ashpard, but was changed by the Indians to Tat-ta-voe-e-tau, or Blue Beads, on account of the string of blue beads which she usually wore around her neck. She was loved and admired by the whole tribe, but particularly by several young chiefs who sought her hand in marriage. Her affections, however, leaned to another direction, and she afterward married W. C. Ross, who owns a large tract of land adjoining the flourishing City of El Reno, the Queen City of the North Canadian. Mrs. Ross is today the mother of a large family of sons and daughters who are a credit to her and an honour to the State of Oklahoma. Even today she delights in telling how she used to enjoy riding out on a bronco, lassoing a wild antelope, or deer, and dragging it back to camp amid the cheers and acclamations of the whole tribe.

W. C. Ross, through his foresight and good business management, succeeded in locating his family allotments in close proximity to the City of El Reno, as I have mentioned above, and his location proved to be one of the most valuable in the Canadian Valley. By its increase in value, due to its location, and by his knowledge of farming, he has placed himself and his family above the reach of want. He is educating his sons and daughters in the Catholic School of El Reno, and they have proved themselves good students. Their native talents developed in such surroundings, show that they are or will be capable of fulfilling the duties of responsible positions in the very near future.

CHAPTER 20

The Adobe Wall Raid

Before setting down in detail the series of events that comprise what is called the 'Adobe Wall' raid, I wish to put forth my reason for undertaking the task of making known to the public an event that will long be remembered, not only by those who took part in the occurrence, but, also, by many of the early settlers of the then far west. So many accounts of the above mentioned raid have been written that it is impossible for the seeker after the truth in the matter to discover what he is looking for, that I deem it proper to narrate the story of the raid as it was told me by one of the most prominent members of the little band who so heroically defended themselves from the murderous assault of the Indian marauders. So much has, also, been written in the past, that sets the real west before the unenlightened in a manner that is misleading, that I think it fitting to give credit to whom credit is due wherever it is due. The ordinary writer from the east is not in a position to narrate the occurrences of the west, because he has no immediate knowledge of events, and, moreover, when he undertakes to set them before the public after receiving them from another, his, narrative will lack the ring of truth because he does not know the environments and the atmosphere of the events he is trying to describe. True, the rank and file of readers may not know the difference, but for those who know the facts of the case, the effort to portray the history of the west by writers who have gleaned their knowledge by hear-say, is pitiful and puerile.

In regard to the narrative of the "Adobe Wall" raid, I shall state again, before proceeding farther, that my authority for the facts to be mentioned hereafter was a member of the fighting squad. I have had the honour of the acquaintance of several of the individuals who took part in the defence of the place, and have had the story related by them, and in its entirety, they all agreed on the most salient features of the narrative, and being men of integrity, their word is sufficient guarantee for the truth of what I write about the matter. The story I tell was related by Jimmie Langton. If the reader wishes any corroboration of my tale, he may refer to R. M. Wright, Charlie Rath, or James Langton, whose addresses I shall append to the end of this article.

The "Adobe Walls" ranch was situated about one hundred miles west of the north line of the Indian Territory, and about thirty-five miles south of what was then called No-Man's-Land, on a little creek, about a mile and a half north of the South Canadian River, in what is now called Hutchinson County, Texas. The settlement consisted of one sod building, a saloon, and a blacksmith shop. The sod building was used as a store and in it occurred the chief events of this narrative. The saloon was owned by a man who went by the name of Jim Hanrahan, and the blacksmith shop was operated by Andrew Johnson, who now resides in Dodge City, Kansas.

The store, or what was then called the "Dobe Walls," was owned by R. M. Wright, Chas. Rath, and James Langton, better known as Jimmie, and who performed the duties of book-keeper for the firm. As I said above, I am indebted to Jimmie for the facts of the story as he was the only one of the partners present in the store at the time of the raid, the others being in Dodge City.

Those who took part in the fight numbered, at most, about fifteen, not fifty or sixty, as some writers have it. In the saloon at the time there were five or six, but their part in the fray was only a minor one, as the Indians did not have any particular purpose in making an attack on that place. In the store were Jimmie Langton, Andy Johnson, Billy Tyler, Miller Scott, A. J. Chappell, Bat Masterson, Mr. and Mrs. Olds, who did the cooking for the ranch, and six or seven other freighters or travellers who happened to be there at the time.

Of the Indians who took part in the raid, I shall enumerate them by tribes, with their chiefs.

Big Bow led the Comanches on the occasion. Quanah Parker was not present, as he was too young to be a participant in the capacity of chief.

The Kiowas took part in the raid under the leadership of Lone Wolf. This gentleman now resides in Hobart, Okla., and has become so much converted to the white man's mode of life that he wears a celluloid collar and a derby hat.

The Cheyennes, who played no small part in the expedition, were led by Red Moon, Chief Mininic, and Gray Beard. Chief Mininic also played the role of Medicine Man, and claimed that his medicine was so strong that the bullets of the white man's gun could not injure him. However, when his horse was shot from under him, he explained the matter by saying that the bullet struck a part of his horse's anatomy where there was no paint.

Besides the above mentioned tribes, there were the Arapahos, who, however, did not have a hand in the fight. True, they had come for the purpose of exterminating the white man from the buffalo-hunting grounds, but when they had arrived at the scene of action, the Comanches informed them that they were not to take part in the annihilation of the pale-faces, but requested them to remain in the distance and see how they, the Comanches and their other friends, would put an end to the intruders on their sacred plains. I believe it was not the mere quest of glory that induced the Comanches to forbid the Arapahos taking a hand in the extermination of the common foe, but rather the knowledge that there were several hundred high power buffalo guns and an abundant supply of ammunition that would be part of the spoils of war when they wiped out the obnoxious white man, and they did not care to have too many on hand when the dividend was to be declared. That they would surely secure such a prize, they had no doubt, but whether they did or not remains to be seen.

The list of the white men killed on the occasion of the raid is comprised of only about half a dozen, and nearly all of them were killed before the raid took place. There were the Scheidler brothers who were slain and mutilated at some distance from the ranch. They had gone off to seek new pasture for the cattle, as that around the ranch house was completely destroyed, both by being eaten off and then being tramped out of the ground by the stock. According to the usual Indian custom, they were also scalped. There was also a Mexican "bull-whacker" who happened to be camping near the Scheidler brothers, and he met the same fate as they, and a negro. The only other death among the white folks, was that of Mr. Olds, who met his end in a very peculiar manner, as will be shown later on in the narrative.

On the morning of June 27th, 1874, the Indians made their descent upon the "Adobe Walls" ranch. There had been rumours of Indian outbreaks in other parts of the country, but those present at the ranch on the occasion had not the remotest idea that there was an Indian within the neighbourhood of fifty miles. As they did not come with the blare of trumpets to announce their arrival, the little party at the ranch did not know that death and destruction was prowling in the neighbourhood until the early hours of the dawn, on the morning of the 27th of June. That was the hour the redskin preferred in making his calls upon his white neighbours, especially if the visit was to be one of a warlike nature, and they were on the war-path on this occasion. There is a good deal of philosophy in the Indian's reason for preferring the early hours of the dawn for his first attack. It gives him an opportunity to steal upon his enemy unawares. He made it his business to hide his approach so that his white foe would fall asleep in apparent security, and then with one fell swoop, rush in upon him and deal death and disaster before the unsuspecting victims could become alive to the dangers of the moment until it was too late. On this occasion, they followed their usual custom and crept silently on the sleeping inhabitants of the little hamlet. The first warning that the sleeping white men had, originated in the screams of the negro who was being done to death at the door of the ranch house. The night was hot, and for the sake of fresh air and whatever coolness he could find, he spent the night in a wagon box at the door of the ranch. Were it not for the coolness and calmness of Miller Scott, the whole party would have suffered the fate of the negro. As soon as he heard the first scream of the unfortunate black, he immediately divined that the Indians were upon them. Without a moment's delay, he seized his gun and through the open door of the ranch poured out such a deadly fusillade of shot that the invaders were compelled to flee. The shouts of the Indians and the roar of the buffalo gun pouring out its relentless fire, soon turned the little peaceful hamlet into a den of confusion. How many there were in the attacking party at that moment he did not know, and apparently did not care, for he was determined to defend himself against all odds or die in the attempt to do so. Apparently the Indians had enough of the entertainment offered on that occasion as they withdrew in a hurried fashion to the protection of the timbers and the hills. Nor was Miller Scott the only one that took a part in giving their unwelcome guests a vigorous welcome, but the others who played their parts were rather slow in getting into action. They had just awakened from a sound sleep and it took some time for them to realize their predicament, but when they did, there was no further delay, but they set out to aid Scott in repelling the attack as vigorously as possible. When the Indians had retreated nursing their discomfiture and several wounds, the first attack was repulsed.

The object the Indians had in view was to get possession of the stock of goods and fire-arms that were in the store. Mr. Langton says that he had more than one hundred buffalo guns, and about eleven thousand rounds of ammunition. Besides these desirable commodities, there were on the outside several horses, mules, and oxen, that attracted the attention of the Indians. There was also the additional reason that they wanted to exterminate the buffalo hunters who had been killing off the game in large quantities, shipping the hides east, and leaving the bulk of the carcasses on the ground to become the food of coyotes, wolves and buzzards. They had laid their plans well, and as far as they could see, they were sure to produce a successful issue, but they had no means of knowing that a negro teamster would offer such strenuous objections to shuffling off the mortal coil that he would arouse the whole neighbourhood in the loudness of his protestations. That the ranch people would be in a position to offer any vigorous resistance, they did not dream. They knew they had that little band of pale faces surrounded, and there remained only the formality of killing them with the usual amount of ferocity, take their goods and return to their camping grounds and plot another raid. For the ranch folks, there was nothing to do but fight like grim death. One thing favoured the little band in the ante-chamber to eternity. The walls of the building were about three feet thick and were impervious to the bullets from such guns as the Indians then had. It was, moreover, impossible to set fire to the building from a distance, as the invaders tried that procedure later on and failed. As far as guns and fire were concerned they were as safe as if they were defended by the Rock of Gibraltar.

Nor were things inside the adobe building very inviting. They all realized that it was no holiday affair. In fact, most of them had just about come to the conclusion that they were about to assist at their own funeral with the flowers and music lacking. Nor could one blame them for feeling that things had a very hopeless appearance. There they were, a mere handful, surrounded by hundreds of hostile Indians in war dress, ready to swoop down upon them at any time, without the least chance of assistance from outside sources. If anything were to be done, it had to be done by themselves, or perish in the attempt. It was certainly critical enough to try the stoutest heart. I have no doubt that, at the first charge, there were not half a dozen of them that were fully aware of what was occurring around them, and whatever they did, they performed on the spur of the moment because they saw others doing it. Some of them became so excitedly helpless that they were unaccountable for what they did, and it was providential that they did not do anything imprudent. Others became nauseated and freely parted with the contents of their stomachs. Mr. Langton confesses that he himself became so overcome with the realization of the horror of the situation that he too parted with his supper of the night before and the only reason why he did not lose his breakfast was that he had not had time to eat it when the first attack was made. He recovered his composure hurriedly, as the exigencies of the situation were such that one could readily forget a little inconvenience when one's life was at stake. After the first display of nervousness had passed he did his duty like a man, and played a very important part in the defence of the ranch. It is not to be imagined that the Indians had not put up some kind of a fight. The fact of the matter is that they did considerable shooting in their own behalf, and that they failed to accomplish anything in the way of killing the white folks was due to the fact that they were rather hurried in their movements. How many of the Indians were killed in this first encounter, it is not possible to say, but the sight of several empty saddles, and several lifeless bodies on the ground around the ranch bore testimony to the fact that the bullets from the buffalo guns had done some execution. Stationed at the one window of the store, stood Miller Scott spiting out death and demoralization from the mouth of his buffalo gun upon the savages as they madly careered around the place on their wiry ponies. *Crack, crack,* as fast as he could push home the charge, went the gun, and another warrior was sent to join his forefathers in the Happy Hunting Grounds. As soon as one gun became too hot to handle, another was put in his hands to carry on the defence. Mr. Langton personally saw to it that he was amply provided with ammunition and guns to perform his duty. Nor were the other members of the party idle all the while. They punched holes in the sides of the building and through the opening did what execution their opportunity afforded them.

It was an appalling situation for a dozen people to be over a hundred miles from civilization, surrounded by five or six hundred, yelling, whooping, devil-daring redskins thirsting for their blood. There they rode, painted in all manner of colours, cavorting like demons around them, roaring defiance, and threatening at every moment to break through the zone of fire and burst in upon them in overwhelming numbers and put them to death mercilessly. It was well for them that they did not lose their nerve completely, as the situation was one to try the stoutest heart. It was well for them that Miller Scott rose to the importance of the occasion and dealt out such a rain of death dealing bullets as to appal the intrepid Indians. Outside roared and ranged the howling mob and inside things were not any too assuring. Poor Mrs. Olds fainted. She was the only woman in the hamlet. Kind hands poured water on her face until she revived. When she recovered her senses, the realization of the predicament in which they all were, and particularly the awful fate that awaited her, if they were overcome, so overpowered her that she tried to commit suicide. She set up a series of yells and screeches in her fright, that the Indians outside must have thought they were killing one another to save themselves from butchery. Strong hands prevented her from doing violence to herself, but there was no way to prevent her screeching, and the only thing to do was to give her freedom to screech until she became exhausted.

In the meantime, the Indians, feeling that their attack was somewhat of a failure withdrew to the shelter of the hills. According to the words of an old timer, the first assault upon the place was not a howling success. But the little party in the ranch knew that they would return, and they made what preparations they could to entertain them on their arrival. They did not seem to be in any particular hurry about making the second attack, as in the distance could be seen Indians riding in pairs, scurrying back and forth on their war ponies, dragging the dead and wounded between them. All of the rider that was visible was an arm and a leg. They made a dash on each side of a fallen victim, and seizing him by the hair, dragged him to a place of safety, either for the attention of the Medicine Man, or for burial. Whenever an opportunity presented itself to the little band of whites to take a shot at them, they did so, and in this manner, if they did not do much damage, they, at least, hastened their movements to a considerable degree.

The little party within the ranch was delighted with the success of the first repulse. None of them had been injured, and beyond the first nervousness, or nausea, suffered nothing. They realized to its fullness the necessity of meeting the marauders when they returned. Every man saw to it that enough weapons were within reach for immediate use, besides having near at hand a dish of cartridges for rapid reloading when the fight was at its zenith. With anxiety and nervousness they awaited the second attack. They did not have long to wait. In less than an hour after the first repulse, they saw them breaking over the hills and descending upon them in dense array. On they came chanting their war songs, or raising their raucous voices in wild war whoops in the weirdest manner possible. For some reason or other, they seemed to halt at some distance from the ranch. Out of their midst rode a chief, who swept on his way chanting wildly, dragging a dry buffalo hide by the tail. Apparently he was trying to incite them on to glory by performing a deed of valour. It may have been that they were a trifle bashful about exposing themselves to the galling fire of the little band entrenched behind the walls. Whatever the reason of their delay, it had no effect upon the lone rider who advanced fearlessly up to the very door of the ranch, gesticulating in a wild manner. He threw the hide upon the ground, and with a spring from his pony landed upon it and began a weird chant to incite his followers to follow his example. To show his contempt for those within, he seized an empty barrel that happened to be standing near and threw it with full force against the door of the building. Just as he let fly the missile, a bullet from Miller Scott's rifle tore its way through his chest. He gave a leap into the air and with a wild shriek fell dead upon the buffalo hide. When his followers saw their chief fall, their enmity was aroused and on they came in one wild charge. Bullets spat upon them as they came, emptying many a saddle in their wild charge. *Pit, pit,* the bullets sank into the three foot walls of the ranch, and *boom, boom* responded the buffalo guns in a roar that was interrupted only for such time as it took to send another charge home, and then they boomed again. Indians were falling thick and fast, dead and dying, men and horses were tumbling about on the open plain in a confused mass. Pitilessly the little band poured out the rain of bullets, until no living being could stand the galling fire. The Indians retreated sullenly before their deadly aim, to the shelter of the hills, once more.

The little incident of throwing the empty barrel against the door, called to the attention of the defenders of the ranch the necessity of barricading it. In the excitement of the first charge they entirely overlooked that important matter, and it was only the foolhardiness of the Indian chief that called the matter to their minds. As soon as they saw how much they were exposed to danger through their oversight, willing hands began to pile sacks of corn and other commodities against the door until there must have been a ton of material stacked up against it. Apparently it was the intention of the chief to break in through the door, and had he succeeded, his followers would have completed the work begun by him. Happily for them, Miller Scott's bullet cut short his career, and probably saved them all from death.

The death of the chief had rather a chilling effect upon the rest of the invaders. Instead of continuing the rush upon the place, they withdrew to a rather safe distance, and contented themselves with doing some long range shooting. The firing became desultory. The Indians had withdrawn for about a mile, and though the buffalo guns would carry that far, it was practically impossible to do any accurate shooting at such a distance. The only chance of doing any execution was possible when any of the Indians gathered in any prominent locality. Then a bullet from a buffalo gun would sing around them, and they would seek safety in the shelter of the hills. Another motive that impelled the besieged to save their ammunition was that they did not know how long they would have to entertain their unwelcome visitors, and it was necessary to keep that thought in mind.

The Indians seemed to have re-organized again, and once more set out to make their third attack on the resolute little band. It was galling to their pride to think that a mere handful of pale-faces were able to withstand their onslaughts so successfully. Besides, it was rather disconcerting to have the principal object of their invasion frustrated just when success seemed to perch upon their banners. The killing of the few inhabitants of the ranch was not so important as securing the arms and ammunition they knew was stored up behind the "Adobe Walls." It was doubly galling to the Comanches to think that they had invited the Arapahos to remain out of the fight to witness the extermination of the hated pale-face, and now they would have to suffer the humiliation of defeat where they expected to return laden with the spoils of victory. On they flew the third time, urging their little ponies to topmost speed, more maniacal than ever in their wild shouts and gestures. Around the little ranch they rode in a fusillade of shots as they passed and repassed, but all to no purpose. Their ranks were thinning through the unflinching fire of the besieged. When a buffalo gun boomed, it was a signal for an Indian to throw up his hands with a screech and fall dead or wounded from the back of his flying steed. The nearer they approached the ranch, the hotter became the fire, until it was impossible to draw sufficiently near to do any damage. They fully realized that their shooting had been in vain. They experienced no diminution in the rapid fire of the little band within those three-foot walls. They felt that it was useless to attempt to take the place by assault, and consequently they withdrew beyond the range of the guns of the besieged, beaten. Three times seemed to satisfy their efforts for pillage and murder. They hovered around at some distance as they did not wish to abandon their dead and wounded. There was no Red Cross Society there to attend to that matter for them, nor was there any flag of truce hoisted to denote a cessation of hostilities. As far as the besieged were concerned, they took good aim and shot to kill whenever an enemy came within range.

Several times during the day they had attempted to recover the body of the chief lying before the door of the ranch, but all their efforts proved futile. They finally gave the matter up for a time, acting as though they thought the whites were using him for a bait to lure them on to destruction. They did not intend, however, to leave him there, for, during the night that followed, under the cover of darkness, they succeeded in removing the body from where it lay. Apparently one of them sneaked up during the night and fastened a rope around it, hitched the other end to a pony and dragged the body off to their encampment. He did not do this without attracting the attention of those within. Anxious ears were listening for every move outside, and when they heard the body begin to drag along the ground, they knew that someone was near, and they immediately poured out a volley upon the rescuer. If they did not hit him, they at least compelled him to hasten his footsteps on his way. They afterwards came to the conclusion that the rescuing party got away successfully as there was no sign of his dead body encumbering the plain the next morning.

As may be imagined, there was no sleep during the night that followed the day of the battle. What the Indians could not do during the light of the day, they might attempt at night, and this thought kept every man alive to the exigencies of the desperate situation. Every man did sentry duty all night long, not on the outside, as that would have been suicidal, but within the walls. When not pacing back and forth across the floor, they strained their ears listening at the openings in the walls for any noise that would indicate the approach of the foe. Light they had none, as they did not dare to so much as burn a match. It was maddening to have to spend the weary hours waiting for they knew not what. They tried to be brave, but it was a difficult matter to do so at such a critical time. There was not a one of them that was not willing to die in defence of the ranch, but the uncertainty of the situation was more galling than the attack itself. Hour followed hour, each one seemed an age, and yet there was no sign of another assault. Wearily, anxiously they waited, each moment dreading what the next might bring.

Morning dawned at last and the little band breathed easier. They felt that there was more than an even chance while daylight lasted. The condition of the place was deplorable. With weary haggard looks they gazed at each other in the pale morning light and tried to smile encouragement to each other but it was a wan effort. The excitement of the previous day, and the anxiety of the night just passed, was plainly visible on their countenances. But one thing remained, they were undaunted and ready to face their foe again if necessary. The sanitary condition of the place resembled the Black Hole of Calcutta in a lesser degree. True, they had food in abundance, but their water supply was exhausted. Fortunately for them, there was a supply of canned goods in the store. Some of these they cut open, and drained off the liquid to quench their thirst. It was not entirely, satisfying as water, but it tided them over a difficulty.

In the meantime the silence from their enemies continued to cause them considerable uneasiness. They could not imagine what new kind of deviltry they were planning to effect the purpose of the raid. They awaited another attack, but apparently it was either being delayed purposely, or the Indians had decided to forego any further attempt on the place. Which of the two it was, they did not know. Finally, when their anxiety became unendurable, Mr. Olds, the husband of the good lady who had stirred up so much excitement in the early part of the fray, volunteered to make a reconnoitre. For this purpose he built a temporary ladder. When the rude implement was constructed, he ascended to the roof of the building. Then he proceeded to make an opening in the sod roof, through which he might make a survey of the country in the neighbourhood. To guard against any attack from nearby, he took a rifle up with him for safety. He looked out through the opening he had so laboriously made, and reported that there was not an Indian in sight. All were overjoyed at this bit of information. Then Mr. Olds began to descend. In some way or other, his gun caught in one of the rounds of the ladder and was discharged when he was about half way down. With a lurch from the ladder he fell heavily to the floor. Whether from the force of the blow as he fell on his head to the hardened earth, or whether it was the bullet that struck him, his brains were scattered round about in gruesome fashion. It was a very unfortunate occurrence, and it cast a gloom over the whole party. Mrs. Olds was heartbroken over the sudden and untimely death of her husband. Needless to say, the other members of the heroic little band offered her what consolation their rough ways would permit. As she had just experienced the fidelity of the manhood around about her, she was much comforted, but it was hard to bear the burden of her loss with the evidence of the accident before her.

When the first duties to the afflicted had been accomplished, others thought of the feasibility of making a more extended reconnoitre from the outside of the ranch. There was also another reason for wishing to breathe again the pure air of the plains. Their water supply needed replenishing, as they were all suffering in some degree from the want of it. With anxious hearts, they removed the barricading sacks from the door and prepared for what might come. Andrew Johnson proposed that some one should go for water, and offered to make the journey himself. To this they all agreed. He took a bucket and as he stepped out, he took a good look around for any possible redskin that might be lurking in hiding. Seeing nothing to indicate the presence of the foe in the neighbourhood, he set out for the creek. His companions covered his journey all the way with their buffalo guns, so that if any Indian put in an appearance, they would have either driven him to flight, or adorned the landscape with his remains. Happily for all, no foe appeared and Mr. Johnson made the journey without molestation. When he returned, he was greeted by his friends in misfortune, with all manner of expressions of gratitude. As there was no indication the presence of the foe, they did not barricade the door again.

The next move was to send out scouts to discover, if possible, whether there was any further danger of attack. Needless to say, they did not wander far afield, as, just then, it was a wise proceeding to be in close proximity to the base of supplies and protection. Those who did not go on the scouting tour, performed the humane task of burying Mr. Olds, and those who had been killed outside the ranch house. With what tenderness their natures possessed they laid away the mortal remains of their companion not far from the spot where they had spent such a heart-rending day and night. As for burying the Indians that lay around them on the plain, they left that part of the duty to the coyotes and the buzzards. At least, I have never heard of any burial service being read over them, on that occasion. Such a method of procedure was common enough in those days, as it seemed to be the usual way in which the enemy regarded the disposal of the remains of his victims. They could not be charged with neglect of duty, as, of all the white men that I have heard of being scalped, murdered, and mutilated in any part of the west, I do not know of one case where the Indian ever took the time and trouble to bury them. There is more truth than poetry in the remark of Gen. Sherman, that "War is Hell," and the little skirmish had a strong resemblance to a section of the infernal regions while it lasted.

The above is the general outline of the fight as it occurred. As I have said in the beginning, my authority for the truth of what I have said was one of the leading men of the battle, if there were any leading men in that terrific struggle where every man stood up to the fight like a 'man.' I have read several accounts of the affray from sources that are unreliable. As a proof of what I say in that regard, though the article purport to be written by some one who had a hand in the affray, it is apparent that they did not write them personally, but left it to some scribe to put down some of the salient features, passing over some of the most important events of the struggle. How would it be possible for a writer who had a share in the battle to forget the important part played by Miller Scott? You say it would be impossible, yet I have seen accounts of the battle in which he is not even mentioned. How could he forget the tragic death of Mr. Olds? However, some writers fail to mention it. How about the killing of the negro in the wagon? And some of them narrate the story in an entirely different manner. I fear that the imagination of many a writer has filled up with fancy when facts of the most thrilling kind were at hand. I know that a writer, in narrating a hair-raising episode under the pressure of excitement is liable to overlook some important feature, nevertheless, for the sake of accuracy and truth, he should revise what he has written and correct the error when discovered if he knows it.

To satisfy the curiosity of the reader in regard to the origin of the Adobe Walls, and how it happened that there were buffalo hunters in that neighbourhood in preference to any other locality, I shall append an explanation as well as mention many of the old-timers who followed that occupation.

In regard to the origin of the Adobe Walls, of which some writers appear to know nothing, I shall narrate the story as told me by those who know. The original walls were built of brick dobe made out of clay and grass, and were sun-dried before being set into place. Under the ordinary care, these walls would have lasted one hundred years or more. These walls were built by the Mexicans before the country was granted its freedom, and long before it entered the union. There was a chain of such structures built across the country to be utilized as trading posts, as well as for fortifications. This chain of little forts extended from the Wichita Mountains down through Texas to Mexico. The reason of their being located so far northward was due to the fact that there were mines in operation in the Wichita range long before the country gained its freedom, and these forts served as protection to the freighters who were engaged in transferring the ore down to Old Mexico. When Texas gained her independence, all these forts and supply stations were abandoned, and in course of time were rubbed and horned down by the countless buffalo that ranged at will over the territory. Then the country became almost a waste, the home of the buffalo, the cougar, and the other wild beasts that grew in number unmolested by man.

About thirty-five years ago I became acquainted with two Mexicans named Romero. They told me that they had freighted ore from the Wichita mountains to old Mexico, and that if I would go with them they would show me where they got it. As I did not know anything about mining I declined the kind offer. Today there are hundreds of men exploring these mountains in search of the precious metal, and if ever they come upon the site of the Mexican mines, their fortune is assured.

In regard to the presence of the buffalo hunters near the Adobe Walls, I am compelled to say that they were there, more by necessity than by choice. The trail passed by the Adobe Walls and offered an opportunity for the hunters to ship their hides into Dodge

City, the only trading post within the radius of over a hundred miles. They were compelled to pitch their camp where they could find water for their stock as well as for themselves. For this reason they located themselves at the head of Wolf Creek, in what is now Ochiltree county, Texas. Others located their outfits in the breaks of Clear Creek, on the south line of No-Man's Land, and a few more were established in the hills on the north side of the South Canadian River, and west of the Adobe Walls. They could not possibly camp on the flats on account of the scarcity of water. There extended there a strip of territory thirty-three miles wide where there was no water except after a prolonged wet-spell, which seldom occurred. Regarding the other conveniences, such as fuel and other things, they had little difficulty, as the buffalo chips supplied the demands in abundance.

As an aftermath of the raid, when the various hunting outfits received word of it, they assembled on Clear Creek for mutual protection, as they did not know when they might receive a visit from the same band who would not be in any friendly mood after the defeat at the Adobe Walls. When they had all assembled, they began to discuss the matter from all angles, and came to the conclusion that the most prudent thing for them to do just then was to move into Dodge City until things became more settled. Having decided what to do, they lost no time in putting the plan into execution. They gathered up their belongings and set out on their hundred mile drive fully alive to the danger of the situation. They crossed Beaver Creek, and slowly trudged along their way over the divide to the Cimarron River. It was a rather difficult journey, and when they crossed the Cimarron they went into camp to give their stock a chance to rest up and enjoy a breathing spell themselves. When the stock had been turned loose to graze, they spread out their bedding to give it a sun-bath. Some of the boys went down to the river to have a swim, and others went off in search of game. They wanted a change of diet as they had been munching buffalo meat three times a day for some time past and the regularity with which it came became monotonous. George Ray and Jim Lane remained at the camp to look after whatever needed attention, and prepare the wagons for the next day's journey. Everything was going along peacefully when Lane happened to look up and he saw an Indian coming out of the mouth of a canyon not more than a hundred yards away. He spoke to George, and they both grabbed their rifles and opened fire. As they were seen by the Indian first, before they had a chance to shoot, there was nothing visible of him but one arm and one leg, for he fell over to the opposite side of his pony and put him on the dead run. The two of them fired three shots each before he could get out of sight into the canyon. They told me afterwards that they did not think that their shooting had any more effect than to speed the Indian on his way.

At the sound of the shooting, the boys who were absent, lost no time in returning to camp. However, they did not lose the object of their hunting expedition as they brought back a fine antelope. When the matter had been discussed, they felt somewhat uneasy, but as no other Indian appeared in the neighbourhood, they did not become unduly alarmed. They spent what remaining time they had before making their departure in cutting up their meat and curing it for future use. They were soon on their way again. They crossed the river, and pulled through the sand hills out on the Adobe Walls trail. Their journey led them across Crooked Creek, then over the divide. On their way they met General Nelson A. Miles at Mulberry. He was leading his troops to the assistance of those men who were at the Adobe Walls, but that was hardly necessary then, as the disturbance caused by the raid had in a great measure subsided. The buffalo hunters pursued their journey to Dodge City, where they waited until matters began to adjust themselves. Some of them then returned to the range, while others went to freighting, some to Fort Supply, others to Fort Ellis, or Mobeetie, Tex.

There were no cow ranches in that territory at the time of the raid, nor for some years afterwards. For the information of the reader, and also to let the old-timers know that they have not been forgotten, I shall give here the names of several of them. I knew the most of them personally and followed their interesting careers with pleasure.

Nelson Cary and Jim Lane, after freighting a few trips, built the first house where Beaver City now stands. They went into the mercantile business and remained at it for years with considerable success. Jack and Bill Combs, George Ray, and Johnny Loughead continued freighting for some time after the Adobe Wall raid. They remained at this occupation until they built what was known as the wild-horse corral, on Crooked Creek, north of the County Seat of Meade County, Kansas. This they maintained for some years and then went back to the old life of hunting and freighting.

Bob and Jim Cader settled down on Pladuro Creek and established a small cow ranch. By close attention to business and industry, they became wealthy.

Ben Jackson, another old-timer, hunter and plainsman, settled on Wolf Creek, about five miles from its source, and went into the business of raising cattle.

I could mention many others, and I knew nearly the whole of them, who were engaged in the business of hunting and freighting in the early days, but their numbers, by no stretch of the imagination, would ever reach two-hundred as some of the narrators of early days would have it.

I shall close this article by giving the present location of some of the principal actors in the drama of the "Adobe Walls."

James Langton, Salt Lake City, Utah. Charlie Rath, A. J. Chappell, El Reno, Oklahoma, R. M. Wright, Dodge City, Kansas, Miller Scott, Santa Fe, New Mexico.

I trust that my readers will see from the internal evidence of the narrative just given, that it rings true, and when reading other so-called accounts of the "Adobe Wall" raid, will be able to sift the truth from the fiction which such writings portray.

CHAPTER 21

The "Dull Knife" Raid

The summer of 1877 found the Indians as active as they had been for some years prior to that date. They had long since come to the realization that if the buffalo hunter continued his destructive work upon their base of supplies, the time would soon come when they would be brought to the verge of want. They had so long considered the buffalo their natural source of sustenance that they could not behold the plains depopulated of the vast herds without offering some kind of protest, and the only one that appealed to him was the rifle, and the tomahawk. Prior to '77 they had levied a heavy toll upon the settlers in varied shapes of depredations. They murdered wantonly, they carried into captivity many wives and daughters of the settlers, they ran off the stock and what they did not take away they destroyed. Things had come to such a pass that the settler had to be protected if the vast plains were to be opened up to agriculture, or ranching. With the removal of the buffalo, the cattle man would have an opportunity of stocking the vast territory with marketable beef, or the farmer would be able to convert the boundless acres of the plains to the production of much needed cereals. Hence it came to pass that the U. S. soldier took a very active part in affording protection not only to the scattering settlers who were brave enough to risk the dangers of Indian incursion, but also, to the cattlemen who were rapidly filling the plains with herds to replace the once numberless buffalo. Miners and freighters also came in for their share of protection from the lawless incursions of the marauding natives of the plains. As a consequence of the activity of the army, several bands of hostile Indians were captured and placed on reservations. Amongst the contingents brought in was Dull Knife with his followers. They were held under surveillance at Red Cloud Agency, Nebraska, until an order was issued by the department to Capt. Lawton, telling him to take charge of the Dull Knife Band, and take them under military escort to Ft. Reno Reservation, Indian Territory. This order was promptly complied with, and he started southwards and located them on the above mentioned reservation without any trouble or annoyance on the part of Dull Knife.

It might be well to interpolate here an assertion of Dull Knife, as it will explain some of his future conduct. He made the claim that he surrendered under a promise, or form of agreement that in case he should become dissatisfied with the Darlington agency at Ft. Reno, he would be allowed return to his northern hunting grounds again. I cannot vouch for the truthfulness of the statement, but will let it pass for what it is worth. The fact of the matter is that he was only a very short time at the Darlington agency before he began fomenting trouble. He managed to render himself obnoxious as possible to every one with whom he had any dealings. John D. Miles was in charge of the Darlington Agency at the time, and Major Misner was in command of Ft. Reno. They each of them kept a close scrutiny on every movement of their distinguished? guest, as his reputation for being a disturber among the Indians as well as amongst the whites had preceded him, and they soon discovered that his change of base did not change his disposition for the better, in fact, it seemed to have the contrary effect upon him. When he was brought into the reservation, the agent located him about nine miles above Reno, close by what was known as Dutch Jake's ranch, and not far from where the present town of Calumet is situated, in the valley of the North Canadian. He was not there very long until he discovered that the whole scheme of creation seemed to be out of harmony with his needs and comfort. He made the startling discovery that the water was no good, that the grass lacked the nutritive qualities necessary to keep his ponies in good condition, and last, but not least, that the agent was stealing his chuckaway and that he, his family and all that was near and dear to him were fast becoming mere shadows of their former selves owing to such scantiness of rations. I do not know whether there

CHIEF DULL KNIFE

was any truth in the claim that the agent, John D. Miles was guilty of the crime charged against him, but this I feel very safe in saying, that a great many of the troubles with the Western Indians had their origin in just such practices, as has often been shown upon investigation. There are usually two sides to every question, but, in the case in discussion, whether there was any truth in the charge, or not, I am safe in remarking that Dull Knife with less provocation, in fact, with only an excuse for provocation, could stir up more strife with less raw material to start on than any Indian I ever knew or heard of, and certainly lived up to the description the Irishman gave of his wife, when he was carried away by his feelings of resentment, "Bad luck to your ould head, ye're never at home only when ye are abroad, and never at peace but when ye are at war."

The condition of which Dull Knife complained with so much petulancy and bitterness continued to exist during the winter. However, when the day arrived for the Indians to draw their rations, he appeared with the rest and took his share. The manner in which the cattle were turned over to them was rather peculiar, but filled the bill to a nicety. At the time appointed, they all adjourned to what was called the "issue" pen where the cattle were turned over to them to kill after their own fashion. As soon as the steer was turned loose the Indians set out in pursuit of him, armed with bows and arrows, with which they endeavoured to despatch him. They rode alongside of him, often times the distance of more than a mile, all the while trying to sink their arrows into some vital spot. Many a wild race they had after some refractory steer goaded to desperation by the wounds inflicted upon him by the arrows. As soon as the beast fell in his track, the pursuers work was done. The attention required to convert the fallen steer into food was given by the squaws who followed the pursuit, some on foot and others on ponies. Arrived at the death scene they immediately set to work with their skinning knives and soon had the steer divested of his hide. That done, they made short work of cutting up the carcass into the portions allotted to each family. Those to whom the meat was distributed looked after the conveyance of it to their quarters in whatever manner suited their taste or convenience. Some wrapped it up in blankets, others hung it from their saddles, others brought into service a gunny sack or any other article that would suit the purpose of transporting their share to their dwellings. In the work of disposing of a steer, they were very economical, as there was very little left of it when they had finished the work of dismembering him. Even the entrails came in for their attention. The smaller intestines they usually relieved of their contents by squeezing between their fingers. When they had them sufficiently cleansed of all foreign matter, they braided them carefully and hung them around the necks of their ponies. If the work happened to take place in warm weather, by the time the work was completed there was usually a halo of flies encircling each squaw to accompany her on her homeward journey. The bucks seldom, if ever, took a hand in the butchering as they considered that work beneath the dignity of a warrior. A few years later this system of disposing of the cattle was abolished by an order issued from the Indian Department at Washington, as the officials considered that manner of killing a beast too barbarous and cruel. To accomplish the end desired, they had the agent select a good marksman to go into the issue, pen and shoot the animal selected for each family. Then the beast was dragged outside and the family to whom it was apportioned, dressed it and made the division of it that suited their fancy. On the day of "issue," I have frequently sat for hours watching the aborigines at their work, and I must say that outside of a few little things, the scene had a certain amount of fascination for me. Here I had an opportunity to study the Indian at close range, and I found it far from uninteresting. However, education and environment has wrought considerable change in the habits and customs of the natives of the plains, though it was a somewhat difficult matter to break away from the mode of life founded upon years of existence under a species of wild and untrammelled freedom such as they enjoyed before they came under the dominion of the white man. I have oftentimes, in my travels over the plains and visits to the different agencies, come upon a family of Indians at their meal. All were seated upon the ground in a circle around the food, each one devoting careful attention to the work of demolishing some choice morsel with a gusto that would make Lucullus envious. Frequently, upon encountering them in such circumstances I discovered young men and young women who had been at Carlyle, or some other institution in the east, I could tell at a glance that they had had the advantage of an educational training, as, upon my arrival they would turn their faces away from me, much embarrassed and somewhat ashamed to be seen in their old habits of life when they had been permitted to enjoy the elevating influences and advantages of higher life. They had not been back from school perhaps, for more than a couple of weeks; perhaps, they were only making a short visit to the old folks on the plains, but they could not conceal their training, and they sought to avoid embarrassment by turning away from the visitor who happened to call upon them. They were wearing the blanket just to please the old people. It was the custom of the early days, and still the mode of life of their parents, and they found it rather difficult to live in a manner different from their people when they were in the midst of them. One who suffered no embarrassment from the visitor was the old buck himself. There he sat munching a piece of raw beef as unconcerned as if no visitor had ever appeared before him. He was apparently oblivious of his surroundings, and it seemed as if the sole purpose in life, just then, was to give his whole time and attention to a quantity of meat, oftentimes of such size that a section of it would be protruding from the corner of his mouth. There he sat and just chewed, like a work ox munching his quid, or a mountain goat contentedly masticating some tough but savoury morsel of food.

 I have digressed considerably from the subject of Dull Knife's doings, but I hope that matter just mentioned has not been uninteresting to the reader as it gives some idea of the manner of life the old rascal led while at the Darlington Agency. To continue the narrative, the agent kept up his mode of procedure in dealing with Dull Knife, and the latter continued to raise objections. He kept the trail between his abode and the agency in a well worn condition owing to his numerous visits to the presiding official. In this manner he managed to put in the whole winter. In other words, he kept the kettle boiling, and one could see that there was something brewing.

 If there is anything that an Indian dislikes, it is to get into any trouble that would force him to leave his camp in the winter time, especially when there is much snow on the ground. Gen.

Phil. Sheridan was aware of this fact when he made his winter campaign on the Washita after Black Kettle, Satanta, and Lone Wolf, and forever settled the outbreaks of the Indians in that section of the country.

When the grass began to spring up along the valley, and his ponies seemed to be putting on some of the much needed flesh, Dull Knife felt the blood pulsing through his heart with greater vigour, and he began to make preparations for war. He made no secret of his intentions to depart at the earliest opportunity from the restraining influences of the reservation. It was quite manifest to all the employees at the agency, and to a great many of the soldiers, that Dull Knife was making his arrangements to part company with his surroundings. News of the intentions of Dull Knife was brought to the agent by an educated half-breed, George Bent. Any rumour that he had of the matter previously was now sufficiently confirmed to warrant his taking what precautionary measures he deemed proper to restrain the war-like ardour of the distinguished guest within his gates. He summoned Dull Knife to his presence and gave peremptory orders to remove his camp from its present location down the river to a position about eight miles east of where the present city of El Reno now stands. It was a good location as there was plenty of water, timber, and grazing, and should have satisfied the demands of Dull Knife for improved conditions, but he immediately put forth all manner of objections to which the agent turned a deaf ear. Reluctantly Dull Knife agreed that the conditions in the new location were much better than where he had been living, but he did not see his way clear just then to make a change in his habitation. The reason he gave for his unwillingness to comply with the wishes of the agent was that there was sickness in his family and consequently it would be extremely dangerous to expose them to the necessity of submitting themselves to a change when it was not absolutely necessary. He promised, however, that as soon as his family was restored to health, he would move them to the new location down the river. The agent permitted the delay suggested by the wily Indian, but as a precautionary measure, had the commanding officer at the fort send a troupe of the fourth cavalry to where he was then camped, to stand guard over him until such time as he would make up his mind to remove to the new site selected for his encampment. The placing of a guard over him, gave Dull Knife another opportunity to raise objections to the general scheme of things, and like a spoiled child who cries because it cannot have the rainbow, he commenced to whine once more. No sooner had the troops taken up their position to guard his actions than he came to the agent to have them removed entirely, or if that was impossible, to have them removed to some distance from his *teepee*. He asserted strongly that the presence of the soldiers so near to him had a tendency to keep his squaws in a state of terror and that, as a consequence, they would not be able to regain their health, at least, as long as the soldiers remained in the neighbourhood. The agent, to put an end to his continual whining, consented to remove the soldiers to a position somewhat removed from Dull Knife's *teepee*, but still near enough to keep some sort of guard over him if they were at all careful in the fulfilment of their duty. The soldiers were rollicking, jolly good fellows, not at all bloodthirsty, and whenever an opportunity presented itself for merriment they entered into the spirit of the occasion with all kinds of ardour. Needless to say, they found the task of acting as guard over one redskin a rather tedious affair, and were compelled to break the monotony of existence by means originating with themselves. They managed to pass the time in running horses, playing cards, and with other diversions. In the meantime the Indians passed back and forth among them with as much freedom as if there had never existed anything like a guard.

In the meantime the summer was passing away, and Dull Knife had not yet changed his residence. The agent was beginning to get somewhat nervous over the matter. He even went so far as to declare that he would leave the agency, but that was a matter that could not be attended to without considerable red tape, and in the meantime he was receiving a good salary where he was. He could not throw up his position without consulting Uncle Sam, as Samuel is rather a harsh task-master when it comes to seeing that his officials fulfil the duties of their position. It was quite evident that Dull Knife was getting on his nerves.

During all this time, Dull Knife was tearing around like a loose cyclone that has recently broken away from its moorings, and his lieutenant, Wild Hog, was not far behind him in activity. He made no secret of what he was doing. Here and there, all over the reservation the wily old villain was meandering for the purpose of getting possession of fire-arms. Anything he had in his possession he was willing to barter for anything in the shape of the utensils of war. Cowboys and soldiers, all were requested to barter something in the nature of guns or ammunition for whatever he could produce. Anything he had was on the market. At times he succeeded in trading a couple of ponies for an old, rusty, six-shooter, but in the general run he was not very successful. As an instance of what he was willing to do, I shall mention one case. James Smith, a teamster for the government at the time, was hauling posts to erect a stockade at the fort. In one of his trips he met Dull Knife. The latter immediately proposed a swap. He saw Smith had his belt full of cartridges, and these seemed to take his fancy. He made a trade with the teamster, giving him a new government overcoat for ten cartridges. This penchant for trading became an obsession with him, and there were times when he rendered himself a nuisance to everyone in the neighbourhood by his continual proposals to make a trade.

Finally, this state of things became very monotonous. They had long since become aware of the fact that Dull Knife had no good intentions in his desire to become possessed of firearms and ammunition. They began to be fearful of him, as they did not know the time he would break out and take the war-path and leave behind him a trail of smoking ruins, with a long list of murdered victims.

On the first of September, 1878, the agent was called up by a family of Indians who informed him that Dull Knife had gone. They said that they had gone with him a short distance, but changed their minds and came back to the reservation. The thing that all had been looking for had come to pass, and they all became anxious for what the near future would make known to them. Something had to be done without delay. The agent immediately summoned Johnny Murphy who had been Gen. Sheridan's confidential ambulance driver during the campaign on the Washita, during the winter of 1868, against the Kiowas, Comanches, and Arapahos, and who was afterwards a reliable despatch bearer between the different posts in that section of the country. The agent explained the situation to Mr. Murphy, and handed him a despatch to forward immediately to the commander at Ft. Reno, telling him of the departure of Dull Knife. When the despatch was handed to the commander, he read it attentively, and asked Mr. Murphy, as a special favour to take it up the river where the troops were still guarding the Dull Knife camp. Murphy again mounted his faithful old steed, Pegasus, and proceeded to bore a hole in the darkness until he arrived at the camp. There he found every one of the soldiers sound asleep while the object of their tender care was on his way to the hunting grounds in the north. It is difficult to account for the somnolent tendencies of the soldiers on this occasion. It does not seem possible that their amusements of the preceding day would have the effect of producing such a lethargic condition. In any case, even the sentinel, whose duty it was, at the expiration of each hour, to shout at the top of his voice and proclaim to the troops in particular and to the whole world in general that "All is well," had surrendered to Morpheus, and was so tightly wrapped in his embrace that Murphy was compelled to roll him out of his blankets and inform him that the commander at the fort, and his country was calling him to duty, and it would be a better procedure to saddle up at once and go to headquarters as soon as possible.

To the average man, the escape of Dull Knife from under the very eyes of his guards, may seem discreditable, but this is a case where truth is stranger than fiction. It seems as if Dull Knife's medicine had hypnotized the guardians of Uncle Sam's peace and dignity. If such were the case, he must have exercised the same powerful influence over the military until he was killed close to the Wyoming line. I cannot blame the reader if he shows a little hesitancy in accepting the statement as a fact, as I myself would have an inclination to question the matter, and begin to look for proof if I were in the same conditions as he, were it not that I am writing this account within a few miles of the locality in which the drama was enacted. I have been over the trail and visited the scenes of some of his brutal massacres. When Dull Knife left the reservation, he had less than one hundred warriors, but had his full complement of squaws and *papooses*, which, all told, would raise the number of the departing contingent to about two hundred and fifty. The fact that he took down his *teepee*, packed all his belongings, and marched off undisturbed by the guard set to watch his every move, would be enough to stagger the mind of any one except some dime-novelist who has the happy faculty of accomplishing marvellous deeds with little or no implements to produce such wonderful results. But, nevertheless, that is what occurred. He had departed unmolested from the midst of his guards, and was on his way to his far off land of promise. When he left the reservation, he continued his march to the Cimarron River without much inconvenience from the military men who were supposed to forestall any such movement on his part. Being that he was poorly provided with munitions of war, or supplies to maintain his command on their journey, he was compelled to seek subsistence by raiding ranches, or killing what stock he met on his way. He did not have much trouble in providing for his future wants, once he came into possession of some beef. This he dried and "jerked," a very easy proceeding, for as soon as the meat was salted and hung out in the sun, it readily cured, and would remain fit for use for a year or more without any further attention.

The day after the departure of Dull Knife and his followers, the soldiers under the command of an old German officer, who had seen service in the army of the Fatherland, Major Randerbrook, set out to arrest the fugitives and bring them back to the reservation. It was manifest to the observer that the major did not relish coming in contact with the rough edges of army life. Here I may pardonably make mention of the fact that this same major, and Captain Gunther, of whom I shall speak later on, were members of the Slumber Squad who were supposed to keep a wakeful eye upon Dull Knife's camp. The old major, when notified by Johnnie Murphy that his captive had vanished, became indignant to think that Murphy, a mere messenger, would have the audacity to disturb his sweet repose. However, realizing that the courier had not acted on his own volition, he summoned up sufficient courage to leave his comfortable bed, and saddle up for the purpose of making a journey to the fort. When he arrived there, he received orders to take charge of the Fourth Cavalry, or that portion of it that was then at the fort, and set out in pursuit. There were several troops of the Fourth Cavalry in that section of the country at the time, as they had been sent down from Fort Sill to keep an eye upon the Kiowas and Comanches if they should show any disposition to foment disturbances. Hence it happened that there was only one troop of the Fourth at the fort at the time of the disappearance of Dull Knife and band. The commander of the fort also sent a courier to Fort Sill telling the commander there that Dull Knife had gone north, and asked him to intercept the Indians if possible.

The fugitive had gone northwards only a short distance when he went into camp in the sand hills which lay north of Dutch Jake's ranch. From his actions it was plainly evident that he was not at all uneasy about the presence of the soldiers, nor did he manifest any fear of them. When he was ready to proceed on his journey, he set out with the same nonchalance as characterized his encamping so near to the scene of his late restraint. He advanced on his route until he arrived at the Antelope Hills, north of the Cimarron River. There he made another encampment. The soldiers had not yet overtaken him, a thing which he seemed anxious for them to do. In fact he became so anxious that they should overtake him that he sent a small band of warriors back to meet them to make inquiries as to the reason of their following him. They were informed by Major Randerbrook that he had been sent out to arrest them and restore them to the reservation. They positively refused to return with the major, and stated plainly that they intended to return to their chief and lay the matter before him. Dull Knife, as might be expected of him, positively refused to consider the return to the reservation, in any light. In order that there might be no mistake about his intentions he began to daub on the war paint in greater abundance than he was decorated with before. He was simply living up to his assertion made previously that he would return to the hunting grounds of the northern territory if the conditions around the reservation did not suit his fancy, and in his present attitude he was fulfilling up to his declarations, and would continue to do so, come what might.

The first evening of the march, Major Randerbrook made the startling discovery that, in the haste and bustle of preparation consequent upon the order to pursue the fleeing Indians, they had forgotten to pack up his feather bed, his davenport, also his writing stand and wall tent. He felt that he could not make a successful journey without these necessary accessories to his personal comfort, and therefore, he detailed Peter F. Weasel, a member of the 16th Infantry, who was acting as teamster at the time, to return to the fort and bring all his belongings (the major's) and overtake the troops the next day. This solemn duty Peter set out to fulfil with proper feelings of submission, but I have never found any evidence to show that the said Peter ever appeared in the presence of the major, laden with his precious feather bed or any of his other belongings.

Do not permit the idea to find lodgement in your head, my reader, that the major was a coward. Far from it, as his later actions showed. Later on, when the Indians refused to surrender when he met them at the Antelope Hills, he ordered the troops to charge upon them in the camp, which they did. After a short skirmish with them, he found that he had lost three soldiers who were killed, and among the injured was the company blacksmith who was crippled by being shot through the hips. After this skirmish the soldiers withdrew from the fray and went into camp. There they buried their dead companions, but when they came to look for the injured blacksmith he was no where to be found. In fact, they never saw him again. The loss on the part of the Indians is unknown, but from what I can learn about the fray, to use the language of the prize ring, that battle might be considered a "draw." Some years afterwards, acting under orders from the department at Washington that all soldiers killed in battle with the Indians on the plains, where their graves were known, their bodies should be exhumed and given a military funeral. This order was complied with in the case of the three soldiers killed in the Antelope Hill fight, and they were later on removed to the fort where they belonged and properly interred. The major himself bore himself in a courageous manner, but he was suffering from the handicap of age. Brave as any man that ever straddled a horse, he wanted to be in the thickest of the fray, but owing to his eyesight being greatly impaired it was not a safe move to permit him to enter so ardently into an engagement, as he could not distinguish friend from foe at even a short range, and the difference between an Indian and any other object at a distance he could by no means make out. The major was thoroughly discouraged with the outcome of the affray, and disgusted with the conduct of his troops on the occasion. He resolved to give up his commission and turn over his command to a younger man. He determined to make his resignation at Camp Supply, but before taking his departure he placed Captain Gunther in charge of the command. This man proved his unfitness for the position of trust confided to him later on at Sand Creek where he displayed the cowardice and worthlessness of his character, which stamped him as one of the most despicable characters who ever disgraced the uniform of an officer since the days of Benedict Arnold. The old major in due time arrived at Camp Supply accompanied by an escort, whilst Dull Knife after carrying off and secreting his dead warriors, started northwards across the Cimarron River, and began a series of depredations on the ranches and cattle in Clarke county, Kansas.

Once he had crossed the river, he did not confine his band to any definite route of travel. In place of an orderly line of march, such as characterizes the trained soldier, his followers scattered out each day in different directions to perpetrate whatever devilment might offer, with the purpose of meeting at night at some appointed rendezvous to plot and plan further rascality to be put in operation on the following day.

There were few stock ranches in the country at the time, and when they had heard that the Indians were on the warpath, and were in the neighbourhood, they began to make preparations to protect themselves and their stock against an expected incursion of the marauding band. They rounded up their horses and kept them under close herd, but that was impossible as regarded the cattle, as they were scattered far and wide, and consequently would afford the Indians an opportunity for obtaining possession of what meat they wanted for their journey. It would have been flying into the teeth of danger to endeavour to round them up just then, as the ranchmen would, in all likelihood, have encountered some of the roving bands of cut-throats in their way, and the result would have been disastrous. However, it was not the nature of the cowboys to remain supinely inactive and permit the Indians to work havoc on the herds at will. They determined to have a hand in the fray, and decided that it was time to give the Indians their first lesson in civilization if they had not received it before. They let the cattle take care of themselves, and set out to deliver their instructions in the only manner that would appeal to the natives of the plains.

The cowboys from Doc Day's ranch, and those from the Driskill ranch, with those of several other outfits, all turned out to take a hand in the fray that was sure to come. They set to work with enthusiasm, and continued it with so much zeal and ardour, that Dull Knife began to fortify himself against their unremitting attention. He selected for this purpose a location on what is called Gypsum Creek. The squaws set to work to dig rifle pits upon the side of the bluffs that overlooks the stream, where the warriors could fire down upon the persistent cowboys if they should have the audacity to follow them into their hiding place.

Everybody was, by this time, on the lookout for the invaders and prepared to give them a warm reception should they appear in the neighbourhood, excepting one man named Sam Kiger. He lived on what is now known as Kiger Creek, so named in his honour. Sam had a little ranch. He lived in a dugout, and had a small herd of cattle, and was busy looking after his own interests. He was so far removed from everybody else, that he did not hear of the danger that was threatening the neighbourhood. It is easy to understand how he was unaware of the menace of the Indians when it is stated that he seldom saw any one, seldom went abroad except when necessity compelled him to do so, and then went to Dodge City which was 45 miles distant, for supplies. He remained in ignorance of his danger until two weeks after the Indians had left that part of the country. That was one case where ignorance was bliss. But another man, Sam Williams, was not so fortunate. He was a sheepman and maintained his flocks on another creek, and had a very close call, in fact, just escaped being murdered by the savages by the narrowest margin. He was herding his sheep all alone at the time. Sam, among the other adornments of nature, was upholstered with a luxuriant crop of whiskers. They were his pride and he spent his spare time in combing them. Never did beauteous maiden bestow so much time and attention upon her personal adornment as Sam spent upon his hirsute appendage. In fact, the care and attention of those whiskers became a sort of obsession with him. Well, the first notice that the aforesaid Sam had of the presence of Indians was when a bullet came singing through the air from behind a sand hill and ploughed a furrow through his highly cultivated whiskers. It did not require any very rapid calculation on his part to tell him that he was living in the midst of alarms, and that he ought to seek the protection of his dugout so as to be secure from further manifestations of hostility on the part of the invisible riflemen. To think was to act, and Sam made the distance between where he was shot at and the dug-out in record breaking time. In fact, he might have shattered the record considerably, had he been timed, but there was no time to look for an official timekeeper then, so his efforts in speed must go unrecorded. Once inside the dug-out he felt comparatively safe, as an Indian would be very careful about approaching it as it was virtually impregnable. There was no mode of assaulting it except from in front, and no wise Indian, with a view to saving his skin from being perforated, would care to approach from that direction, as he would be compelled to take that direction if he wished to create any impression on the occupant of the dug-out. In the meantime, the proprietor of the place, acting on the law of self-preservation, would likely be cutting the dust from around the said Indian's moccasins, if not making a more successful effort to convert his assailant into what is called a "good Indian." Usually, as the besieging party came to realize that he could not set fire to the place, nor make any success of shooting into it, he would abandon his undertaking for some other more tractable victim. But, the fact that he could not kill his victim, did not prevent his turning his attention to some other mode of deviltry at which the Indian was usually adept. In this case, they rounded up the sheep belonging to Williams and drove them into a water-hole where six hundred of them were drowned.

While prowling among the Sand Hills, the Indians chanced upon and, after a running fight, killed a man, named La Force, a brother of Perry La Force who was foreman on the Diamond F. ranch, owned by the Franklin Land and Cattle Co., and managed by B. B. Groom, part owner of the stock. He was a fine type of Kentucky gentleman, actuated by the highest ideals, and one who ran true to the standard of the highest kind of hospitality. When the ranchman became aware of the absence of La Force, as he had not returned from his tour of inspection, or whatever duty took him away from the remainder of the party for the day, they organized a search party to discover his whereabouts. They probably had more than a suspicion that he had met with something more than an accident, as they were aware of the fact that the Indians were on the rampage, but it would not be according to the ethics of their mode of life to abandon him unless they were positive that he had met death. For weeks they maintained the search, but with no success. Finally, in one of their excursions, they came across a skeleton, or what was left of it, as the bones had been disjointed and scattered in all directions. They were not yet positive that it was the remains of their friend. However, they were not long left in their uncertainty for they discovered La Force's six-shooter. Every chamber of it was empty, which went to show that he had not yielded tamely to his fate, but fought manfully against whatever odds he had encountered. How many there were opposed to him, the searching party had no idea of calculating, but there was no doubt in their minds that he had accounted for more than one of his foes. The condition of his remains was due to the fact that they had left his body where he had fallen, and the coyotes had gnawed every particle of flesh from the bones. They gathered up what bones they could find and bore them to the ranch and buried them with all the tributes of respect that could be shown to one who had been not only a friend, but who had held a very exalted place in their regard. They then notified his brother Perry La Force, of the untimely death of his brother, giving him what information they could of his tragic end. He came from the Panhandle where he was living at the time and had the remains exhumed and took them to Mobeetie, Texas, where he laid them in their last resting place.

Whilst these acts of thievery, murder, and other rascality were being perpetrated on the Cimarron, and Big, and Little Sand creeks, a small contingent paid a visit to a personal friend of mine, named Charles Coe. He, at the time, was holding a herd of beef cattle in the south-western part of Ford county, awaiting an opportunity to ship them from Dodge City. The herd was owned by Tuttle and Chapman. In his employment he had a negro who performed the duties of cook, as well as acting as chore boy around the outfit. This same Charlie Coe was afterwards bookkeeper for the George S. Emerson Mercantile Co. in Dodge City, Kan. At the time I mention he was what was termed a tenderfoot, and along with being inexperienced in the ways of the west, had little or no knowledge of the Indians mode of existence, especially on the warpath. Anything he happened to know of them, he had gleaned from rumour and reading. His tent was located not far from Crooked Creek. When the Indians came upon him, decked out in their war regalia, he was in a quandary what to do. It would have been useless for him to endeavour to seek shelter behind the bank of the creek, as the distance was rather far just then, and his tent would offer no protection from the bullets of the enemy. Plainly he was confronting a proposition the like of which he had never encountered before. It did not take him long to realize the danger of the situation, and he saw at a glance that it was death or glory for him, no matter which horn of the dilemma he chose to take. Instead of seeking safety in flight, he preferred to break a long established precedent of running away, and faced the danger unflinchingly. He seized his gun and stepped outside and waited the coming of his foes. As soon as they came within range, he took careful aim and fired. His first shot brought to earth the horse of the leader of the band. Indications showed that he wrought some damage upon the rider also, as he had to be assisted by his comrades in rascality. They picked him off the ground where he lay, and placed him on a pony behind another redskin. The bold front shown by the white man had the effect of halting the marauders in their mad career, and at the same time had a stimulating effect upon young Coe. He continued to fire at them as long as they remained within range. The reception they had received was wholly unexpected by the Indians, and after firing several random shots at him, without inflicting any damage, turned their horses around and withdrew to the Sand Hills about a mile distant. As soon as they had departed the young tenderfoot entered his tent to take stock of his means of defence. A brief glance at his small supply of ammunition showed him that he was not in a position to stand much of the siege. In fact he had very few cartridges left, and considering prudence the better part of valour decided to make an improvement in his conditions by seeking safety in flight. He gave orders to his stable attendant to hitch up the horses and they would set out for Dodge, which was about thirty miles away. He told the negro the condition of affairs and showed him that they would likely lose their scalps and their lives if the Indians should make another descent upon their camp.

To the proposal to abandon the place, the negro made reply, "No, sah, I ain't agwine to leave Marse Tuttle's mules heah for dem pestificatin red debils to get. Ise agwine to take dem along."

Having delivered himself of this proclamation of loyalty, he started to hitch up. Coe could not persuade him that he was exposing himself to unnecessary danger, and while Mr. Tuttle would appreciate his feelings of loyalty to his interests, at the same time he was not cruel enough to wish to expose him to the danger of losing his life. This and all other arguments that Coe could urge, were of no avail. He had determined to follow his own course in the matter, and nothing could move him from that determination. He had a strong liking for that team of mules, and a very strong affection for Mr. Tuttle, and in less than an hour later he lost his life through his fidelity to his master's interests. Reluctantly Coe started off for Dodge City. Sharp eyes were watching every move he made. From the Sand Hills they had noticed the preparations made at the tent, and saw the paleface ride away in the direction of the city. They felt that it was useless to follow him, as they knew he was well armed, and they remembered too well the manner of reception he tendered them but an hour before, and knew that he would be prompt to repeat it if they offered him another opportunity. They had no desire to lose any members of their band, and they felt that it would be a certainty that they would suffer some loss if they pursued him, so they let him proceed on his way. Not so did they show any consideration for the negro. When they saw him set out they started in pursuit. They rode down from the Hills, gradually converging to a point in which the darkey and the team of mules was the centre of attraction. When the negro saw them coming with the evident intention of intercepting him, he put the mules to a gallop, but it was impossible for the team dragging the heavy wagon to outrun the war ponies of the Indians. When they were drawing down upon him they began to shout and shoot at the same time. The poor darkey was terrified. The mules were stampeded and ran away. They overturned the wagon in their flight. In their mad career, the driver had been shot in the back several times and was killed outright. They overtook the mules and unhitching them, led them back to the Sand Hills where Dull Knife had now established his temporary headquarters. They did not scalp the negro, nor burn the wagon as was their custom. Evidently they must have come to the conclusion that the team of mules and the plunder of the tent was sufficient for one day. The darkey was later found and buried by some cowmen, and his grave for a long time was used as a landmark for travellers along the Jones and Plummer trail. Mr. Tuttle was in Dodge City at the time his faithful attendant gave up his life for his interests. Naturally he felt the loss of his servant rather keenly. When the news was brought to him that his wagon was still out there along the trail where it had been upset, he hired Hoodoo Brown, an old scout, to go out and bring it into Dodge, for repairs. The old scout often told me of his experience upon that dangerous journey.

It was late in the afternoon when he had the wagon fixed up in such a fashion that he could haul it into the city. He made the return trip the same night as he did not care to expose himself to the danger of meeting the same or worse fate than the negro. He said that he imagined he could see an Indian hiding behind every sage brush, or cactus in the country. But as it proved to be nothing more real than a fancy of the imagination, he had no difficulty in making the journey, for which Mr. Tuttle paid him handsomely.

This band that had just perpetrated the deviltry, had returned to Sand Creek just in time to avoid a posse of cowboys who were in pursuit of them. They had but recently run the rest of the Dull Knife band into the canyon which they had fortified, and it would have gone hard with the battle contingent that had just come from murdering the negro if the cowboys had a chance to meet them before they sought shelter in the rifle pits the squaws had recently dug.

By this time, the whole country was well aware that Captain Gunther and Dull Knife had been playing a game of "hide and seek" for the past ten days. The cowmen became weary of such dilatory tactics, and determined to go into the canyon and fight it out with the Indians. At this time Captain Gunther had arrived on the scene with the 4th Cavalry, and demanded that the cowmen withdraw from the sight as he was going to take that matter into his own hands. He said that the Indians were well fortified and that he would have considerable trouble in dislodging them. He stated that he intended to place sentinels around the canyon so that none of them could escape, and intended to hold a conference with Dull Knife in the morning. He assured the cowmen that he was well acquainted with the old warrior and felt certain that he would have no difficulty in persuading him to return to the reservation with all his followers.

After the captain had arranged his guards around the canyon in such a manner as he thought would preclude the possibility of the Indians making their escape, he busied himself with preparations for encamping down the creek. While he was thus engaged, he was approached by Ben Jackson, the noted scout and buffalo hunter, who saluted him in military fashion, as far as his knowledge of that accomplishment would permit, and proposed that he, the captain, give him a despatch to be delivered to the commander at Fort Dodge requesting him to send more troops to aid in capturing the Indians. This despatch he promised to deliver within a few hours. The captain, not knowing the resourcefulness of the man making the request, replied that he could not spare an escort for the undertaking. To which the scout replied that he did not need an escort as he was well acquainted with the country and did not have any fears about the prompt delivery of the message. The captain answered that such a course of proceedings was unnecessary, as he was well acquainted with Dull Knife personally. He said that he intended to hold the conference with him the next morning, and that when matters were set before him in the proper light, there would be no further trouble in the case, as he was positive the Indians would be perfectly satisfied and return to the agency without any further difficulty. When this short interview had been completed, the captain proceeded down the creek and went into camp. In the meantime the pickets were on duty around the canyon, or rather were supposed to be, but, in some manner or other, Dull Knife's medicine hypnotized them as it did on the former occasion when he escaped from the North Canadian. I am not going to make any remarks about the private soldiers of this campaign, as they were ever ready and willing to do their duty if they had a proper officer to lead them; nor am I going to make any comments, nor pretend to fix the blame where it belongs, but will state the facts and let the reader judge for himself who was culpable in the matter; but it seems incredible that 250 Indians could come out of that canyon, supposedly well guarded, and pass through a cordon of pickets without a gun being fired. Incredible it is, but, nevertheless, that is the unvarnished truth of the matter. When dawn appeared the following morning, the Indians had vanished, as if they had been swallowed up by the earth. Their trail indicated that they had gone northward. They pursued their line of flight to Crooked Creek, in Meade County, Kansas, and after crossing that stream near what is called the "Three Bends," they came to a hay camp that was conducted by G. S. Emerson. Here they did not give themselves up to their usual depredations, but contented themselves with taking some provisions and cutting up a pair of calf skin boots belonging to the proprietor. That they did not commit any murders, was due to the fact that the men of the outfit were absent. From there they proceeded to what was intended to be the county seat of Meade county, which development did not extend further than the erection of a story-and-a-half frame building, with an unfinished well nearby, at which the city fathers were working when the Indians arrived. They immediately set out to explore the contents of the house and surroundings. Their efforts were not rewarded very highly, but one thing attracted their attention, a grindstone standing near at hand. The sole occupant of the dwelling, Captain French, was compelled to perform the task of turning the grindstone while they were sharpening their knives. To test the acuteness of the finish they had put on their weapons, they contented themselves with drawing them across the captain's throat. To show him further that they were not at all unselfish in their attentions to him, the squaws lent a hand in pulling and hauling him around and inflicting all manners of abuse upon him, but they did not attempt to kill him. I asked the captain shortly afterwards why they did not take his life, and he replied that they knew better than try that. He stated that he had a picture of George Washington hanging on the wall of his dwelling, and they knew that if they killed him the government would soon be in pursuit of them. Poor old cap! He did not know that the government was on their trail at the time.

Although there were four or five men working at the well at the time the Indians devoted their attention to the captain. They did not molest them but continued on their way northward. On their route they encountered a man, Wash Connors, who had been to Dodge City to do some trading. He had spent the previous night with a friend of mine, C. M. Rice, and set out early in the morning so as to reach his destination in good time, as he had some material for those who were digging the well at the new town-site. Mr. Rice urged him to remain and have breakfast with him, but he said that he was in a hurry and would attend to that duly when he reached his destination. With a good team of mules hitched to his lumber wagon, he started off in good spirits, little thinking he would never reach the end of his journey. He was proceeding on his way in a brisk fashion and had come in sight of the town-site when the members of Dull Knife's band met him. They stopped him without any ceremony and attacked him before he could get out of his wagon. They cut his throat, tore the harness off his mules and went their way taking his team. The well-diggers saw the whole proceedings, but were unable to render assistance as they were not in a position to do so.

Leaving the victim of their murderous assault dying in his wagon, they set out toward the north again. Between the scene of their latest crime and the Arkansas they committed no further depredation. They crossed the river west of Dodge City, not far from where the present station of Cimarron is located on the Santa Fe railroad. Their depredations after crossing the river were few, as there was little to attract their attention, excepting some wild cattle and the accompanying cowboys. They did not molest the latter as they had a wholesome respect for that individual by reason of the fact that he was generally armed with a brace of six-shooters and a Winchester rifle, and was an expert in the use of both. Meeting a cow-puncher under such conditions was a hazardous thing, as the Indian knew the cowboy would not trade even. They had no doubt about their ability to eventually kill him, but the price to be paid was too great, as he usually sent three or four of the wily redskins across the Great Divide before succumbing to their prowess, and they did not usually care to pay the price.

By this time the whole country was aroused. The news was heralded abroad on the wings of the wind. The newspapers, as is their custom, in glaring headlines, magnified the extent of the depredations, and gave alarming accounts of the atrocities committed by the Indians. Everybody was on the lookout, those in the neigh-

1. General N. M. Crook
   Formerly 7th U.S. Cavalry
2. Black Wolf. 4. Wooden Leg.
3. Little Wolf. 5. Willis Rowland
All Northern Cheyennes. (M.T.)

bourhood fearing a visitation of the marauders, and those far away living in expectation of the next savage depredation. The excitement reached such a high degree of intensity that the department ordered Lieutenant-Colonel Lewis to take charge of the field of action, which for some time had been a field of inaction as the gentleman who was supposed to be at the head of the movement against the Indians was but a poor apology for a successful military commander. It may be well to remark that this man was soon relegated to the military scrap-heap in disgrace.

When Lieut.-Col. Lewis was notified of the appointment, he responded with alacrity. He set out at once from Dodge City with his command. He soon was on the trail of the Indians. A short journey westward brought him to the point where the band had crossed the Arkansas on their way northward.

In the meantime the Indians were pursuing their way with considerable speed. They may have realized that another expedition would be organized to follow on their trail, or another commander would be put in charge of the one they had left so unceremoniously on the night of their escape, but whatever their conclusions were, they did not stop to commit any more outrages until they reached the North Beaver, or Sand Creek. On their arrival there, they saw they were about to have a fight on their hands, as the lieutenant-colonel had followed their trail with such speed that he was almost upon them. Escape for the time being was out of the question, and they resolved to fight. Lewis did not want to kill them, but preferred to have them surrender and return to the reservation. Such idea did not enter into Dull Knife's calculations, and he decided to fight rather than return to the place of his recent abode.

It was now getting late in the afternoon. Considerable sharp-shooting had been done on both sides for some time, and then a skirmish took place. Each party was doing what execution it could without exposing itself to any more danger than was necessary. The Indians endeavoured to make every shot count as their ammunition was getting scarce, and the soldiers were employing the same mode of warfare as their opponents, though it was not the scarcity of powder, but rather the desire to preserve their anatomy from the missiles of the enemy that induced them to seek shelter behind every bush and hillock. The lieutenant-colonel was a busy man, directing the operations of his troops, and looking after things in general. The battle lagged along until evening, without much evidence of success for either party. Towards evening Lewis rode out to the firing line to get a closer view of things and to lend his men the encouragement of his presence. When he reached the zone of fire, one of the Indian scouts approached him and advised him to dismount from his horse as he would very probably be shot if he remained exposed in such a manner to the fire of the enemy. The lieutenant-colonel did not heed the advice so freely given by his scout, and in less than ten minutes he received a bullet in the thigh. The missile struck an artery, and as a result, the lieutenant-colonel died a few hours later from loss of blood, (My authority for the above statement is G.W. Brown, who was lying not twenty feet away when the scout gave the warning of danger.) He piloted the ambulance bearing the lieutenant colonel under the command of Lieutenant Gardner and escort to Fort Wallace that same night, as he was familiar with that part of the country owing to the fact that he had hunted buffalo all through that section of the country in the early days. After the escort had proceeded on its journey for about six miles, a rider returned to the lieutenant and told him that the lieutenant-colonel had died. This sad news was a shock to the company, as he was a man of the highest type of bravery, and his demise was regretted by every man in the command. When the news was first broken to the troops a look of grim determination settled upon the countenance of every man, which meant that at the first opportunity they would avenge the death of him who they loved so well. The fortunes of war averted the blow for the present, for, during the night, Dull Knife and his followers fled, leaving nothing behind but the embers of his camp fires to show where he had taken his stand. The soldiers started in hot pursuit, as they did not want their enemies to go unpunished. They had not followed the trail very far when they learned that the Indians had divided their forces and gone in different directions. Wild Hog, the chief adviser of Dull Knife went towards the north-east, over to Sappa Creek, where he and his followers murdered over forty persons, pillaged their stock and burned what they could not conveniently carry off. Dull Knife with the rest of the band headed due north. This division of the Indians compelled the soldiers to adopt the same method of procedure. They were accordingly organized into two divisions and set off in hot pursuit of their wily foes. From this time onward the expedition assumed the character of a running fight. This system of pillage, and plunder, on the part of the Indians, with the pursuit on the part of the soldiers, was maintained until the 7th Cavalry, under General Samuel D. Sturgis succeeded in capturing both bands on the Niobrara River in the vicinity of the place in which Camp Niobrara was built, and about 15 miles east of Camp Sheridan. This event occurred in the month of October, 1878, but I cannot give the exact date of the occurrence. The captives were then taken as prisoners of war to Fort Robinson, Neb., or, as it was then called, Camp Robinson. They were placed in the guard house and held there until New Year's night, 1879, when they broke out, killed the guards and made their escape through the sand hills until they had almost reached the Wyoming line.

When the news was brought that Dull Knife had killed his guards and made his escape, everything was in a flutter of excitement. Preparations were immediately made for pursuit. At dawn, as soon as it was possible to observe the direction of the trail, the bugle sounded and the Third Cavalry mounted their horses and set out in pursuit of the wily old villain who had so often eluded them. They followed hastily all forenoon and the further they advanced, the clearer the signs manifested to them the fact that they were close upon the fleeing Indians. In the afternoon they overtook the band in the said hills close to the border line of Wyoming. When Captain Wessels rode up to them, he immediately ordered them to surrender. Dull Knife's reply to this was a rifle shot that killed an Indian scout belonging to the cavalry. He repeated with another shot at Captain Wessels. The bullet struck the captain but did not inflict a mortal wound. The action of Dull Knife was a sufficient guarantee that he did not intend to surrender, and immediately the troops poured a succession of volleys into the foe. When the smoke of battle cleared away, and the few who remained alive surrendered, it was discovered that Dull Knife himself, his daughter who was present, and about two thirds of his followers had all gone to the Happy Hunting Grounds together. After giving the proper attention to the wounded, and burying the dead, the troops with the prisoners returned to Camp Robinson. Among the number returning to the fort were Wild Hog and many other leading spirits of the movement. They were held there until the spring of 1879, when the leaders were sent to Dodge City, Ford county, Kansas to be tried for murder and other crimes.

I called upon those notable characters while they were supposed to be in durance vile, and found them the most conspicuous and best entertained men in prison. The representatives of different illustrated newspapers were there, sketching their pictures, and treating them to cigars. It was certainly a very novel sight to me, and I thought it strange that the citizens of Dodge City had not formed a necktie party for the entertainment of the whole party of savages, for they were well aware of the characters of their guests and well acquainted with the amount of crime and rascality they had perpetrated almost within view of the town itself. However, everything seemed to be following along the even tenor of its way, and I came to the conclusion that Dodge City was a very law abiding city, and was a good town to live in (especially when one is acquainted with the early history of the place). I cannot refrain from remarking that, if a white man, or a body of white men, had been guilty of one-tenth of the crimes perpetrated by the Indians who were then sojourning in their town, they would have been hanged as high as they could be raised on a lariat rope, or shot to pieces in the streets. Strange are the dealings of man with man.

Chapter 22

Buffalo Hunters

When the first railroad construction train started west from the Missouri River, with its gangs of graders, tie-slingers, and track layers, the sound of the locomotive whistle proclaimed to the Indian more plainly than any language could do, that the days of his activity over that vast expanse of country were about to terminate, peaceably if possible, but forcibly if necessary. The company kept in its employ one or more buffalo hunters to supply the boarding car with fresh meat which was plentiful on the prairie in those days. The engineers had staked out the right-of-way, and established the different grades in advance, and everything was kept in good shape for the speedy progress of the work. The Indian saw all this. He also saw the graders, the tracklayers, the spike drivers, and heard the locomotive whistle. He saw the engineers and the buffalo hunters, but he failed to see the real cause of his trouble. He could not see the promoters of that great undertaking and enterprise, because they were beyond the reach of his limited vision. They were in their luxurious offices figuring on the possibilities and probabilities of one day declaring large dividends on that stupendous undertaking that was to reach out to the gold mines of Colorado and on through the mountains to the Pacific coast. The promoters could see at a glance that it was useless to expect any great returns from the capital invested if they were to be dependent on any freight or traffic from the Indian. They needed not to be told that he was not an agriculturist. He was not a stockman and had no use for agricultural implements such as threshers, sulky ploughs, fanning mills or corn shellers. He made his living by hunting and fishing and was to a certain extent self supporting and independent of all railroads. He was not accustomed to take his squaw and *papooses* to any foreign watering place to spend the summer. Whenever he felt like taking a few days' recreation, he bundled his camp equipage and with his family started for some creek where there were plenty of fish and there remained until his visit was completed. Sometimes several families went together and had a big time talking over Indian customs and the ways of the white man. This had been their custom from time immemorial and any act performed by the white man to disturb his equanimity or distract him, was looked upon as an outrage and sacrilege, and any who did such things were served with summary punishment.

The capitalists could see at a glance that the Indians were not a class of people to build up a profitable industry and felt it their duty to remove them from that section of the country in order to induce stockmen and farmers to occupy it. As a step in that direction they created a market for buffalo hides, which seemed to have the desired effect, for it was but a short time until many adventurous spirits who could gather together enough money to buy a span of ponies, a wagon and ammunition for the purpose, were engaged in the business, some as hunters, others as skinners. As soon as they had a load of hide they shipped them to market and with the proceeds prepared for another trip to the range again. Few but the hardiest and bravest young men could stand the dangers, trials, and exposure which they confronted in all kinds of weather.

There was one young man that I feel a pardonable pride in mentioning as engaged in that undertaking, namely W. F. Cody, who by his dexterity with the rifle had acquired the title of "Buffalo Bill," and who had become famous as an Indian scout and had established an international reputation as the greatest marksman and horseback rider in the western plains. He was also chief of scouts and confidential friend of General Phil Sheridan, and at this writing is the owner and proprietor of Buffalo Bill's Wild West Show. His was a plain case of 'survival of the fittest.' The Indian looked upon his kind as trespassers and intruders and as he had no navy or war department behind him other than the tribal medicine man who decided the war movements of his tribe by incantations or by observation of the way the smoke blew from his camp fire, after deliberating on the general condition of the country, the signs of the moon, as well as the inroads the hunters were making on the buffalo which he considered his private property, decided to go on the warpath and kill off a few buffalo hunters and discourage any future invasion of what he felt was his private right. When he began his undertaking he soon learned that hunting the buffalo hunter was entirely different from hunting the buffalo, and it was a work that two could engage in from opposite angles, at the same time, with the advantage greatly in favour of the buffalo hunter as he was always well armed, and an expert marksman; and in this particular they soon learned to have a high regard for Buffalo Bill. To such a degree did they come to admire him that they looked upon him as a being of a higher order, and not of the common clay. Things came to such a pass after some experience with the buffalo hunter, that the Indian never took any chances with him, but when the hunter pointed to a distant horizon, the aborigines usually followed the direction without further parley.

Prior to the time of which I write, the Quaker sect came into close touch with the Indian Department in Washington, D. C., and formed what was called the Indian Bureau. They urged the only sane and proper way to civilize the Indian was to educate him and teach him agriculture. General Hazen was placed at the head of the movement and a conference was called at Medicine Lodge, Kansas, which the Comanches, Kiowas, Cheyennes, and Arapahos were invited to attend. General Harney presided, surrounded by reporters, interpreters and such other attendants as were required to lend dignity to a court of such magnitude. After several days of vexation and worry, they succeeded in formulating a treaty which was supposed to be signed by all the chiefs of those different tribes, by which they agreed, for certain considerations made and provided, to vacate all that country lying between the Platte and Arkansas Rivers and go southward to take up their permanent abode in what was then known as Indian Territory. The Comanches and Kiowas were located on Red River and in the vicinity of the Wichita mountains. The Arapahos were located south of the North Canadian. The Cheyennes were allotted the country along Pond Creek, in what was known as Cherokee strip. The Quakers were not slow to learn that they had made a fatal mistake in locating the

Cheyennes so close to the state line of Kansas, as the State of Kansas at that time was not governed by prohibition laws and the bootlegger was abroad in the land, and unless some steps were taken very speedily it would be a question of only a short time before the bootlegger would have all the Indians' portable possessions over in the State of Kansas. I happen to be personally acquainted with a man who was engaged in that business and he told me that at one time he had traded a boot full of whiskey for nine head of ponies. He had no jug and rather than lose the deal, he pulled off his boot and filled it from his keg and then started off with his ponies for Kansas. The agent left in charge readily saw that such conditions could not hold out long. There were marshals who had been appointed to guard and protect the interests of the Indians, but some of them were in secret collusion with the bootlegger and received a share of the gain. As a consequence of this condition the agent decided to remove the Cheyennes southward to the North Canadian where a permanent agency was established and put under the control and management of Mr. Darling and even to this day is known as the Darlington Agency. A large portion of the Cheyenne tribe settled there and adopted the white man's way of farming. After they drew their allotments, the government employed white men to go among them and instruct them in the management of their affairs, and how to sow and cultivate their crops. Women were also sent as matrons among them to instruct the squaws in the art of fulfilling household and social duties. Schools were built and teachers employed, and the advance they have made is really surprising.

The treaty of Medicine Lodge, it was hoped, would put an end to all hostilities between the Indians and the whites and bring about a settled condition of affairs, but such was not to be the case, for a large percent of the Cheyennes and a considerable portion of the Arapahos became disgruntled and claimed they had not signed the treaty, and others claimed that the interpreters did not properly translate their wishes and said they were not going south to the territory and would not comply with any of the requirements of the treaty, or, in other words, they were going to stay where they were, and go and come as they pleased regardless of the white man's feelings in the matter. The leaders of this discontented branch of the different tribes were Roman Nose, Black Kettle, Turkey Leg, and

Dull Knife, with a few smaller chiefs. These bands of Indians kept roaming back and forth between the Platte River on the north and the Cimarron River on the south and west to the Rocky Mountains, and at one time went eastward as far as Council Grove, Kansas, where the Kaw Indians, a peaceable tribe, were located. They raided them and after killing a few of them, ran off their stock and returned to their favourite hunting grounds.

This was kept up continually for years. Robbing stage coaches, killing freighters, raiding stock ranches, or murdering the frontier settlers seemed to be a favourite pastime with them. Ever since the treaty of Medicine Lodge, they kept growing bolder and more threatening. Brigadier General Sully who was in command at Fort Larned at that time, called their attention to the fact that there had to be a change in their attitude toward the whites, or he would be compelled to take action against them. When they received this notice a delegation of the leaders called on the general for a conference. They reported that all the mischief had been perpetrated by some young Indians that were dissatisfied with the treaty, and had acted entirely contrary to the wishes of their leaders. They begged him to supply them with ammunition and arms, and assured him that there would be no more trouble along that line. The foxy old bucks knew that they were lying and if the old general had been educated on the plains instead of a military academy, he would have known it too but he was one of those good-natured, easy-going old fogies who were much more intended to take charge of a Sunday school class than of a branch of the army. At all events, after a good deal of palavering and soft-soaping the old general issued an order for the agent to turn over to them the firearms with the understanding that they should return to the reservation and behave themselves and commit no further depredations on any person; all of which they meekly agreed to perform. It was not 24 hours after receiving the arms until old Black Kettle with a few of his confederates were making medicine on the Pawnee and Walnut Creeks. The band started north to the Saline River and commenced the most atrocious murders, rapes, and other acts too abominable to be placed in print. They did not stop there to complete their work of plunder and pillage, but hastened on until they reached the Solomon River where their villainous and blood-thirsty designs were carried out in full force and effect. They murdered about fifteen farmers and two women, and committed other depredations and horrors too hideous to repeat here. They carried off all the stock they could find, besides taking away two little girls who were never heard of afterwards. On their return to the Saline River they started in to complete the work of destruction they had only partly accomplished on their way to the Solomon. By this time the farmers had congregated at a farm house and were making ready to fight them when they should arrive. They did not have long to wait, for they were hardly inside the farm house when the Indians appeared and began their *pow-wow* and war cry and firing into the dwelling. Just about the time they were getting under headway with the work of pillage and plunder, Captain Benteen heard the firing and came to the rescue of the settlers. He had heard at Fort Zarah that the Indians were on the war-path and how they had treated two women who were afterwards taken to the fort for care and protection after their bitter experience with the noble red man. He started out with a troop of cavalry and reached the besieged just in time to save them from the horrors which they would be compelled to face if captured. There were 200 Cheyennes on that raid and when Captain Benteen appeared on the scene, they scattered like a flock of quail. These Indians drifted back in the direction whence they had come and remained a short while with the Black Kettle band on the Walnut and finally crossed the Arkansas and went southward toward the Cimarron River.

The old brigadier general had by this time awakened from his lethargy and found that he had been out-generalled by the Indians. He decided to take immediate steps to punish them for their treachery and deception. There was a large body of Indians operating between the Arkansas and Cimarron, and Brigadier General Sully concluded to go out and give them a good thrashing to settle accounts for their past treachery and misdeeds. These Indians were a mixed body of different tribes and seemed as anxious to meet the general as he was to meet them. After three different engagements in which the general was defeated, he was compelled to return to Fort Dodge to avoid being captured by them.

Chapter 23

Custer's and the Indians

About this time General Phil. H. Sheridan made his appearance in the Indian country, bringing some additional soldiers under the command of General Custer. He also asked for a regiment of Kansas volunteers. His request was granted and the recruits were placed under the command of Colonel Crawford with orders to meet General Sheridan at the junction of Wolf and Beaver Creeks, or what is now known as Camp Supply.

When the regiment had been enrolled and the men were ready and anxious to make the journey, General Sheridan, in order to facilitate matters and avoid any disappointment, sent two guides to pilot the new recruits to their destination. It was now getting late in the year and each day brought its quota of snow, rain, or sleet, but in spite of such unfavourable conditions, the boys made no complaint, but rode patiently along their tedious journey. After they had been out a few days the colonel seemed to grow impatient and irritable, and began to dictate to the guides and volunteered his advice as to the direction they should pursue. He wanted to turn to the left and cross the Cimarron River and insisted on his idea to such a degree that the guides, or scouts, withdrew their services then and there and left him to select when and where he would elect to ford the river. The weather being stormy the colonel lost his way and through his impatience finally lost his head and did not know where he was. The brakes and canyons on the north side of the river were filled with snow that had drifted in from the prairie. In his desperation he started to cross the stream and spent several days floundering around through the snow banks and drifts. After he succeeded in crossing the river he found it as hard to get out of the difficulty as it was to get into it. To add to his misfortune, he had neglected to bring along sufficient food for horses or men. However, he succeeded in getting out and up on the flats south of the river at the expense of a great number of horses, but was fortunate enough not to lose a single man. The situation was not improved in any measure as he did not know where he was. He continued southward until he reached the North Canadian River. Here his remaining horses kept themselves alive by browsing in the timber while the men were compelled to live on what hackberries they could find.

As Colonel Crawford did not arrive at the expected time, nor for several days afterward, General Sheridan became anxious for his safety and sent out scouts to see if any trace of him could be found. With much risk and effort they found the colonel and what was left of his cavalry about twenty miles below the designated place of meeting. To say they were in a deplorable condition, would be putting it mildly. The moment General Sheridan received word of the disaster that had befallen Colonel Crawford's command, he sent out men and teams to their relief with instructions to bring them into camp. The relief party did not arrive any too soon as the men and horses were in a very sorry plight, owing to their lack of nourishing food. One thing alone was in their favour in their present deplorable condition and that was the abundant supply of dead timber at hand which afforded them an opportunity to keep warm, or rather keep from freezing, a thing which was entirely lacking on the Cimarron. I may as well say that they were all afoot by this time, as the horses that were still alive, were reduced to such a state of weakness that they were unable to carry their riders. It took two days to get them into camp, owing to their enfeebled condition. General Sheridan's headquarters was then located on the north bank of the North Canadian River about four or five miles south east of where the present city of Woodward, Okla., is situated. On the departure of the command from Topeka the newspapers in flaming headlines announced the affair to the world, but their great expectations were converted into "Crawford's Calamity."

In the face of all this vexatious delay, awaiting re-enforcements from Colonel Crawford, General Sheridan did not relax his energy in the least. He kept everybody at work fixing up a base of supplies that would be in his reach until the termination of that campaign which he intended to settle during the winter months whilst the Indian ponies were poor and weak and unable to transport belongings any distance. He also knew that if he delayed matters until warm weather when there would be plenty of grass, he would have to fight those Indians from the British possessions to Texas. He was down there to fight those Indians or make them return to their reservations to remain there and behave themselves and stop prowling all over the country committing depredations. He had no time to engage in peace treaties and had no guns to turn over to them, and there was no chance for any trickery or treachery with him. He did not want to smoke the pipe of peace with them and then be shot in the back and killed as Turkey Legs and his band did with his scouts Comstock and Glover. He was there for permanent peace or a permanent fight and the choice rested with them. There was no swapping of horses or palavering. He meant business.

By this time General Sheridan's headquarters very much resembled a Canadian north-west logging camp. Everybody was kept busy, some hauling logs, others digging trenches for the stockades, others were bringing poles and brush to cover rude pole sheds for the purpose of affording a temporary shelter for the stock. If there was anybody idle, it was some one who was too ill to work, or who had hidden in the brush to avoid work. The scouts were kept busy scouring the country in search of some trail or sign of the Indians and finally were rewarded by the discovery of a trail leading southward, which showed a large body of Indians had gone in that direction. On receiving that information General Custer asked permission from General Sheridan to fit out an expedition to follow them. The request was readily granted by General Sheridan, as he was anxious to bring the campaign to a close as speedily as possible. As soon as Custer had his troops in proper shape he set out in the direction indicated by the scouts. After crossing Wolf Creek and getting well up on the divide he discovered the trail, but found it very difficult to follow owing to the snow having drifted and covered any marks they had left behind them. Occasionally, where the wind had blown the snow from some high place he found all evidence required to justify him in keeping up the pursuit. He maintained his route until he reached the north brakes of the South Canadian and went into camp for the night in the least protected place he could find and made things as comfortable as circumstances would permit. Next morning after taking a survey of the situation he found himself confronted with a great and dangerous undertaking through having to ford the river. As every man who has ever crossed it with a loaded wagon knows, it is one of the most treacherous streams to ford, in the south-west; and to add to the miry condition of the river it was frozen over, but the ice was not of sufficient thickness to bear the weight of the horses, much less the heavy wagons that were to follow them. General Custer, a persevering and an energetic man, was not daunted by this present difficulty. He sloped down the bank of the river and set his men to work cutting a channel across and clearing the ice from it, so that it would not cut or injure the stock in crossing. After passing the cavalry back and forth several times to settle the quicksand, he sent forward the freight and supply wagons and with great difficulty succeeded in landing on the south side. Here he stopped for dinner as it was after twelve o'clock when the last wagon passed up the bank. After dinner they hooked up and started on their perilous under taking of climbing and winding their dangerous way through the canyons and sand hills until they reached the flats that divide the South Canadian and Washita Rivers. The distance travelled that afternoon was not very great but the difficulties and obstacles to be overcome were very trying. The general decided to have an early supper and after a consultation with his officers determined to make a night drive as the moon shone brightly and the trail was now becoming so plain that the scouts felt there would be no difficulty in following it. Accordingly they hitched up after their slight rest and set out under the leadership of two Osage Indian scouts together with California Joe, a white man who had been on the frontier all his life and who understood the language of the different tribes. Custer had learned from his scouts that it was the intention of the Indians to go into winter quarters on the Washita, but was not certain of the exact locality. Consequently he had to use great caution in trying to discover their whereabouts. He found some smouldering campfires, which showed that they were not very far in advance. The scouts did not proceed very much farther until one of them on looking over a bluff discovered the main camp and then hastened back and made the fact known to the general. Custer then and there stopped the outfit and went into consultation with his officers. It was now past twelve o'clock and he decided to make no attack until after daybreak. He arranged to divide his force into four different sections, each squad to be under the command of an officer, and at daylight, at the sound of the bugle, they were to make a charge. All was carried out as planned, with the precision of clockwork. At dawn the bugle sounded and the band struck up the tune of *Garry Owen* and the troops dashed in on the gallop. When they reached the camp from the different directions, the battle began. At the first volley fired, the Indians tried to escape, and some of them, succeeded in getting away, but the most of them, were shot down, either in their *teepees*, or as they were fleeing to some place of safety; others dropped behind trees or logs and fought like demons, but it was useless as they were overmatched. When the smoke of battle cleared away there were over one hundred dead Indians lying on the camp ground.

It was General Sherman, I believe, who said "war is hell," a statement which, proved to be absolutely correct in this instance for the wailing of the squaws and the screaming of the papooses together with the groans of the dying made a weird accompaniment to the cracking of rifles and the commands of the officers. After the flurry of the battle had somewhat subsided, Custer ordered all that were alive, squaws and *papooses*, to be taken prisoners and put in charge of a squad of soldiers, whilst the remainder busied themselves burning the *teepees*, provisions, and other camp equipage found there. When the work of destruction was completed he ordered all their ponies, about two hundred in number, to be brought in and shot. To the reader this may appear cruel and inhuman, but it was only a just retribution for the deeds this same band had committed on the Saline and Solomon Rivers in Kansas, where they spared neither age nor sex, but perpetrated outrages on women that are too beastly for publication, and this was a small instalment on what was due them. On roll call it was found that Major Elliot and fifteen men were missing.

The Kiowas and the Comanche tribes were camped but three or four miles below where the battle took place, and it did not take them very long to make their appearance about five or six thousand strong. Here was a fresh problem for Custer to solve. If he was looking for a fight with the Indians, they were at hand. Why did he not attack them? Why did they not attack him? Why did not Custer make an effort to find out what had become of Major Elliot and the fifteen missing men who had been with him. I shall explain that as I see it from my point of view. There is no doubt in my mind that General Custer was afraid to attack those two tribes, and was also afraid to make an attempt to find Major Elliot and his companions, as his conduct that evening abundantly proves. He had sent his scout, California Joe, with a dispatch telling Sheridan of his condition and asking him to send re-enforcements at once. That afternoon he held a consultation with his officers and decided to return to Camp Supply to reorganize his men and get more forces to engage in battle with those two tribes. Now the question might be asked, why did not the Indians attack him? There was but one reason and that was that they were afraid. They had force enough to defeat Custer, but there was something else to take into consideration. They knew General Sheridan was someplace in the country and was, perhaps, at that time waiting to catch them in a trap. They were not afraid of Custer and his command, but they knew that if Sheridan ever got them in a tight place, it would be goodbye, Mr. Indian, for there would be nothing left of him. It was a plain case of where Custer was afraid and the other 'dassent,' it averted, as a result, one of the worst slaughters that ever occurred in the Indian Territory.

In looking over the dead, Chief Black Kettle was identified. He had been instrumental in starting out the band that had committed all the depredations in the Saline and Solomon valleys, and but a few months prior to this time had defiantly refused, when asked by General Sheridan to come into Fort Dodge with the promise that he would be properly cared for. He declared that he was going on the warpath and made good his declaration as the battle on the Washita will show.

Chapter 24

Sheridan's Camp

The night of the battle, Custer started for Camp Supply and very nearly overtook his scout, California Joe, as the latter had to hide so much on the way to avoid being caught by the Indians; and I believe that Custer made a record trip, as he was afraid of the same thing. When he returned and Major Elliot's absence was not satisfactorily explained, General Sheridan showed great dissatisfaction. He issued an order to get everything in readiness at once and decided to take a hand in that business himself to see if he could not discover what had become of Elliot. The Kansas volunteers having lost most of their horses in the snow banks on the Cimarron River, with the remainder unfit for service, were organized as infantry and taken along. In fact, every available man was taken from Camp Supply except those who were required to guard the provisions and look after the stock. Although Sheridan was a graduate of West Point, he never encumbered himself with any West Point tactics in fighting Indians. He just put on his fighting clothes and set out to whip them into subjection regardless of any military parade, and usually accomplished what he set out to do. There was one feature of all his expeditions which he never neglected, and that was that he never failed to keep in touch with the best and most reliable scouts and guides to be found, and once he had secured them he never failed to be governed by their instructions, as he was well aware that such men understood the topography of the country much better than some titled professor of a military academy. Such scouts he found on this occasion. He took along as his guide and chief of scouts, one Ben Clark, because

Ben was married into the Cheyenne tribe and understood and spoke the tribal languages fluently. He also took along California Joe, as he was a good scout and was familiar with all the customs and habits of the Indians, having lived and dealt with them all the way from California to Texas. He was invaluable as a scout and guide, but had one fault, of which I shall speak later on, that tried the patience of the general sorely at times, but still Sheridan could not afford to part with him. Those two, with the addition to two Osage Indian scouts, were all that he brought into service. When everything was in readiness the general set out with the firm determination to settle the Indian trouble for once and for all time to come, if possible. He took General Custer with him, as he was familiar with the route and also with the locality of the recent battle. He took as his ambulance driver Johnny Murphy, a lad scarcely out of his teens and who acted in that capacity until the close of the campaign. The first night out they camped on the south bank of Wolf Creek where they found an abundance of timber and living water, two essentials at that time as the weather was hovering around the zero mark. The men were becoming accustomed to the cold and stood up in it like Eskimos. Next morning they were up and away to cross the divide to the South Canadian. The snow was still quite deep on the flats and the moisture had softened the soil which had not frozen sufficiently to hold up the heavy freight wagons, which made it a tedious and toilsome trip to reach the river. Clark being acquainted with the country guided them down a canyon where they found timber and a fair shelter. There they went into camp for the night. Next morning one of the real trials of the journey confronted them. The river had to be forded and they were forced to repeat the labours that Custer had performed on the former occasion and as the ice was not thick enough to bear a heavy weight. They had to cut a channel and remove the ice from it and trample the quicksand with the cavalry to make it fordable for the wagons. They accomplished the crossing with a great deal of difficulty and hardships, as most of them were wet from trampling through the stream or assisting the lumbering wagons on their way. When the last team had crossed they were glad to know that this difficulty had been overcome. (The reader sitting on a balcony, viewing troops of cavalry prancing along the paved streets seems to enjoy the spectacle and can easily come to imagine that the cavalry man's life is one continual round of pleasure, but let him change his location and go and sit with me on the south porch of a snow bank and see those same soldiers fording a treacherous stream in the winter season and his impressions of the gay and happy life will be suddenly changed.) When out of the brakes and the canyons they were on the last lap of their journey to the battle ground where Custer had wound up the wild and turbulent career of Black Kettle and his band of Cheyenne warriors. This day was but a repetition of the day before except that at noon they camped long enough to feed the stock some grain, as the mules were becoming tired and jaded from the bad condition of the prairie. After dinner they resumed their journey and that evening went into camp about two miles from the scene of Custer's fight with the Cheyennes a few days previous. Next morning they set out and in a short time arrived at the battle ground. They stopped to examine the place which gave every evidence of a severe conflict. After Sheridan had examined the field he sent out scouts and squads of soldiers to scour the surrounding country in search of Major Elliott and the fifteen missing men. They were found about two miles from the battle ground, dead, and stripped of their clothing and mutilated in the most horrible manner. The mutilation was the work of the squaws. They had not been scalped and their bodies lay not very far apart and the number of empty shells lying near each body showed the desperate defence they had made. It was learned afterward that Major Elliott had followed a band of fugitives and captured them, and when returning was met and overpowered by a large band of Kiowas and their dead bodies were left there for the squaws to mutilate. When this discovery was made and the news brought to Gen. Sheridan, he was in no frame of mind to adopt any conciliatory measures towards the Indians, besides it had a strong tendency to lessen his respect for Gen. Custer for not making some effort to learn what had become of Major Elliot and his fifteen companions. Sheridan was now in the right humour for a fight. He wanted to fight and was going to have a fight or a footrace with the first Indians he met. He started down the Washita, where the Kiowas and the Comanches had their headquarters. His progress was closely watched by the Indians. They pulled up everything and moved on in advance of him, but well out of his reach. They were certainly in a predicament as they could not cover up their trail by scattering out over the plain, as they would do in summer time, as the snow on the prairie gave evidence of every move they made and things were in such a shape that it was either fight or surrender. Gen. Sheridan did not seem to care which. They continued to move down stream with Sheridan in pursuit until the third day when they sent a messenger back carrying a white flag and a letter from Gen. Hazen, chairman of the peace committee, asking for a conference with the general. The reader can readily see about how Sheridan felt on the subject. He sent back word to them that there was but one way in which he would recognize Hazen's request for a conference and that was that he would give them twenty-four hours to surrender and come in as prisoners of war, or a fight would start at the expiration of that time. He was compelled to acknowledge the flag of truce and the Indians were well aware of that fact. Reluctantly he gave them the 24 hours to surrender or prepare for battle, as the recent outrages on the settlers on the Saline and Solomon Rivers, the barbarous treatment of Major Elliot and his companions were fresh in the mind of Sheridan. The Indian, aware of the value of the flag of truce used it always to his advantage when in a tight place, though they had no respect for it in their own dealings with others. Sheridan was waiting anxiously for the expiration of the time of truce, but the Indians forestalled the allotted time by about four hours. If the thing was to be done over again, I do not believe that Sheridan would have paid any attention to the flag of truce, as the first sight that met the general's eye after he had marched into their camp and taken Chief Lone Wolf and Chief Satanta prisoners, was the body of a white woman who had been kidnapped from near Fort Lyon by Satanta and kept to gratify his savage lust. When he found escape impossible, he shot her to avoid giving her up to her rescuers and took her white child by the feet and dashed its brains out against a tree. When the fiend shot the woman, whose name was Mrs. Blynn, he held the gun so close to her that her face was powder-burned. In her death, I imagine that there was relief brought to one poor tortured soul.

During the armistice, which did not last twenty-four hours, the

Indians killed all their ponies rather than turn them over to their conquerors. After the preliminaries of surrender were completed, they were ordered back to Ft. Cobb and accordingly started back to fulfil their agreement. Any one familiar with the lay of that country can begin to appreciate the difficulty Gen. Sheridan had on hand. Moreover, the reluctance of the Indians to return made the journey all the more difficult. They had a thousand different excuses to delay the journey, but it availed them nothing. They were kept on the move and closely watched. In spite of the vigilance exercised by the troops, some of the Indians managed to escape. At every opportunity some of them would dodge through the brush along the way and make their escape. Satanta seeing the success of his companions, made a dash for liberty also. He was immediately captured by the soldiers and put in handcuffs. To show no partiality in the matter, Chief Lone Wolf was also manacled. To give further proof of his intentions to compel them to submit, he told Lone Wolf and Satanta that unless those Indians who had made their escape did not return very soon, he would hang the two of them without ceremony. That put a different complexion on things. The two chiefs immediately communicated with their followers, who at once sent out runners in different directions to bring back the escaped prisoners. They succeeded in bringing in most of them in fact enough of them returned to move Sheridan to defer the hanging of the two chiefs.

It is my belief that Sheridan afterward regretted that he did not hang the two of them, as they richly deserved it for their past atrocities. I had the pleasure last year, 1912, of seeing old Chief Lone Wolf strutting around the streets of Hobart, Okla., wearing a celluloid collar and derby hat, breaking himself into the habits and customs of the white man. The sight of him caused me to wonder if he ever stopped to consider how near he came to having his neck cracked by Gen. Sheridan and how richly he deserved it.

After carefully looking over the situation in all its different aspects, Sheridan concluded that Fort Cobb was not the proper place to establish his headquarters. He decided to take all his prisoners over to Cache Creek where he would have more and better material to construct a small fort for the protection of the frontier of Texas. This part had been subjected to the raids of the Indians very frequently in the past and they were likely to make an incursion at any time. When he had brought most of the Indians there, he set to work building temporary headquarters and gave the place the name of Fort Sill, after one of his old schoolmates. He held Satanta, Lone Wolf; Little Robe, and several other lesser chiefs as hostages for the faithful performance of all the conditions of the surrender with the explicit understanding that any violation of any of the terms of it would mean the hanging of the whole party. This understanding had a very salutary effect and a strong tendency to establish order and discipline. These acts may seem to show Sheridan to be a cruel man, but I will say, judging from his action in caring for the remains of Mrs. Blynn and her child who had been so brutally murdered, in taking them to Fort Arbuckle and giving them a Christian burial, he has shown that his heart was in the right place.

Chapter 25

Expedition to Panhandle

Previously to the time of which I am writing, the general had sent a bunch of cavalry horses to Fort Arbuckle where he had made arrangements for their keep. The Chickasaw and Choctaw Indians raised some crops and had feed to spare and agreed to look after the horses. The general thought by this time they would be sufficiently recuperated to be of service to him in his present needs. Consequently he fitted up an escort and an ambulance and took California Joe along as scout and guide to go and get them. (I promised the reader to tell him of Joe's one fault and will take this opportunity of doing so.) When they had arrived at Ft. Arbuckle, they found everything in better shape than they had expected. The general began making preparations for his return to Fort Sill. When everything was ready he found to his surprise and amazement that California Joe was gloriously drunk. As the prohibitory law in regard to the sale of intoxicants was in full force, in the Indian Territory, he could not account for Joe's condition. He thought he would remain over a day or so to give Joe a chance to sleep off the effects of his overdose of liquid joy. The next day found Joe as happy as a clam in high water and there was no indication of a scarcity of liquor. The general was face to face with a difficulty. He could not remain longer at Ft. Arbuckle, and he could not go on without Joe, as he might need his services at any time. Patience ceased to be a virtue and he bundled Joe into the ambulance, jumped in himself and started off. They all reached Fort Sill the next day safe and sober. In the meantime the general had not learned where his scout had obtained the liquor to make him drunk. Joe himself told me years afterwards that he had obtained access to the general's jug.

Upon his arrival at the fort, he found everything in as good condition as the circumstances might warrant. It was a city of soldiers and Indians. The habitations consisted of *teepees* and tents, while dug-outs were in course of construction in case of a storm.

As it was one of Gen. Sheridan's principles to allow no guilty man to escape, he ordered Gen. Custer to take a company of men, mounted on the horses he had brought from Ft. Arbuckle, with some scouts among whom was to be found California Joe, and proceed to the head of the Red River and bring back those Indians who had escaped after the surrender when returning to Ft. Cobb.

After Gen. Custer had taken his departure, Gen. Sheridan made provision for the policing and government of the camp, also for the distribution of rations to the Indians during his absence. As soon as he had completed these regulations in a satisfactory manner, he began his own preparations for a trip to Camp Supply. All these things took time and caused him no little vexation, but he was equal to the emergency, and as soon as the work was done he took his escort and full camp equipage and set out. It was now getting along toward the first of March and the soft soil made the wheeling of all vehicles a slavish task for man and beast. In spite of this difficulty, he proceeded on his way and crossed the Washita above Ft. Cobb and continued in a northerly direction until he reached the South Canadian where to his great surprise he found the water very low, and what was more pleasing, he found that the ice was all gone. The season was not far enough advanced to thaw the snow on the mountains and consequently, the river being almost dry, was easily forded. It is unnecessary for me to go into details of that journey as it was but a repetition of his former trip to Fort Sill, except for the floundering around in the snow banks and the cutting of a passage through the ice to make a crossing possible. These latter difficulties he escaped, owing to the lateness of the season. Difficult passages through bad canyons were also avoided owing to Ben Clark's thorough knowledge of the country. At best, it was a tedious journey and on the seventh day after leaving Fort Sill, he crossed the North Canadian just below the junction where the Beaver and Wolf Creeks form the headquarters of the North Canadian. From there he proceeded to Camp Supply, which was only a short distance away. When Sheridan arrived at the camp, he found a message awaiting him, which had been brought from Fort Dodge, Kansas, by stage. The despatch contained the announcement of his promotion to the position of lieut. general of the army and requested him to proceed at once to Washington, D. C. Sheridan did not seem much surprised at his promotion, and continued to perform his usual duties of looking after the Indians and ordering supplies. (He saw to it that those old squaws who had mangled and mutilated his soldier-comrades should be properly cared for as prisoners of war.) (In fact, he was about the busiest man in camp.)

Before Gen. Sheridan had left Camp Sill, Gen. Custer had returned from his trip to the head of Red River, which he had made at his own request. He reported that he had found nothing but a bleak waste. He stated that there was no sign of animal or vegetable life to be seen and that he did not think it possible for the Indians to subsist there. On hearing this report Gen. Sheridan said nothing but took the matter into consideration and, after revolving the affair in his own mind for some time, it was plain to be seen that he was dissatisfied with the report. He ordered Gen. Custer to increase his force by taking the Kansas volunteers and mounting them on the horses he had brought from Fort Arbuckle, to refit and refurnish them thirty days rations and return. He also ordered him to take a full complement of scouts and scour the country until he did find the Indians and bring them into Camp Supply, or whip them into subjection, with all of which Custer was ready to cheerfully comply. The camp was now alive, each soldier fitting up his belongings for a return trip. Gen. Sheridan told Custer that he had to return to Supply and that he wanted the Indian business closed up as soon as possible and for all time to come; that he did not want the band left at liberty until the grass was green as they would then be self-supporting and could prey upon the stockmen and the settlers at will; that it was his duty to prevent this and he would, regardless of consequences.

It did not take long to make the proper preparations for the return trip, and Custer took a sufficient number of men to overpower any ordinary band of Indians, and on the following morning set out for the Panhandle country. Gen. Sheridan intended to set out the same day, but as he said he had neglected his correspondence, he thought it better to take another day to devote to that matter and arrange everything of that nature before leaving.

On the second day afterwards he had his baggage and other effects packed ready for the trip and went down to the corral to bid his old comrades and teamsters goodbye. He made them a short talk, thanking them for their faithful services they had always so readily rendered. He said that whilst he did not ever expect to return to that post again, that he would be glad to meet any of them, at any time or place. After shaking hands with all the boys he started for the ambulance which was to take him away. When he met Johnny Murphy, his tried and trusty teamster all through the campaign, he said, "Well, Johnnie, I am going to leave you. Be a good boy, and if you should ever come to Washington, call on me. I shall always be glad to meet you." He shook hands with him and when he had gone a short distance, he turned and shouted back, "Now, Johnnie, do not fail to call on me." At his departure there could be seen on the cheeks of more than one of those old battle-scarred veterans, a glistening tear, the true token of deep-seated regret. It was a sorrowful parting as these men had followed him through the din of battle for four years during the rebellion and through the Indian campaigns and had come to look upon him as their dearest friend for whom it was a pleasure to shed their blood in the performance of duty. But such was life in the west. When he had gone, each turned to his duty and tried to forget his sorrow. It was such little traits as this that made Sheridan loved by his own men, revered by his friends, and admired and respected by his enemies.

The general had hoped to be able to reach Washington to lead his old command in the Inaugural parade on March 4th, but such was not to be, as his duties in the territory delayed him, too long, as it was now March 2nd. He set out as soon as it was possible for him to leave his command. If there was any bad weather, it seemed to be his luck to be out in it. It sleeted and as scout and guide to go and get them. I promised the rained all during the journey to Bluff Creek and continued to do the same all the way to Dodge City.

Gen. Custer, a very energetic man and strict disciplinarian, too strict in fact to always retain the respect of his men, kept everybody and everything on the move. The snow was now fast disappearing from the territory, but the mud and slush caused by the thawing snow, made travelling a slavish task. Each day was a repetition of the preceding one and such it continued to be until they reached the Panhandle country where they found more snow and less protection from the winds. They still advanced keeping the scouts well to the fore to escape any chance of being taken by surprise. Each day brought the same routine of duties and the same results until it became monotonous, so much so that the boys said that they would like to have a little fight just for a change and to liven things up a little. On and on they went across the dreary desolate plain, with not even a buffalo to be seen as they had been driven from the flats by the severe storms that swept that part of the country prior to the trip. A gray wolf might be seen occasionally, or perhaps an antelope, but that was about all as the wild horses or mustangs had sought shelter in the canyons or brakes. Desolation reigned supreme and were it not for the company they found in each other they wouldn't have been able to endure the loneliness of the place. Duty urged them on, and forward they went well out on the Staked Plains. One day the scouts returned with the information that they had discovered an Indian village. Such news was music to their ears and each and all began to prepare for the impending conflict. Strange as it may seem, those Indians were aware of the approach of the scouts and fully realized their danger. The scouts had scarcely returned to camp when Custer saw through his fieldglasses a lively movement among the Indians. He knew that he had sufficient force to crush them, but hesitated to do so as he had learned that they held two white women as captives, and thought it best to parley with them, for if he attacked them they might repeat the act of cruelty and cold-blooded murder that was perpetrated by Satanta on the Washita rather than deliver her up to her rescuers. They did not have to wait, for it was a short time until the white flag which the Indian always kept within easy reach, was brought forth. When well out from the village and not far distant from the train, the general and his staff with an interpreter went out to meet them. It did not take long to arrange the preliminaries as they were anxious to surrender, or more so, than he was to capture them. Whilst the negotiations were being conducted for their surrender and return to Camp Supply, Chief Tall Bull made his escape with a few followers and was not heard of until a year later when the report was made that General Parr had made a final settlement with him and sent him "where the wicked cease from troubling", and "the weary are at rest," up on the Republican River in Colorado.

About the first request made by these Indians was for chuckaway as they were almost famished for want of something to eat. Custer readily acceded to their demand and gave them a liberal supply of rations. Then they made ready to move. They had no pianos, sewing machines, or bric-a-brac to pack and crate, but they had a good quantity of buffalo robes, blankets, tanned buckskin, pots, skillets, and other belongings of an Indian camp and it took some time to get them in readiness for transportation. To a person who has never witnessed such a thing, it is very interesting. The *teepees* had to be taken down and put in shape to be packed on ponies. In fact, everything had to be packed on ponies as a wagon was an unknown thing to them. They had a substitute for the wagon which they made from a green cow hide. This while soft and pliable they fastened by each corner to a post and weighted down the centre until it assumed the form of a large dish. When it became dry and hard, they attached it to two long *teepee* poles fastened one on each side of a pony. Into the hide they then put anything they wished to transport and turned the pony loose with the rest of the herd. I have seen them place *papooses* in this rude vehicle and the old pony wandered at will over the prairie. The *teepee* poles were made of cedar and were very light. Sometimes as many as a dozen poles would be fastened to a pony with other luggage fastened on his back. The young babies, or small *papooses*, were strapped to the squaws shoulders where she usually carried it in all kinds of weather. The older children climbed on the back of a pony, as that is about the first thing they learned, and were ready for any kind of a journey. The Indian ponies are usually very docile as they are broken to handle from colthood. It is a very rare thing to see one of them bucking or running away, and consequently we seldom hear of an accident to an Indian caused by a vicious horse.

When everything was in readiness, the general gave orders to set out and off they started on their return trip to Camp Supply. Their progress was necessarily very slow owing to the starved condition of their ponies, but Custer urged them on to the limit of their endurance as he had now a great many new boarders on hand and he feared that he might run short of supplies. Each day of the journey was like the other. One thing was favourable, the weather was warmer and the ground was not so soft and muddy as on their advance into that country. One day one of the soldiers shot a buffalo and he and his comrades cut off the hump and one hind quarter to divide among his companions. He told the Indians to help themselves to the rest. The general called a halt to give the Indians a chance to attend to the remnant of the buffalo and put the cook to work preparing some of the hump for himself. They also fed the stock some grain and by the time the general finished his slice of hump there was not enough of that buffalo left to bait a mouse trap. There was nothing left but the horns, hooves, and bones. Even the entrails did not escape their ravenous appetite. Nevertheless, the buffalo saved the general's commissary the necessity of providing one good meal and that was quite a consideration at that particular time, as provisions were beginning to get low. Each day brought its quota of petty annoyances. Sometimes a wagon would bog down in the creek, or a whiffle-tree would break or a mule balk. But that is all the part of a journey. On they went until they came to the South Canadian River where they expected to meet the greatest difficulty of their trip, but to the surprise of all parties, the water was very low and they succeeded in crossing it with much less trouble than they had to contend with in crossing some of the smaller streams. The quicksand was their greatest obstacle to be encountered in the way. The Indian ponies, as I have said, being very poor and weak, one of them would frequently fall and flounder around in the quicksand throwing his burden, a squaw and her *papoose*. There they struggled with the treacherous sands until a soldier equal to the emergency would gallantly go to their rescue and bring them back to safety on the opposite bank. The bucks faced the ordeal very reluctantly, but seeing that it was a case of the 'devil take the hindmost' they removed their moccasins, blankets, and in many cases reduced themselves to a state of primitive simplicity, and made their way across as best they could. Much to the relief of the commanding officer the last of them, after a good deal of struggling and snorting, landed on the north bank of the treacherous stream in safety. The general in his eagerness to proceed, did not wait for them to arrange their toilets, but pushed on through the brakes and canyons until he reached the flats where he went into camp. He was eager to reach his destination to unload his responsibility and one cannot blame him for that feeling after performing such an arduous task. It took three more days to reach Camp Supply where Gen. Custer turned over his charge to the Indian Department and in due course of time discharged the regiment that had rendered such valuable service. During that expedition Custer had brought back those renegades and turned them over to the department without firing a gun except at game on the way.

CHAPTER 26

Murder of a Freighter

At this time the Quakers were largely in control of the Indian Department and were indorsed in their views by Pres. U. S. Grant. They believed the Indian could be civilized and kept under control by moral suasion by the erection of school houses for his children, and by imparting a knowledge of the proper system of agriculture. Under their influence, rations were issued and blankets distributed among them. They were also given wagons, ploughs, and other farm implements which they knew nothing about. They would not ride on a spring seat, nor sit in a wagon box, but for some reason best known to themselves, they would remove the box and place *teepee* poles on the wagon bolsters and all climb in when they were ready for a trip. The ploughs and other implements which were sent out among them to encourage them to farm, I have seen suspended from trees. I cannot understand why they did so, unless it was to show contempt for the white man's way. It is true, some of them raised small patches of corn, which with the rations issued by the agency and the game they killed, kept the wolf from the door, or rather the flaps of their *teepees*. Occasionally a small band of them would get a permit from the fort commander to go on a hunt, with the understanding that they were to return at a stipulated time and behave themselves during their absence and not commit any depredations. All this they complied with. I have met these hunting parties up in No Man's Land and other places and never heard of their perpetrating any mischief on persons or stock whilst out under a permit.

The squaws, when not busy in the corn patch or in their little garden, were engaged in making ornaments or other fancy needlework at which they were experts. These articles they afterwards sold to tourists from the east, at the agency, as souvenirs of their trip among the Indians. Some of this kind of work had a real intrinsic value far above the ornamental part of it. I knew one chief's daughter who had a blanket ornamented with elk's teeth and shells, that was valued at $1500. She was taken ill and died, and the blanket which she loved to wear at festivals was used as a shroud. A few days afterwards, some person passing by noticed that the grave had been disturbed. He notified her people and an investigation being made, they found that some white man or men had been there and had stolen the blanket or robe in which she was wrapped. If they were ever captured, I am not aware of it. I said that white men did it, because a negro is too superstitious to do it, and I do not believe there is an Indian in the territory who would stoop to such a ghoulish act; so I shall give some white animal the credit for the deed.

The government also built large corrals or cowpens where the cattle were issued to the Indians. On the size of the family depended the size of the cow or steer issued. The agent had the name of each family and the number of persons comprising it. When a steer was selected a cowpuncher rode among the herd and cut out the desired animal and rushed him through the gate of the corral where the Indians were waiting with bows and arrows to kill him. They seldom killed him at the first or second shot. More frequently a dozen shots were required before they struck a vital spot. When the beast fell, the squaws, *papooses* and dogs came along to do the skinning and oversee the division of the meat. Each one came in for a share. After the killing, the lordly old buck would seek out the shelter of some tree or other shady place to rest his manly form until the animal was dressed and ready for consumption; then he would return and fill his capacious stomach with *wohaw*. The government shortly changed the arrow shooting feat as it considered that such a practice had no civilizing influence on the Indian and, besides, it wanted them to forget their old habits as soon as possible. Thereafter, when on issuing day a beef was selected, a man was there to shoot it in the corral and the Indian entered with his ponies to drag away the carcass to dress it outside.

After some time the department decided to remove a large number of the Indians at Camp Supply to the Darlington Agency which is located about 140 miles south-east of Supply on the north bank of the North Canadian River, and about two miles from Fort Reno. Here they settled down submissively and appeared to be content with their existing condition. At times there were some small complaints about the agent, which upon investigation proved oftentimes to be correct. On the other hand there was a disturbing element. This thing is not common to the Indian alone, but may be found among civilized folks who are not at peace with themselves or the world at large. Taking everything into consideration, they were doing about as well as could be expected under the circumstances.

The other band of Cheyennes who had located on Pond Creek, were also brought down to the Darlington Agency. This left the Cherokee Strip comparatively deserted, but it did not remain so long as the cowmen entered there and built ranches and stocked them with cattle under leases from the Indians. There were the Turkey Track, the Box T. R-S, Bull Foot and other ranches too numerous to mention, all located in the Cherokee Strip.

Everything moved along smoothly with but little trouble from the Indians until the year 1874, when the spirit of unrest seized them again and extended to all the Indians over the western plains. Some had one grievance and some had another. They began making medicine, which to a man acquainted with the Indians meant trouble sooner or later. At that time, supplies to Anadarko, Ft. Reno, and the Darlington Agency were freighted from Wichita, Kansas, and distributed to the different bands at these places. As there were no railroads in this country, it gave employment to hundreds of men and teams on the trails to enable them to keep up the supplies. The freighting business was a great boon to the early settlers of Kansas as the grasshoppers had destroyed everything in the form of vegetation and the settlers who had teams went to Wichita and engaged in freighting for the government. Even the white folks at this time were reduced to a great state of privation and had to depend on the bounty of the outside world. The more fortunate in the older states responded to their appeal and tided them over their distress until prosperity placed them beyond the reach of want.

About this time small bands of discontented Cheyennes began prowling around over the country and occasionally went beyond the limit allowed them by the agent, and then returned to draw their rations with the other Indians at the agency. They continued to do this for some time and finally began to make depredations on stock or anything else that came within their reach. The agent prone to avoid trouble with them, treated them leniently, but the more leniency he showed, the bolder they became until a small band under the leadership of Tall Meat, a petty chief, went north as far as Buffalo Springs on the south line of the Cherokee Strip. There they could see the freight wagons in the distance laden with government supplies heading for Anadarko, and came to the immediate decision of raiding the train. They withdrew into a canyon on the side of the trail so as to be out of sight when the train arrived. They intended to murder the teamsters and plunder their goods of whatever they wanted and then make their escape. A man named Patrick Hennessey was driving the lead wagon of one of the trains. He was trudging along on foot beside his team without the slightest suspicion of any danger. As soon as he had passed where they were hiding they shot him in the back. When the shooting took place the team stampeded and dragged Hennessey in his dying condition along the ground. The wagon upset and a bag of grain fell across Hennessey's lower limbs and there he lay dead. In the meantime the drivers of the other wagons together with a passenger who was working his way down the country, abandoned their teams and wagons and fled. Next day the Indian agent with an escort happened to pass that way and discovered the work of destruction of the day previous. They found the remnants of the wagon which had been set on fire. Some of the oats which comprised part of the load were still burning, and the sack that had fallen across poor Hennessey's limbs in burning had charred his legs to a crisp. The agent, John D. Miles, and his escort, Billy Mulally, dug a kind of temporary grave to protect the remains from the coyotes and the buzzards and marked the place with a few rocks. Every freighter that passed that way felt it his duty to see that the grave was kept in as good condition as circumstances would permit. The resting place of Pat Hennessey became a landmark for all travellers in that section until the Rock

Island railroad was built, when the remains were removed to their present place of rest. The city of Hennessey, one of the most prosperous little cities in the state is named in his honour. I have since been told that the women of Hennessey have erected a monument with suitable inscription at his grave. The other teamsters who fled when the first shot was fired were overtaken and killed at some distance from where Hennessey fell.

This little band of highwaymen could not expect to be allowed to pursue their murderous way with impunity. They had no following, as such acts would be condemned by the best Indians of their tribe, and again they were surrounded by forts. Supply on the north, Elliot on the west, Sill on the south, and Reno at home. A small band of white men might escape under such conditions as it would be possible for them to avoid detection, but not for Indians of the kind, as their approach would be a signal to begin shooting. It was a very short time until they were captured and brought into the agency. Several others were rounded up at the same time. Then an official investigation was made and after a great deal of red tape ceremonies and other preliminaries, it was thought best for the interests of the Indians, as well as for the safety of the white settlers, to transport them to the Dry Tortugas. I have never visited that locality, but from what I have learned from persons who did, it was not a very desirable place to locate a people who might expect any great degree of personal comfort. I had been told by a man who spent some time there, that if the government sent those folks there to confine and punish them, it had struck the exact spot where everything had a tendency to add to human misery, and he believed it was located so close to the region of the lost that he could hear old Cerberus barking across the dead line.

To show the reader a fine sense of filial affection and brotherly attachment is not a stranger to the savage breast, I must mention a little circumstance that occurred. When all that were to be sent off were standing around and their friends were giving their farewell greetings, one young Indian stepped forward and asked the officer in command if he were going to take his brother away where maybe so he not come back some time. The officer replied that such was the present intention, but modified his remark by saying that at some time in the future they might regain their liberty if they were good Indians. The young Indian hesitated a moment and then said, "Well, me go too. Me not want for stay here and my brother he take away some place I not know and maybe so he not come back at all sometime. Me go, too." The commanding officer granted his request and gave him transportation along with his brother to the Dry Tortugas, situated 175 miles west of Key West in the Gulf of Mexico.

When the Indians were removed, in a short time everything dropped back into peaceful channels and ran along in a comparatively smoother fashion until Chief Dull Knife became uneasy and wanted to return to the Black Hill country. His outbreak will form the subject of another chapter.

Since writing the above I have had occasion to visit one of the public schools of El Reno, where I found a history of Oklahoma written by Joseph B. Thoburn, former secretary of agriculture, and Isaac M. Holcomb, former superintendent of Oklahoma City schools. On page 133 I found a brief history of the tragic death of Pat. Hennessey on July 3rd, 1874, and what a brave defence he made against such odds and when captured was bound to a wagon wheel and burned alive. Also, there was a foot-note stating that it was reported and generally believed that it was the deed of white men disguised as Indians, in order to have it charged up to the Indians. Such was not the case and the above statement is misleading and incorrect, and for the benefit of the school children of the State of Oklahoma, as well as in justice to the Indian I shall set down the correct statement of the case.

My authority for my version of the affair are the following gentlemen: John Murphy of El Reno, and H. A. Todd of Calumet, brother-in-law of Billy Mulally who assisted John D. Miles, Indian agent at Darlington, to bury Pat. Hennessey, while on their way to Wichita, Kansas. Their version of the affair is as follows:

Patrick Hennessey in the lead of a wagon train was going from Wichita, Kansas, to Anadarko, I. T. loaded with grain and other supplies for the government. He had been warned at Buffalo Springs ranch, kept by a man named Mosher, that the Cheyenne Indians were on the war-path, and was advised to go no farther. He persisted in going and in like manner did the two other teams of the train. With them was a passenger who was working his way with them. When not far from where Hennessey, Okla. is now located, a band a Cheyenne Indians, under the leadership of Bear Shield and Tall Meat, came out of a draw and shot Hennessey in the back. The commotion caused by them stampeded the mules Hennessey was driving. He in his dying condition hung on to the lines and was dragged along the ground, as he had been walking alongside the wagon. Presently the wagon upset and a sack of oats fell across Hennessey's prostrate form and pinned him to the ground. He was dead. The other drivers with their passenger leaped from their wagons and ran north-east in the direction of Skeleton Creek where they were followed by the Cheyennes and killed, and were afterwards buried by the cowboys and Mosher. This accounts for their not being buried with Hennessey. The burning of Hennessey cannot be attributed to the Cheyennes as the Osages happened along about this time and the Cheyennes fled. The Osages after plundering the wagons of all they wanted, set fire to what they could not carry away. The following forenoon, John D. Miles, Indian agent at Darlington, accompanied by Billy Mulally, a cowman on his way to Kansas, came across the wreckage. The grain was still burning and Pat Hennessey's body lay partly under a sack of grain which was still smouldering, and not tied to the wagon wheel as the history has it. From, there they removed him and buried him in a temporary grave. From this resting place he was afterwards removed to what is now called Hennessey, Okla., where there stands a splendid monument erected to his memory by the women of Oklahoma.

Note—This correction is only one of many that might be made in our present day history which pretend to set forth a correct idea of the early days of our state. For any further reference to such matters, living witnesses are at hand to give a correct version of many erroneous statements that have crept into our text books and other writings.

CHAPTER 27

Custer's Massacre

For several years, I might say the whole decade from 1870 to 1880, the Indians occupied the attention of the public. In the northwest they were very active. The Utes, Apaches, Cheyennes, and the Sioux were almost continuously on the warpath, and their activities were so widespread and far-reaching that, at times, they almost blocked the progress of the wheels of commerce, and made trade and travel a very dangerous proceeding. The movement on the part of the Indian developed a corresponding activity on the part of the military department. Gen. P. H. Sheridan, Gen. Crook, Gen. Custer, and Gen. Nelson A. Miles and many other men high up in military affairs devoted their time and attention to the pressing condition of affairs and took up their position in localities where they would be able to suppress the movements of the Indians and bring about a peaceable solution of their difficulties.

The various bands of Indians adopted practically the same mode of procedure in their warlike movements. Each spring and summer, when there was plenty of green grass and abundance of water, usually found them opening up a new campaign against the encroachments of the white population. It was very galling for them to stand by and see the source of their supplies, the buffalo, exterminated without making any contrary movement. In fact, they did not propose to do so, but set out to exterminate the hunters who were intent on making a desert of the plains that teemed with millions of their favourite game. Their efforts were sometimes crowned with success, and frequently they encountered disaster. In spite of the reverses they suffered, as at the Chivington massacre on Sand Creek, Colorado, they did not abandon their efforts to retain their rights to the land they had so long retained as their lawful hunting ground. The fact that he had practically no further means of gaining a livelihood, made them all the more determined to fight to the finish with those whom they considered usurpers of their ancestral kingdom.

To add to his difficulties in the way of the encroachments of the whites, an unexpected circumstances arose that made conditions much more difficult to bear. Gold had been discovered in the Black Hills. There was a rush made upon the gold-bearing district, which stirred the Indians to greater excitement. Immigrant trains from Missouri, Kansas, Nebraska, and as far east as Ohio and Michigan, began to wind their long sinuous way across the plains in the direction of the new gold fields. They were not entirely unacquainted with the excited condition of the territory through which they were compelled to travel, and consequently made preparations to meet the difficulties and dangers of the way. They were well aware that the Indians were on the warpath and ready to give them a warm reception on their invasion on the Indians' domain. To meet the perils of such a journey as they were compelled to make, each wagon train consisting of numerous outfits, was under the guidance of some experienced plainsman. He showed them the proper manner of procedure in the method of self-defence in case they were subjected to an attack from the marauding bands of red-men on the way. It was well, as far as their own safety was concerned, that they learned how to corral their wagons and stock in the time of danger, as more than one wagon train was attacked and completely destroyed and the members of the party massacred on their way across the plains. In justice to the Indians, I wish to remark that all the massacres and plunderings of the early days were not wrought by the Indians. It is a well-known fact that the Mormons in Utah played a part in such inhuman affairs, as is evidenced by the actions of John D. Lee and his followers, disguised as Indians, when they perpetrated the Mountain Meadow massacre. To leave the impression that it was the work of the tribesmen they scalped their victims, ran off their stock, and burned their wagons. There are several other instances that might be mentioned, wherein the white man in the guise of the Indian, performed deeds of deviltry and endeavoured to cast the blame upon the red man. While charging the Indian with his crimes, let us not forget to give him credit for his virtues also, or as Theodore Roosevelt would say, "let us give him a square deal."

Time passed on, each year bringing its quota of trouble and disaster, without any indication or improvement in the general condition of affairs. All the frontier posts were supplied with soldiers who seemed anxious for something to turn up to relieve the monotony of camp life. They finally had their wishes fulfilled, for in the spring of 1876, Sitting Bull, the Napoleon of the Sioux tribe, succeeded in concentrating his whole force in the valley of the Little Big Horn. No opportunity was more desired by the whites for putting an end to the activity of the Indians. Gen. Custer lost not a moment in taking the field against him. His past successes in fighting the savages seemed to guarantee him victory in his present undertaking. In his impetuosity he set out flushed with the thought of the success that was to perch upon his arms. In his ardour lay his crushing defeat. Custer had about 700 men—only 256 with him in actual fight where he fell, every man killed except Curley the Crow scout who escaped. Reno and Benteen were already held in check on the hill they retreated to when attacked before Custer engaged the Indians. The Indians had 3600 braves or warriors. Sitting Bull was the Bismark of the Sioux and Gall the Von Molkte. Custer and Terry had been informed by Indian agent at Standing Rock that only 800 braves were to be engaged. Sitting Bull had defeated General Crook a few days before he encountered Custer. Sitting Bull fearing also General Gibbons and Crook at any minute to reinforce the Seventh Cavalry hastened to make his escape to Canada, otherwise he would have annihilated Reno and the balance of the Seventh Cavalry. These Indians in 1881 returned to the United States and I helped put them on steam boats at Fort Buford and Fort Keogh, or Miles City now, and sent them to Standing Rock agency, Rain in the Face's band being at Keogh. Sitting Bull, by strategy, succeeded in decoying General Custer, with his entire command, into a position that was suicidal. The wily Indian chief, with about nine thousand warriors, on the 25th of June, 1876, attacked him and annihilated the whole command, carrying off all Custer's munitions of war as trophies of victory. Acting on the principle that "to the victor belong the spoils," Sitting Bull, by the total annihilation of the enemy was able to replenish his larder at the expense of Uncle Sam. It was a veritable windfall for him, as the supplies of food, guns, ammunition, horses, blankets, and everything that was needed for comfort and safety, were very much in demand about that time, as the Indian's resources were almost at the vanishing point at the time. It is not my purpose here to offer any explanation of Custer's failure, but it was commonly reported that General Reno had been expected to take part in the engagement, but did not do so. Others lay the disaster to Custer's impetuosity, not waiting for his auxiliaries to arrive. I am not prepared to say who was to blame for the calamity.

In the death of General Custer, the country lost one of the bravest men that ever donned the uniform of the soldier. He had his faults but cowardice was not one of them. He was true to his country and his flag and his fall where the fight was thickest, was an indication of his military character.

I thought it proper to write this short sketch in order to show the influence it exercised on succeeding events. It was several days before the results of the day's disaster became known to the general public. There were several reasons for the delay. First, those who were to join Custer in his attack on the Indians did not arrive for some time after the battle and as there was not a living soul left to tell the tale of the deeds of heroism performed in that desperate encounter, nor give any inkling as to the whereabouts of the dead bodies of the slain, it was more by chance than design that their location was discovered as soon as it was. Even to those who came upon them where they lay stiff and cold in death, it did not seem possible that there could be such a complete massacre that not a living man was left to relate what happened. Again, the means of communication with the world at large were very meagre. There was the pony express, a very slow method at its best. However, the news was finally forwarded to the country at large, and as usual, the newspapers went into glaring accounts of the disaster, calling upon imagination for what they lacked from authoritative sources. The whole country was aroused.

When the other Indian tribes had learned of Sitting Bull's successful annihilation of the hated pale-face command, their enthusiasm knew no bounds. They began to see at last the extermination of the white man. No more would the buffalo hunter deprive them of their means of subsistence. No more would the freighter and the settler occupy the lands that belonged to the Indian long before the white man had set his foot on American soil. The prophecy of the Messiah was coming true, and they were ready and willing to have a share in hastening the day of their deliverance from the white usurper. Naturally, they began to make their war medicine and prepare themselves to aid in freeing their beloved plains from the objectionable intruder. Herein, they reckoned without Uncle Sam. No sooner had the news of Custer's defeat and annihilation been brought to him, than he began to make preparations for another expedition against them, determined to wipe out the stain of recent defeat. The purpose of the new expedition was probable more comprehensive than the former efforts of a like nature. The government began to realize that it was face to face with no common danger. The forts were put in proper condition to resist any attack that the Indian might contemplate making upon them. New forts were established at different points of vantage and men enlisted for the purpose of bringing the defence up to a proper footing, as well as to afford protection for the trade and commerce of that disturbed region.

The year of 1877 was but a repetition of the preceding years with very few exceptions. The Indian was becoming accustomed to the ways of the white man, especially in the art of making war. Whenever and wherever possible he discarded his primitive weapons, the bow and arrow, for the more up-to-date and efficient firearms. These they acquired, sometimes by barter and frequently by successful engagements in battle, as in the case of the Custer massacre where they obtained sufficient munitions of war to make them feel rather bold in their dealings with the boys in blue.

One thing noticeable about this time, was the change in the method of conducting warfare by the organized forces of Uncle Sam. The old army method of fighting was improved by adopting the strategy of the enemy while fighting on his native heath.

Heretofore they had followed the tactics of civilized warfare acquired by experience in the years of the Great Rebellion, but they were glad to adopt the latter and improved method of bringing the battle to the Indians in the manner that was more conductive to personal safety and at the same time offered opportunities for personal initiative. The change seemed to be more agreeable to the men in the ranks, for they seemed to enjoy mounting a horse and scurrying over the plains in free-lance fashion. One great drawback to their success was their ignorance of the topography of the country in which they were operating. They were oftentimes compelled to rely upon the knowledge of scouts who were frequently as ignorant as themselves. Since so much depended on the accurate information given by the guide, one may imagine the plight of a body of men guided by an unreliable scout in an expedition through the mountains or over the plains. Happily, men of such character were the exception and not the rule. The rank and file of the scouts were composed of men whose knowledge of the plains seemed almost uncanny, whose personal courage was on a par with that of the bravest of men, and who could be relied upon to accomplish their undertakings with prudence and despatch. Such men as Ben Clark, Buffalo Bill, Amos Chapman, W. F. Brannan, Jack Stillwell, Billy Dixon, and others too numerous to mention filled all the requirements for a successful scout, and rendered service to the country that can not be properly estimated or fitly described within the limits of a short narrative. Some of them I am acquainted with personally, and I feel myself honoured by it. They were the men that guided the U. S. troops through the most difficult and dangerous campaigns, blazing the highways for them, and making civilization possible on the western plains.

The summer of 1877 passed away in very much the same fashion as the preceding seasons of Indian warfare. The first snow fall was a harbinger of peace, as the tribesmen do not favour the winter time as one fitted for the activities of warfare. They preferred to sit around the camp fire in their winter quarters and wait till the grass was green and the plains free from snow before taking the warpath again. They were never known to break the custom of generations, until General Phil. H. Sheridan arrived at the conclusion that it was not advantageous to allow the Indians to go into winter quarters to wait for another season of warfare. That looked too much like allowing the enemy to say when, where, and how they would fight, and that was contrary to the notions Sheridan had of conducting a successful campaign. He it was who ordered the winter campaign against the Kiowas, Comanches, and Cheyennes, which proved successful and paved the way to permanent peace with those tribes. Nelson A. Miles adopted the same plan and drove Sitting Bull through the snow banks across the boundary into the Dominion of Canada, where he was quite willing to promise to behave himself in the future if permitted to return to the land of his fathers. I know for a certainty that he lived up to his promises, though I do not know how far he would have done so if he had not lost his power as a medicine man with the Sioux. He was shortly after his return shot and killed by the Indian police. His death removed one of the greatest leaders and warriors that ever led the Sioux tribe into battle, and conduced to the establishment of permanent peace with that nation.

Custer's Last Battle

The 7th U. S. Cavalry, 700 men and 28 officers, 2 companies of the 17th U. S. Infantry, 1 company 6th U. S. Infantry—8 officers and 135 men; One Platoon of Gatling guns, 2 officers and 32 men, of the 20th U. S. Infantry and 40 Ree scouts, the 7th Cavalry being commanded by General Geo. A. Custer, and the expeditionary forces under command of Brigadier General Alfred H. Terry, at the sounding of the "general" at 5 o'clock in the morning of may 17th, 1876 proceeded to march to the camp of Sitting Bull in the Little Big Horn country, by 7 a. m. the 7th Cavalry was marching in column of platoons through the post and around the parade ground, of Fort A. Lincoln, the band mounted on white horses playing *Garry Owen* the Seventh's battle tune, first used when this gallant regiment charged at the battle of Washita. The column halted just outside of the garrison and dismounted where their wives and members of the families came out and bid their husbands and fathers goodbye, many of whom they would see no more, after the farewells, the signals "mount" and "forward" were sounded and the

General H. M. Creel

command headed by the Gallant Seventh, marched away the band playing *The Girl I Left Behind Me*.

The command proceeded until on the Rosebud, Indian trails were discovered June 19th. The mouth of the Rosebud was reached June 21st, where preparations were made for the battle that followed on the Little Big Horn June 25th and 26th, 1876.

The Indians attacked in this campaign were various Sioux tribes, also Northern Cheyennes and Arapahos, the leading chiefs being Sitting Bull, Rain in the Face, Crow King, Low Dog, Big Road, Spotted Eagle and Little Horse of the Northern Cheyennes—Gall, Crow King, and Crazy Horse were the three ruling fighting chiefs; the total fighting strength of the combined Indian forces was 3000.

General Custer was ordered by General Terry to engage the Indians, reports from the Indian agencies leading him to believe that there were only about 800 bucks in the field.

General Crook had engaged Sitting Bull's command before on June 17th and was badly defeated by the Indians, indeed glad to escape without total annihilation. General Gibbons was near, but the three commands operated independently of each other while had they co-operated together, attacking as a whole, the Custer massacre as it is called would never have occurred.

On June 25th, 1876, the Indians were attacked by one battalion under Major Reno, consisting of Troop "M"; Captain French, Troop "A"; Captain Moylan, Troop "G", Lieutenant McIntosh, the Indian scouts under Lieutenants Varnum and Hare and Interpreter Girard, Lieutenant Hodson acting adjutant, Doctors DeWolf and Porter Medical officers, this battalion marched down a valley that developed into a small tributary to the Little Big Horn, now called Sundance or Benteen's Creek, where they reached the river, and crossing were routed by the Indians in great force and retreated across the river to the bluffs loosing three officers and 29 enlisted men killed, seven enlisted men and one officer wounded, one officer and fourteen enlisted men missing, the Ree scouts ran away and continued their flight until outside of the danger zone. Some Crow scouts remained with the troops.

The battalion commanded by General Custer, consisted of Troop, "I", Captain Keogh, Lieutenant Porter, Troop "F", Captain Yates, Lieutenant Relly; Troop "C", Captain Tom Custer and Lieutenant Harrington; Troop "E", Lieutenants Smith and Strugis, troop "L", Lieutenants Calhoun and Crittenden; Lieutenant Cook was adjutant, Dr. G. E. Lord, Medical officer.

The third battalion was under Captain Benteen, the ranking captain of the Seventh Cavalry, consisted of Troop "H", Benteen, captain, Lieutenant Gibson; Troop "D", Captain Weir and Lieutenant Edgerly; and Troop "K", Lieutenant Godfrey. The pack train was in command of Lieutenant Mathey, escorted by Troop "B", Captain McDougall, this battalion was to proceed to the right and supposed to cut off Indians routed by Reno, but on coming into view of the Little Big Horn Valley succeeded in joining Reno on the hills where he was being engaged by the Indians; while Gall was leading the attack against Reno, Iron Cedar, one of his warriors, announced that more soldiers were coming, which was the battalion under General Custer, the Indians withdrawing from attack on Reno concentrated on Custer, who never forded the river but being attacked by overwhelming forces made his stand on a ridge where he and every one of his command went down to defeat, not one man escaped to tell the tale—212 bodies were buried on the battle field, all stripped and mutilated except General Custer who was shot in the temple and left side. The bodies of Dr. Lord and Lieutenant Porter, Harrington and Sturgis were never found, at least not recognized, the clothing of Lieutenant Porter and Sturgis was found in the debris, and showed they had been killed. The total killed of the entire command was 265, wounded 52. Little plots of wild sun flowers mark the graves of those resting here who died on that memorable June 25th, 1876, no one will ever know the heroic death they met or the terrible scenes enacted but they attest the services of the Gallant Seventh Cavalry who did more to clear the country in the early days from Mexico to Canada than almost all the other regiments combined. *Garry Owen* can not awake them to glory again, and the girls they left behind will mourn until death shall enable them let us hope, to join their departed dead never seen after that fatal parting, May 17, 1876, at old Fort Abraham Lincoln on the banks of the historical Missouri River.

General H. M. Creel

CHAPTER 28

Trouble With the Northern Cheyennes

The year 1878 found the Northern Cheyennes up in arms and on the warpath, as were the other tribes on the plains and in the mountains. Prominent among the roving bands of warriors was the Little Chief band of Northern Cheyennes. They were very active and indications seemed to point out that they were likely to make things very disagreeable for the troops as well as for the ranch man in that section. Little Chief and his band were brought to Fort A. Lincoln in December 1877 and remained there until July 24th, 1878, when they left with the 7th cavalry for the Black Hills to locate a fort, named later Meade. The fortunes of war proved very unfavourable for him and he was forced to surrender early in the season. His whole band consisting of 375 warriors, with the Little Chief himself at their head, was taken to fort Abraham Lincoln as prisoners of war and placed in charge of Major Tilford who was in command of the place at that time. They remained there till the latter part of July, when he selected Ben Clark, General Sheridan's chief of scouts and Indian interpreter, to take charge of them and take them under military escort from thence to their destination at Fort Reno reservation, in the Indian Territory. I herewith give Clark's commission in full.

Headquarters
Fort Abraham
Lincoln, Dakota
July 20th, 1878.
To Mr. Ben Clark, in charge of the Cheyenne Indians.
Sir: I am directed by the commanding officer to inform you

that it is his intention to have the Cheyenne Indians, prisoners of war, leave this post for their destination early next week, and that you will make the necessary arrangements for their departure at that time. If you need any assistance or information in this connection, you will report to the commanding officer in person. Very respectfully,
Your Obedient Servant,
F. M. Gibson
1st Lieutenant 7th Cavalry, Post Adjutant

Ben Clark accepted the appointment and at once began to make the preparations necessary for the removal of the Indians to their destination at Fort Reno, I.T. It was a perilous undertaking at that season of the year as the plains were alive with hostile Indians. Another incident arose about the time to make the journey more hazardous than usual, *viz.*, the report that Dull Knife had left the reservation at Fort Reno and was on his way northward to his former hunting grounds. In other words, Dull Knife was on the warpath and as explained in a former chapter, was committing all kinds of depredations. It may be easily imagined what would occur if the tribe that had just broken away from Reno reservation were to join forces with the Little Chief band on their way to the place the other had just quitted. Naturally the tensity of the situation exercised its influence on the whole force accompanying the Little Chief band. At this juncture Ben Clark received the following telegram:

Headquarters
Fort Abraham
Lincoln
July 24th, 1878
Special Order, No. 175.
Companies H and L, 7th Cavalry, will move into camp on the hill in the rear of the post at one o'clock, p. m., preparatory to taking the field tomorrow, the 25th of July, 1878, to join troops operating from Bear Buttes, Dakota, Ter. The Cheyenne Indian prisoners will leave this post with this command *en route* to Camp Robinson under the charge of Ben Clark who will draw for these Indians thirty-two days Indian ra-

tions, and will attend to the loading, hauling, and issuing of the same during the march. By command, Major Tilford,
F. M. Gibson
1st Lieutenant, 7th Cavalry
Post Adjutant

When everything was in readiness, and there was considerable difficulty in the task just accomplished, the expedition set out for Bear Buttes. General Sam D. Sturgis, Colonel of the Seventh Cavalry, in command. Captain Benteen, in command of the escort. The journey was rather tedious as the distance to be travelled each day was limited by Ben Clark to 15 miles. When they reached Bear Buttes they were met by Second Lieutenant H. M. Creel, of K troop of the 7th Cavalry, and Captain Mathey, who took charge of the escort from that place to Fort Robinson. Everything went along as well as the trying conditions of the march would permit, and through the watchfulness of Ben Clark the Indians had little cause to murmur, as he looked after their interests and comfort in a manner that reflects great credit upon him. When they reached Sidney Barracks farther south, the following telegram was awaiting them.

Omaha Barracks
Nebraska
Sept. 14th, 1878, 12:35 p. m.
To Ben Clark, in charge of Cheyenne Indians, In care of Commanding Officer, Sidney Barracks, Neb.
As the Northern Cheyenne Indians who were at Fort Reno, I. T., have left there and are trying to make their way back north, the department commander desires to know if you think it advisable for the Indians under your charge to continue their journey south at present. Is there any likelihood of their trying to join those who have left Fort Reno? Where do you think those who have left Fort Reno will try to cross the Union Pacific Railroad? Telegraph reply to this and any other information or opinion regarding movements of those from Fort Reno which may be useful. By command of Gen. Crook.
R. Williams
Ass't Adjut. General

Major Mauck took charge of the escort under Ben Clark at Sidney Barracks. Things went along according to the usual routine until they reached the vicinity of the Red Cloud agency. The close proximity of that agency to the present position of the prisoners of war, no doubt, had some influence on the Little Chief band, as they used to belong to that section of the territory. At this place, Iron Shirt and Black Wolf, chiefs of no mean repute, decided that they would go no further. They declared that they preferred to go to the Red Cloud agency and did not want to go any further south. For a time it seemed as if there was going to be some difficulty in getting the expedition under way again as Iron Shirt, in particular, who was looked upon as a military genius by his followers, was quite determined in his attitude against any further advance towards Reno. However, the matter was promptly adjusted by the commanding officer, by the use of a little diplomacy, as he explained matters to them through the interpreter and put the affair in such a light that it seemed satisfactory to all concerned. The Indians had been rather loathe to leave Fort Abraham Lincoln and would in all probably openly resisted were it not for an agreement made between them and General P. H. Sheridan wherein he promised them good locations, plenty of rations, good hunting on the North Canadian, and besides, gave them permission to retain their firearms as there was an abundance of game in the land to which they were going. The reader will discover later on how this agreement was respected by the war department.

The expedition journeyed along from Sidney Barracks under command of Major Mauck, *via* Fort Wallace, Fort Dodge, and Camp Supply, without any interruption of any importance, though it was a very ticklish situation all the way as they knew not at what time or place they might encounter the Dull Knife band. It took all the wariness of Ben Clark to keep the band out of all possibility of meeting their kinsmen who were then on the warpath. That he did it successfully, is to his credit, and for it he deserves the highest commendation of not only those immediately concerned with the expedition, but of the country at large, for if those two bands of Cheyennes united, there would have ensued another massacre appalling in its execution.

Little Chief and his band escorted by four troops of the fourth cavalry under Major Mauck arrived at Camp Supply, I. T., in December, 1878, after a few days' rest started for Fort Reno, the first day's march brought them to the junction of Wolf and Beaver Creek, forming the North Fork Canadian River, where the command camped, the next morning in the midst of a heavy snow storm Major Mauck came to Lieutenant Creel's tent about five o'clock with a telegraphic order from General Pope commanding department of Missouri directing him to disarm and dismount the Northern Cheyennes in his charge and *en route* for Fort Reno, as the interior department at the instigation of the Indian office refused to allow the Indians to enter the territory unless this was done—this was done to prevent a repetition of the Dull Knife raid of that year. General Pope being entirely ignorant of the promises made by General Sheridan to these Indians that they should retain their arms and ammunition and he had called their attention to the excellent hunting in the Indian Territory. Now on this morning the Indians expected to start out on a great hunt and had asked Lieutenant Creel to go with them, but immediately after reveille and breakfast were confronted with the four troops of the Fourth Cavalry mounted and asked to deliver up their arms and ponies. Lieutenant Creel told Major Mauck of the promises made the Indians by General Sheridan and pointed to the interpretation that would be placed upon such treatment and asked Major Mauck if he could not defer action until they could get into communication with General Sheridan, Division commander, but due to poor means of communication Major Mauck was afraid to assume the responsibility. Later when General Sheridan learned of this action on request of the Indian office, it is needless to say he was much incensed and it was due to this fact that he in a short time affected the transfer of all Northern Cheyennes in this band who desired, to return to their old hunting grounds in Montana.

On the arrival of the expedition at Camp Supply, they were confronted with a dispatch from the war department through General Pope, demanding the immediate disarmament of the Indians. When the order was made known to Little Chief, he at once objected to its enforcement, and with his band, stood with arms drawn and ready to rebel against such open violation of their treaty with General Sheridan.

The Indians when asked to surrender their arms and ponies refused, and formed in battle line in semicircular formation, the women and children in the centre. Iron Shirt exhorting them to die fighting for their rights, telling them that they had been lied to long enough, during this time had one gun gone off, it would have been the commencement of a bloody massacre of women and children. All the women and children that could crowd into Lieutenant Creel's two tents, thinking that when the firing commenced they would be immune. Until eleven o'clock the Indians maintained a bold and relenting attitude, their guns in hand, they stood immovable not yielding one inch; during this tense interval when any moment one shot would have precipitated a bloody fight, Lieutenant Creel remained with the Indians in their midst, walking quietly up and down their line urging carefulness and pleading for the lives of their women and children until they finally surrendered. The Northern Cheyennes as Little Wolf said at Washington in the winter of 1913, had made him an adopted member of their tribe, and the history of the Cheyenne nation or people would not be complete without his name in it, that no white man, an officer in the gallant Seventh Cavalry had when death was near, stood with the Indians in their midst, and on their side as he had done, every other white man had left the Indian camp including William Roland, a half-breed Cheyenne interpreter for these Indians, saying there was going to be a massacre.

It was certainly a very trying situation. There was not a man of the whole command who did not admit the justice of the Indian Chief's refusal to turn over the arms which he had been promised to be allowed to keep as he would need them in his new location for the purpose of killing game. The cavalry were ordered to mount and enforce the unjust order. At this point there occurred one of those little incidents that oftentimes raises a man above his fellows and marks him for all time as one to whom the regard for justice is paramount above all things, even life itself.

The troops had mounted and were holding themselves in readiness for further orders, when H. M. Creel, second lieutenant of K troop, indignant at the injustice of the order, went to

BEN CLARK, GEN. P. H. SHERIDAN'S CHIEF OF SCOUTS

the Indians and urged them to refrain from bringing on an engagement which would prove disastrous to themselves and cause a massacre of their women and children. As the lieutenant could speak the Cheyenne tongue fluently, and was familiar with the customs and habits of the tribe, he received a hearing that was respectful. He succeeded in bringing about a conciliation by becoming personally responsible for their firearms and anything else which they might have that was considered contraband of war. By his course of action in the matter, he at once won the undying gratitude of the Cheyennes, which endures to this day, and will continue to do so as long as the traditions of the Cheyenne are handed down to posterity.

The trouble being averted, the escort started on its way again, Ben Clark guiding them down the river. But the danger was not yet past. General Pope insisted on the order being carried out in spite of the fact that justice and decency forbade it. However, he succeeded in having it fulfilled, but when it was carried into effect there were not enough guns of any value to arm a corporal's guard. I have always been under the impression that the Indians during the march from where the trouble arose to the place where they were disarmed, succeeded in secreting the best of their arms, which was not very difficult as the soldiers were not too strict in trying to prevent their doing so as they saw that an injustice was being done to their charges. I do not know what General Sheridan thought or said when he learned how his treaty of peace with the Indians had been observed by the war department, but, I am under the impression, that if one could have taken a kaleidoscopic view of his thoughts at the time, there would likely have been a very lurid tint about them.

Once the Indians were disarmed, the work trials of the expedition were practically at an end. It was a very short march down the North Canadian to the place of their future abode. Ben Clark saw to it that things were carried out, as far as possible, to the satisfaction of all.

Nor did Lieutenant Creel leave the wards of the government at once. In fact he remained with them for a considerable length of time in the capacity of agent, and the confidence they had in him is shown by the results of his tenure of office among them. He came to be looked upon as a father to all of them, to whom they might go to have all wrongs righted, and their rights preserved. The result of such confidential relationship between Lieutenant Creel and the Indians is manifest today in the high-class of citizenship that exists among the wards of the government, and their advancement in the various pursuits of life according to the white man's ways.

Creel was the man of the hour. He devoted his time, talents, and energy to the elevation of the children of the plains. He set out to improve their educational facilities. He wrote a grammar and a dictionary of the Cheyenne tongue, of which he had a complete mastery. Also work on the sign language of the North American Indians. His work in this regard was of such a high order as to be preserved in the Smithsonian Institute in Washington, D. C.

CHAPTER 29

Ben Clark & General Creel

In concluding the little work, I deem it impossible to close without paying tribute to two men who have done so much in the way of settling the difficulties of the west, and making it possible for the white settlers to live in peace and prosperity, freed entirely from the haunting spectre of an Indian raid. Many have contributed their share to the important work, and credit must be given them, nevertheless in any undertaking, there are men who seem by nature to be better adapted to the work than others; so it was in the closing days of the Indian troubles of the west, when the Indian had good cause for looking on the white man with suspicion, and the result as shown in those numerous raids upon the white settlements during the decade of 1870 and 1880.

In the long array of men who endeavoured to bring the difficulties that disturbed the west to a satisfactory close, we find two who played an important part within the scope of their opportunities, and the results of their work are manifest at this date.

Ben Clark was a scout. The term to the ordinary man of affairs does not mean much, but if one could ask General Sheridan's opinion of the man and scout, he would place him in the very first rank of all scouts of the west. He was a man particularly gifted by nature with the endowments requisite to achieve success in his calling. He seemed to have an uncanny knowledge of the plains. Like an open book he read her every mood. On his knowledge of that vast trackless plain depended the success of many an expedition, and there yet remains no failure to mar the brilliant record of his achievements. Not only soldiers, but generals placed themselves unreservedly in his hands and felt safe. He was not a soldier, but no soldier ever showed greater qualities of generalship than he. Generals commanded the armies, he commanded the generals and they gladly obeyed him. Amid all the trials and vicissitudes of his life of hardship, he ever maintained an evenness of temperament that carried him down to the present day, to a ripe old age, after more than fifty years of service in the army, not a soldier, but as a scout, respected and retaining the confidence of the men with whom he spent days and years of hardship on the plains.

Associated with Ben Clark in the later days was one who has risen by dint of devotion to duty to a very high position in the sphere of military affairs. I refer to General Creel, as he is now called. Among the many positions that General Creel has held was that of adjutant general of his state, North Dakota, where he raised the national guard of his state from chaos to such a degree of efficiency that the war department after full inspection and field manoeuvre of the guard with regulars declared ninety per cent fit for duty in the field on a par with the regular army. General Creel on his own request was highly complimented by the governor for his distinguished services, and retired with the rank of major general as provided by law. Of his soldierly qualities there is not much need of making the record here, as it is open to all who wish to consult the archives of the army. Fighting qualities are expected in a soldier, otherwise he would be out of place in the ranks, but there are other qualities that set a man apart from his fellows. Some men have administrative ability, some diplomacy, others skill in various lines, but a man must have a special adaptation by nature who can take the rough, untamed spirits of the plains away from their native heaths, from all that is dear to them, and at the same time make them love him. Some could do it by force, but the result would not be lasting, as is instanced in the case of Dull Knife; others could do it by love of justice and fair play and convert the savage into a high-class citizen of the state. The latter was the method used by General Creel, and to show that they have not forgotten the spirit of fairness that characterized the man, one would but have to visit the Darlington Agency, Oklahoma, when the general makes a trip to the scene of his early efforts as an Indian pacifier, and see how they gather around him and show marks not merely of respect, but of real affection. To the work of his office he added occupations of his own choice. He devoted himself to a thorough study of the Cheyenne tongue, and his efforts resulted in a grammar and dictionary of that language. Not only is the general an authority on the Cheyenne dialect, but his work on the sign language is masterly. He is not only a man well versed in Indian affairs, though that itself would be sufficient for most men, but is one of the directors of the 1914 Chatauqua institute. One would be inclined to think that with all the successes that attend his efforts, and the title of general that he bears, that he would be inclined to be swelled with the sense of his own importance, but not so. You will not find a more modest man in the whole range of activity than the general. He is the last man that you would take to be one of the great geniuses of the west if you were to estimate him by his general behaviour.

In conclusion, much might be written about the complex nature of the Indian and the trouble he created for the white man during the last half century. But if the white man were to put himself in the place of the Indian I doubt if he would act differently. One cannot see an intruder come into one's domain and lay waste the very foundation of one's existence without finding that trouble has originated that is likely to be far reaching. That was the situation. The Indian had been master of the plains from time immemorial, and like every possessor of territory; he had no idea of yielding up his home, his life, without a struggle. He had not admitted the sovereignty of the government when the white man came among the tribes. Any territorial extension that had been made on the part of the government was made by treaty, and any one conversant with history well knows how faithlessly the truces and pacts with the Indians have been kept. In fact, it is one of the standing disgraces to our country that so many of the agreements with the original holders of the land have been broken. It looks as if the principle that "might makes right" were the only one in vogue when dealing with the Indian. He has not only been deceived frequently in the past, and treaties with him violated, but he has also been plundered in ruthless fashion by those whom the government sent to look after his affairs. Scandal upon scandal has occurred among the agents in charge of the different reservations, with the result that the Indians not only became disgusted with the treatment they received, but broke away from their locations and went on the warpath. If the different tribes that surrendered had been treated with the proper amount of justice, half or more of the blood-curdling atrocities of the latter part of the decade of 1870 would not have occurred. What was wanted was more men like General Sheridan, and General Creel, and less of the grafters and boodlers who looked upon the Indian as lawful prey to be robbed and pillaged with ruthless abandon.

The government, I have no doubt was willing to do the right thing, but was frequently unfortunate in the choice of the means adopted. The Quakers who came upon the scene early in the management of Indian affairs, meant well, but their peaceful measures were not adapted to the nature and character of the tribes of the plains. They did not understand the nature of the Indians who were wont to travel with unrestrained freedom over the vast plains, living their lives according to their lights and traditions. The Quaker method of curbing their dauntless spirit was about as effective as trying to tame a wildcat by saying, "pussy." As I said, they meant well, did their best, but their efforts caused the Indian to smile on more than one occasion.

The methods frequently used by the war office to bring the Indians into subjection did not always meet with the success that the efforts exerted would warrant. True, it was a novel kind of warfare for civilized men to undertake, but I do not think that the utmost care was always exercised in carrying out the different campaigns. There is much to show that there must have been considerable laxity in different places, as is shown in the ease with which Dull Knife marched, by, past, and around, different forts in his way north, and with a mere handful of men set at naught the efforts of several regiments. There is no question about the willingness of the private soldier to do his duty, for he was usually found at his post and fighting to the last ditch, but there were men wearing the garb of officers who did not exercise the judgment of skilled fighters in handling a difficult situation, or in following an efficient plan of campaign. All this naturally tended to give the Indian an opportunity he was looking for, and the blows he dealt in return were of considerable heft.

The day is coming slowly but surely when the last red man will have disappeared from the domain wherein he roamed a monarch. He does not seem to be able to thrive on the white man's mode of life. It may be that the veneer of civilization that he had acquired in recent years is more of a restraint than a benefit to him. The vices of the white man have had their effect upon him also. Whatever the causes, the race seems to be doomed to extinction, the buffalo and the Indian seemed to be an essential part of the plains. The buffalo is practically only a memory, and the red man is following his trail toward the setting sun, soon to disappear over the horizon of time.

Afterword

Before taking leave of my readers, I cannot refrain from expressing the appreciation I feel for the assistance I have received from numerous reliable sources. The best authority for an account of any happening is the chief actor in the drama, and this is undoubtedly true when the authors themselves are men of integrity, reliability, modesty and truth. Men of this type necessarily leave the impression of truthfulness and reliability, on any narration of events they may make. Such men I have consulted in my work to guarantee the authenticity and veracity of my narrative. I take a great pleasure in acknowledging my indebtedness to General H. M. Creel, Ben Clark and Mr. John Murphy. Others who have assisted me in compiling the preceding chapters, I have mentioned in various parts of the book, but those I enumerate here, have assisted me in a special manner and I feel it a duty to thank them abundantly for their favour in directing me in setting down the correct narrative of events described. As these gentlemen are still living, it is a very easy matter for any one to consult them in regard to the historical events of the preceding chapters, but any one who knows the character of these gentlemen will deem it sufficient that they have placed the stamp of their approval on the pages of the preceding work.

To my wife, who so faithfully kept the light in the window as a beacon to insure my safe return, this little volume is most respectfully dedicated.

The Author

ALSO FROM LEONAUR
AVAILABLE IN SOFTCOVER OR HARDCOVER WITH DUST JACKET

A HISTORY OF THE FRENCH & INDIAN WAR *by Arthur G. Bradley*—The Seven Years War as it was fought in the New World has always fascinated students of military history—here is the story of that confrontation.

WASHINGTON'S EARLY CAMPAIGNS *by James Hadden*—The French Post Expedition, Great Meadows and Braddock's Defeat—including Braddock's Orderly Books.

BOUQUET & THE OHIO INDIAN WAR *by Cyrus Cort & William Smith*—Two Accounts of the Campaigns of 1763-1764: Bouquet's Campaigns by Cyrus Cort & The History of Bouquet's Expeditions by William Smith.

NARRATIVES OF THE FRENCH & INDIAN WAR: 2 *by David Holden, Samuel Jenks, Lemuel Lyon, Mary Cochrane Rogers & Henry T. Blake*—Contains The Diary of Sergeant David Holden, Captain Samuel Jenks' Journal, The Journal of Lemuel Lyon, Journal of a French Officer at the Siege of Quebec, A Battle Fought on Snowshoes & The Battle of Lake George.

NARRATIVES OF THE FRENCH & INDIAN WAR *by Brown, Eastburn, Hawks & Putnam*—Ranger Brown's Narrative, The Adventures of Robert Eastburn, The Journal of Rufus Putnam—Provincial Infantry & Orderly Book and Journal of Major John Hawks on the Ticonderoga-Crown Point Campaign.

THE 7TH (QUEEN'S OWN) HUSSARS: Volume 1—1688-1792 *by C. R. B. Barrett*—As Dragoons During the Flanders Campaign, War of the Austrian Succession and the Seven Years War.

INDIA'S FREE LANCES *by H. G. Keene*—European Mercenary Commanders in Hindustan 1770-1820.

THE BENGAL EUROPEAN REGIMENT *by P. R. Innes*—An Elite Regiment of the Honourable East India Company 1756-1858.

MUSKET & TOMAHAWK *by Francis Parkman*—A Military History of the French & Indian War, 1753-1760.

THE BLACK WATCH AT TICONDEROGA *by Frederick B. Richards*—Campaigns in the French & Indian War.

QUEEN'S RANGERS *by Frederick B. Richards*—John Simcoe and his Rangers During the Revolutionary War for America.

AVAILABLE ONLINE AT www.leonaur.com
AND FROM ALL GOOD BOOK STORES

LEONAUR
ALSO FROM LEONAUR
AVAILABLE IN SOFTCOVER OR HARDCOVER WITH DUST JACKET

JOURNALS OF ROBERT ROGERS OF THE RANGERS by *Robert Rogers*—The exploits of Rogers & the Rangers in his own words during 1755-1761 in the French & Indian War.

GALLOPING GUNS by *James Young*—The Experiences of an Officer of the Bengal Horse Artillery During the Second Maratha War 1804-1805.

GORDON by *Demetrius Charles Boulger*—The Career of Gordon of Khartoum.

THE BATTLE OF NEW ORLEANS by *Zachary F. Smith*—The final major engagement of the War of 1812.

THE TWO WARS OF MRS DUBERLY by *Frances Isabella Duberly*—An Intrepid Victorian Lady's Experience of the Crimea and Indian Mutiny.

WITH THE GUARDS' BRIGADE DURING THE BOER WAR by *Edward P. Lowry*—On Campaign from Bloemfontein to Koomati Poort and Back.

THE REBELLIOUS DUCHESS by *Paul F. S. Dermoncourt*—The Adventures of the Duchess of Berri and Her Attempt to Overthrow French Monarchy.

MEN OF THE MUTINY by *John Tulloch Nash & Henry Metcalfe*—Two Accounts of the Great Indian Mutiny of 1857: Fighting with the Bengal Yeomanry Cavalry & Private Metcalfe at Lucknow.

CAMPAIGN IN THE CRIMEA by *George Shuldham Peard*—The Recollections of an Officer of the 20th Regiment of Foot.

WITHIN SEBASTOPOL by *K. Hodasevich*—A Narrative of the Campaign in the Crimea, and of the Events of the Siege.

WITH THE CAVALRY TO AFGHANISTAN by *William Taylor*—The Experiences of a Trooper of H. M. 4th Light Dragoons During the First Afghan War.

THE CAWNPORE MAN by *Mowbray Thompson*—A First Hand Account of the Siege and Massacre During the Indian Mutiny By One of Four Survivors.

BRIGADE COMMANDER: AFGHANISTAN by *Henry Brooke*—The Journal of the Commander of the 2nd Infantry Brigade, Kandahar Field Force During the Second Afghan War.

BANCROFT OF THE BENGAL HORSE ARTILLERY by *N. W. Bancroft*—An Account of the First Sikh War 1845-1846.

AVAILABLE ONLINE AT www.leonaur.com
AND FROM ALL GOOD BOOK STORES

ALSO FROM LEONAUR
AVAILABLE IN SOFTCOVER OR HARDCOVER WITH DUST JACKET

AFGHANISTAN: THE BELEAGUERED BRIGADE *by G. R. Gleig*—An Account of Sale's Brigade During the First Afghan War.

IN THE RANKS OF THE C. I. V *by Erskine Childers*—With the City Imperial Volunteer Battery (Honourable Artillery Company) in the Second Boer War.

THE BENGAL NATIVE ARMY *by F. G. Cardew*—An Invaluable Reference Resource.

THE 7TH (QUEEN'S OWN) HUSSARS: Volume 4—1688-1914 *by C. R. B. Barrett*—Uniforms, Equipment, Weapons, Traditions, the Services of Notable Officers and Men & the Appendices to All Volumes—Volume 4: 1688-1914.

THE SWORD OF THE CROWN *by Eric W. Sheppard*—A History of the British Army to 1914.

THE 7TH (QUEEN'S OWN) HUSSARS: Volume 3—1818-1914 *by C. R. B. Barrett*—On Campaign During the Canadian Rebellion, the Indian Mutiny, the Sudan, Matabeleland, Mashonaland and the Boer War Volume 3: 1818-1914.

THE KHARTOUM CAMPAIGN *by Bennet Burleigh*—A Special Correspondent's View of the Reconquest of the Sudan by British and Egyptian Forces under Kitchener—1898.

EL PUCHERO *by Richard McSherry*—The Letters of a Surgeon of Volunteers During Scott's Campaign of the American-Mexican War 1847-1848.

RIFLEMAN SAHIB *by E. Maude*—The Recollections of an Officer of the Bombay Rifles During the Southern Mahratta Campaign, Second Sikh War, Persian Campaign and Indian Mutiny.

THE KING'S HUSSAR *by Edwin Mole*—The Recollections of a 14th (King's) Hussar During the Victorian Era.

JOHN COMPANY'S CAVALRYMAN *by William Johnson*—The Experiences of a British Soldier in the Crimea, the Persian Campaign and the Indian Mutiny.

COLENSO & DURNFORD'S ZULU WAR *by Frances E. Colenso & Edward Durnford*—The first and possibly the most important history of the Zulu War.

U. S. DRAGOON *by Samuel E. Chamberlain*—Experiences in the Mexican War 1846-48 and on the South Western Frontier.

AVAILABLE ONLINE AT **www.leonaur.com**
AND FROM ALL GOOD BOOK STORES

ALSO FROM LEONAUR
AVAILABLE IN SOFTCOVER OR HARDCOVER WITH DUST JACKET

THE 2ND MAORI WAR: 1860-1861 by *Robert Carey*—The Second Maori War, or First Taranaki War, one more bloody instalment of the conflicts between European settlers and the indigenous Maori people.

A JOURNAL OF THE SECOND SIKH WAR by *Daniel A. Sandford*—The Experiences of an Ensign of the 2nd Bengal European Regiment During the Campaign in the Punjab, India, 1848-49.

THE LIGHT INFANTRY OFFICER by *John H. Cooke*—The Experiences of an Officer of the 43rd Light Infantry in America During the War of 1812.

BUSHVELDT CARBINEERS by *George Witton*—The War Against the Boers in South Africa and the 'Breaker' Morant Incident.

LAKE'S CAMPAIGNS IN INDIA by *Hugh Pearse*—The Second Anglo Maratha War, 1803-1807.

BRITAIN IN AFGHANISTAN 1: THE FIRST AFGHAN WAR 1839-42 by *Archibald Forbes*—From invasion to destruction-a British military disaster.

BRITAIN IN AFGHANISTAN 2: THE SECOND AFGHAN WAR 1878-80 by *Archibald Forbes*—This is the history of the Second Afghan War-another episode of British military history typified by savagery, massacre, siege and battles.

UP AMONG THE PANDIES by *Vivian Dering Majendie*—Experiences of a British Officer on Campaign During the Indian Mutiny, 1857-1858.

MUTINY: 1857 by *James Humphries*—Authentic Voices from the Indian Mutiny-First Hand Accounts of Battles, Sieges and Personal Hardships.

BLOW THE BUGLE, DRAW THE SWORD by *W. H. G. Kingston*—The Wars, Campaigns, Regiments and Soldiers of the British & Indian Armies During the Victorian Era, 1839-1898.

WAR BEYOND THE DRAGON PAGODA by *Major J. J. Snodgrass*—A Personal Narrative of the First Anglo-Burmese War 1824 - 1826.

THE HERO OF ALIWAL by *James Humphries*—The Campaigns of Sir Harry Smith in India, 1843-1846, During the Gwalior War & the First Sikh War.

ALL FOR A SHILLING A DAY by *Donald F. Featherstone*—The story of H.M. 16th, the Queen's Lancers During the first Sikh War 1845-1846.

AVAILABLE ONLINE AT **www.leonaur.com**
AND FROM ALL GOOD BOOK STORES

ALSO FROM LEONAUR
AVAILABLE IN SOFTCOVER OR HARDCOVER WITH DUST JACKET

THE FALL OF THE MOGHUL EMPIRE OF HINDUSTAN by H. G. Keene—By the beginning of the nineteenth century, as British and Indian armies under Lake and Wellesley dominated the scene, a little over half a century of conflict brought the Moghul Empire to its knees.

LADY SALE'S AFGHANISTAN by Florentia Sale—An Indomitable Victorian Lady's Account of the Retreat from Kabul During the First Afghan War.

THE CAMPAIGN OF MAGENTA AND SOLFERINO 1859 by Harold Carmichael Wylly—The Decisive Conflict for the Unification of Italy.

FRENCH'S CAVALRY CAMPAIGN by J. G. Maydon—A Special Correspondent's View of British Army Mounted Troops During the Boer War.

CAVALRY AT WATERLOO by Sir Evelyn Wood—British Mounted Troops During the Campaign of 1815.

THE SUBALTERN by George Robert Gleig—The Experiences of an Officer of the 85th Light Infantry During the Peninsular War.

NAPOLEON AT BAY, 1814 by F. Loraine Petre—The Campaigns to the Fall of the First Empire.

NAPOLEON AND THE CAMPAIGN OF 1806 by Colonel Vachée—The Napoleonic Method of Organisation and Command to the Battles of Jena & Auerstädt.

THE COMPLETE ADVENTURES IN THE CONNAUGHT RANGERS by William Grattan—The 88th Regiment during the Napoleonic Wars by a Serving Officer.

BUGLER AND OFFICER OF THE RIFLES by William Green & Harry Smith—With the 95th (Rifles) during the Peninsular & Waterloo Campaigns of the Napoleonic Wars.

NAPOLEONIC WAR STORIES by Sir Arthur Quiller-Couch—Tales of soldiers, spies, battles & sieges from the Peninsular & Waterloo campaingns.

CAPTAIN OF THE 95TH (RIFLES) by Jonathan Leach—An officer of Wellington's sharpshooters during the Peninsular, South of France and Waterloo campaigns of the Napoleonic wars.

RIFLEMAN COSTELLO by Edward Costello—The adventures of a soldier of the 95th (Rifles) in the Peninsular & Waterloo Campaigns of the Napoleonic wars.

AVAILABLE ONLINE AT **www.leonaur.com**
AND FROM ALL GOOD BOOK STORES

ALSO FROM LEONAUR
AVAILABLE IN SOFTCOVER OR HARDCOVER WITH DUST JACKET

AT THEM WITH THE BAYONET by *Donald F. Featherstone*—The first Anglo-Sikh War 1845-1846.

STEPHEN CRANE'S BATTLES by *Stephen Crane*—Nine Decisive Battles Recounted by the Author of 'The Red Badge of Courage'.

THE GURKHA WAR by *H. T. Prinsep*—The Anglo-Nepalese Conflict in North East India 1814-1816.

FIRE & BLOOD by *G. R. Gleig*—The burning of Washington & the battle of New Orleans, 1814, through the eyes of a young British soldier.

SOUND ADVANCE! by *Joseph Anderson*—Experiences of an officer of HM 50th regiment in Australia, Burma & the Gwalior war.

THE CAMPAIGN OF THE INDUS by *Thomas Holdsworth*—Experiences of a British Officer of the 2nd (Queen's Royal) Regiment in the Campaign to Place Shah Shuja on the Throne of Afghanistan 1838 - 1840.

WITH THE MADRAS EUROPEAN REGIMENT IN BURMA by *John Butler*—The Experiences of an Officer of the Honourable East India Company's Army During the First Anglo-Burmese War 1824 - 1826.

IN ZULULAND WITH THE BRITISH ARMY by *Charles L. Norris-Newman*—The Anglo-Zulu war of 1879 through the first-hand experiences of a special correspondent.

BESIEGED IN LUCKNOW by *Martin Richard Gubbins*—The first Anglo-Sikh War 1845-1846.

A TIGER ON HORSEBACK by *L. March Phillips*—The Experiences of a Trooper & Officer of Rimington's Guides - The Tigers - during the Anglo-Boer war 1899 - 1902.

SEPOYS, SIEGE & STORM by *Charles John Griffiths*—The Experiences of a young officer of H.M.'s 61st Regiment at Ferozepore, Delhi ridge and at the fall of Delhi during the Indian mutiny 1857.

CAMPAIGNING IN ZULULAND by *W. E. Montague*—Experiences on campaign during the Zulu war of 1879 with the 94th Regiment.

THE STORY OF THE GUIDES by *G.J. Younghusband*—The Exploits of the Soldiers of the famous Indian Army Regiment from the northwest frontier 1847 - 1900.

AVAILABLE ONLINE AT **www.leonaur.com**
AND FROM ALL GOOD BOOK STORES

ALSO FROM LEONAUR
AVAILABLE IN SOFTCOVER OR HARDCOVER WITH DUST JACKET

ZULU:1879 *by D.C.F. Moodie & the Leonaur Editors*—The Anglo-Zulu War of 1879 from contemporary sources: First Hand Accounts, Interviews, Dispatches, Official Documents & Newspaper Reports.

THE RED DRAGOON *by W.J. Adams*—With the 7th Dragoon Guards in the Cape of Good Hope against the Boers & the Kaffir tribes during the 'war of the axe' 1843-48'.

THE RECOLLECTIONS OF SKINNER OF SKINNER'S HORSE *by James Skinner*—James Skinner and his 'Yellow Boys' Irregular cavalry in the wars of India between the British, Mahratta, Rajput, Mogul, Sikh & Pindarree Forces.

A CAVALRY OFFICER DURING THE SEPOY REVOLT *by A. R. D. Mackenzie*—Experiences with the 3rd Bengal Light Cavalry, the Guides and Sikh Irregular Cavalry from the outbreak to Delhi and Lucknow.

A NORFOLK SOLDIER IN THE FIRST SIKH WAR *by J W Baldwin*—Experiences of a private of H.M. 9th Regiment of Foot in the battles for the Punjab, India 1845-6.

TOMMY ATKINS' WAR STORIES: 14 FIRST HAND ACCOUNTS—Fourteen first hand accounts from the ranks of the British Army during Queen Victoria's Empire.

THE WATERLOO LETTERS *by H. T. Siborne*—Accounts of the Battle by British Officers for its Foremost Historian.

NEY: GENERAL OF CAVALRY VOLUME 1—1769-1799 *by Antoine Bulos*—The Early Career of a Marshal of the First Empire.

NEY: MARSHAL OF FRANCE VOLUME 2—1799-1805 *by Antoine Bulos*—The Early Career of a Marshal of the First Empire.

AIDE-DE-CAMP TO NAPOLEON *by Philippe-Paul de Ségur*—For anyone interested in the Napoleonic Wars this book, written by one who was intimate with the strategies and machinations of the Emperor, will be essential reading.

TWILIGHT OF EMPIRE *by Sir Thomas Ussher & Sir George Cockburn*—Two accounts of Napoleon's Journeys in Exile to Elba and St. Helena: Narrative of Events by Sir Thomas Ussher & Napoleon's Last Voyage: Extract of a diary by Sir George Cockburn.

PRIVATE WHEELER *by William Wheeler*—The letters of a soldier of the 51st Light Infantry during the Peninsular War & at Waterloo.

AVAILABLE ONLINE AT **www.leonaur.com**
AND FROM ALL GOOD BOOK STORES

ALSO FROM LEONAUR
AVAILABLE IN SOFTCOVER OR HARDCOVER WITH DUST JACKET

OFFICERS & GENTLEMEN *by Peter Hawker & William Graham*—Two Accounts of British Officers During the Peninsula War: Officer of Light Dragoons by Peter Hawker & Campaign in Portugal and Spain by William Graham .

THE WALCHEREN EXPEDITION *by Anonymous*—The Experiences of a British Officer of the 81st Regt. During the Campaign in the Low Countries of 1809.

LADIES OF WATERLOO *by Charlotte A. Eaton, Magdalene de Lancey & Juana Smith*—The Experiences of Three Women During the Campaign of 1815: Waterloo Days by Charlotte A. Eaton, A Week at Waterloo by Magdalene de Lancey & Juana's Story by Juana Smith.

JOURNAL OF AN OFFICER IN THE KING'S GERMAN LEGION *by John Frederick Hering*—Recollections of Campaigning During the Napoleonic Wars.

JOURNAL OF AN ARMY SURGEON IN THE PENINSULAR WAR *by Charles Boutflower*—The Recollections of a British Army Medical Man on Campaign During the Napoleonic Wars.

ON CAMPAIGN WITH MOORE AND WELLINGTON *by Anthony Hamilton*—The Experiences of a Soldier of the 43rd Regiment During the Peninsular War.

THE ROAD TO AUSTERLITZ *by R. G. Burton*—Napoleon's Campaign of 1805.

SOLDIERS OF NAPOLEON *by A. J. Doisy De Villargennes & Arthur Chuquet*—The Experiences of the Men of the French First Empire: Under the Eagles by A. J. Doisy De Villargennes & Voices of 1812 by Arthur Chuquet .

INVASION OF FRANCE, 1814 *by F. W. O. Maycock*—The Final Battles of the Napoleonic First Empire.

LEIPZIG—A CONFLICT OF TITANS *by Frederic Shoberl*—A Personal Experience of the 'Battle of the Nations' During the Napoleonic Wars, October 14th-19th, 1813.

SLASHERS *by Charles Cadell*—The Campaigns of the 28th Regiment of Foot During the Napoleonic Wars by a Serving Officer.

BATTLE IMPERIAL *by Charles William Vane*—The Campaigns in Germany & France for the Defeat of Napoleon 1813-1814.

SWIFT & BOLD *by Gibbes Rigaud*—The 60th Rifles During the Peninsula War.

AVAILABLE ONLINE AT **www.leonaur.com**
AND FROM ALL GOOD BOOK STORES

ALSO FROM LEONAUR
AVAILABLE IN SOFTCOVER OR HARDCOVER WITH DUST JACKET

ADVENTURES OF A YOUNG RIFLEMAN by *Johann Christian Maempel*—The Experiences of a Saxon in the French & British Armies During the Napoleonic Wars.

THE HUSSAR by *Norbert Landsheit & G. R. Gleig*—A German Cavalryman in British Service Throughout the Napoleonic Wars.

RECOLLECTIONS OF THE PENINSULA by *Moyle Sherer*—An Officer of the 34th Regiment of Foot—'The Cumberland Gentlemen'—on Campaign Against Napoleon's French Army in Spain.

MARINE OF REVOLUTION & CONSULATE by *Moreau de Jonnès*—The Recollections of a French Soldier of the Revolutionary Wars 1791-1804.

GENTLEMEN IN RED by *John Dobbs & Robert Knowles*—Two Accounts of British Infantry Officers During the Peninsular War Recollections of an Old 52nd Man by John Dobbs An Officer of Fusiliers by Robert Knowles.

CORPORAL BROWN'S CAMPAIGNS IN THE LOW COUNTRIES by *Robert Brown*—Recollections of a Coldstream Guard in the Early Campaigns Against Revolutionary France 1793-1795.

THE 7TH (QUEENS OWN) HUSSARS: Volume 2—1793-1815 by *C. R. B. Barrett*—During the Campaigns in the Low Countries & the Peninsula and Waterloo Campaigns of the Napoleonic Wars. Volume 2: 1793-1815.

THE MARENGO CAMPAIGN 1800 by *Herbert H. Sargent*—The Victory that Completed the Austrian Defeat in Italy.

DONALDSON OF THE 94TH—SCOTS BRIGADE by *Joseph Donaldson*—The Recollections of a Soldier During the Peninsula & South of France Campaigns of the Napoleonic Wars.

A CONSCRIPT FOR EMPIRE by *Philippe as told to Johann Christian Maempel*—The Experiences of a Young German Conscript During the Napoleonic Wars.

JOURNAL OF THE CAMPAIGN OF 1815 by *Alexander Cavalié Mercer*—The Experiences of an Officer of the Royal Horse Artillery During the Waterloo Campaign.

NAPOLEON'S CAMPAIGNS IN POLAND 1806-7 by *Robert Wilson*—The campaign in Poland from the Russian side of the conflict.

AVAILABLE ONLINE AT **www.leonaur.com**
AND FROM ALL GOOD BOOK STORES

ALSO FROM LEONAUR
AVAILABLE IN SOFTCOVER OR HARDCOVER WITH DUST JACKET

OMPTEDA OF THE KING'S GERMAN LEGION by *Christian von Ompteda*—A Hanoverian Officer on Campaign Against Napoleon.

LIEUTENANT SIMMONS OF THE 95TH (RIFLES) by *George Simmons*—Recollections of the Peninsula, South of France & Waterloo Campaigns of the Napoleonic Wars.

A HORSEMAN FOR THE EMPEROR by *Jean Baptiste Gazzola*—A Cavalryman of Napoleon's Army on Campaign Throughout the Napoleonic Wars.

SERGEANT LAWRENCE by *William Lawrence*—With the 40th Regt. of Foot in South America, the Peninsular War & at Waterloo.

CAMPAIGNS WITH THE FIELD TRAIN by *Richard D. Henegan*—Experiences of a British Officer During the Peninsula and Waterloo Campaigns of the Napoleonic Wars.

CAVALRY SURGEON by *S. D. Broughton*—On Campaign Against Napoleon in the Peninsula & South of France During the Napoleonic Wars 1812-1814.

MEN OF THE RIFLES by *Thomas Knight, Henry Curling & Jonathan Leach*—The Reminiscences of Thomas Knight of the 95th (Rifles) by Thomas Knight, Henry Curling's Anecdotes by Henry Curling & The Field Services of the Rifle Brigade from its Formation to Waterloo by Jonathan Leach.

THE ULM CAMPAIGN 1805 by *F. N. Maude*—Napoleon and the Defeat of the Austrian Army During the 'War of the Third Coalition'.

SOLDIERING WITH THE 'DIVISION' by *Thomas Garrety*—The Military Experiences of an Infantryman of the 43rd Regiment During the Napoleonic Wars.

SERGEANT MORRIS OF THE 73RD FOOT by *Thomas Morris*—The Experiences of a British Infantryman During the Napoleonic Wars-Including Campaigns in Germany and at Waterloo.

A VOICE FROM WATERLOO by *Edward Cotton*—The Personal Experiences of a British Cavalryman Who Became a Battlefield Guide and Authority on the Campaign of 1815.

NAPOLEON AND HIS MARSHALS by *J. T. Headley*—The Men of the First Empire.

ALSO FROM LEONAUR
AVAILABLE IN SOFTCOVER OR HARDCOVER WITH DUST JACKET

COLBORNE: A SINGULAR TALENT FOR WAR *by John Colborne*—The Napoleonic Wars Career of One of Wellington's Most Highly Valued Officers in Egypt, Holland, Italy, the Peninsula and at Waterloo.

NAPOLEON'S RUSSIAN CAMPAIGN *by Philippe Henri de Segur*—The Invasion, Battles and Retreat by an Aide-de-Camp on the Emperor's Staff.

WITH THE LIGHT DIVISION *by John H. Cooke*—The Experiences of an Officer of the 43rd Light Infantry in the Peninsula and South of France During the Napoleonic Wars.

WELLINGTON AND THE PYRENEES CAMPAIGN VOLUME I: FROM VITORIA TO THE BIDASSOA *by F. C. Beatson*—The final phase of the campaign in the Iberian Peninsula.

WELLINGTON AND THE INVASION OF FRANCE VOLUME II: THE BIDASSOA TO THE BATTLE OF THE NIVELLE *by F. C. Beatson*—The final phase of the campaign in the Iberian Peninsula.

WELLINGTON AND THE FALL OF FRANCE VOLUME III: THE GAVES AND THE BATTLE OF ORTHEZ *by F. C. Beatson*—The final phase of the campaign in the Iberian Peninsula.

NAPOLEON'S IMPERIAL GUARD: FROM MARENGO TO WATERLOO *by J. T. Headley*—The story of Napoleon's Imperial Guard and the men who commanded them.

BATTLES & SIEGES OF THE PENINSULAR WAR *by W. H. Fitchett*—Corunna, Busaco, Albuera, Ciudad Rodrigo, Badajos, Salamanca, San Sebastian & Others.

SERGEANT GUILLEMARD: THE MAN WHO SHOT NELSON? *by Robert Guillemard*—A Soldier of the Infantry of the French Army of Napoleon on Campaign Throughout Europe.

WITH THE GUARDS ACROSS THE PYRENEES *by Robert Batty*—The Experiences of a British Officer of Wellington's Army During the Battles for the Fall of Napoleonic France, 1813.

A STAFF OFFICER IN THE PENINSULA *by E. W. Buckham*—An Officer of the British Staff Corps Cavalry During the Peninsula Campaign of the Napoleonic Wars.

THE LEIPZIG CAMPAIGN: 1813—NAPOLEON AND THE "BATTLE OF THE NATIONS" *by F. N. Maude*—Colonel Maude's analysis of Napoleon's campaign of 1813 around Leipzig.

AVAILABLE ONLINE AT **www.leonaur.com**
AND FROM ALL GOOD BOOK STORES

ALSO FROM LEONAUR
AVAILABLE IN SOFTCOVER OR HARDCOVER WITH DUST JACKET

BUGEAUD: A PACK WITH A BATON *by Thomas Robert Bugeaud*—The Early Campaigns of a Soldier of Napoleon's Army Who Would Become a Marshal of France.

WATERLOO RECOLLECTIONS *by Frederick Llewellyn*—Rare First Hand Accounts, Letters, Reports and Retellings from the Campaign of 1815.

SERGEANT NICOL *by Daniel Nicol*—The Experiences of a Gordon Highlander During the Napoleonic Wars in Egypt, the Peninsula and France.

THE JENA CAMPAIGN: 1806 *by F. N. Maude*—The Twin Battles of Jena & Auerstadt Between Napoleon's French and the Prussian Army.

PRIVATE O'NEIL *by Charles O'Neil*—The recollections of an Irish Rogue of H. M. 28th Regt.—The Slashers—during the Peninsula & Waterloo campaigns of the Napoleonic war.

ROYAL HIGHLANDER *by James Anton*—A soldier of H.M 42nd (Royal) Highlanders during the Peninsular, South of France & Waterloo Campaigns of the Napoleonic Wars.

CAPTAIN BLAZE *by Elzéar Blaze*—Life in Napoleons Army.

LEJEUNE VOLUME 1 *by Louis-François Lejeune*—The Napoleonic Wars through the Experiences of an Officer on Berthier's Staff.

LEJEUNE VOLUME 2 *by Louis-François Lejeune*—The Napoleonic Wars through the Experiences of an Officer on Berthier's Staff.

CAPTAIN COIGNET *by Jean-Roch Coignet*—A Soldier of Napoleon's Imperial Guard from the Italian Campaign to Russia and Waterloo.

FUSILIER COOPER *by John S. Cooper*—Experiences in the 7th (Royal) Fusiliers During the Peninsular Campaign of the Napoleonic Wars and the American Campaign to New Orleans.

FIGHTING NAPOLEON'S EMPIRE *by Joseph Anderson*—The Campaigns of a British Infantryman in Italy, Egypt, the Peninsular & the West Indies During the Napoleonic Wars.

CHASSEUR BARRES *by Jean-Baptiste Barres*—The experiences of a French Infantryman of the Imperial Guard at Austerlitz, Jena, Eylau, Friedland, in the Peninsular, Lutzen, Bautzen, Zinnwald and Hanau during the Napoleonic Wars.

AVAILABLE ONLINE AT **www.leonaur.com**
AND FROM ALL GOOD BOOK STORES

ALSO FROM LEONAUR
AVAILABLE IN SOFTCOVER OR HARDCOVER WITH DUST JACKET

CAPTAIN COIGNET *by Jean-Roch Coignet*—A Soldier of Napoleon's Imperial Guard from the Italian Campaign to Russia and Waterloo.

HUSSAR ROCCA *by Albert Jean Michel de Rocca*—A French cavalry officer's experiences of the Napoleonic Wars and his views on the Peninsular Campaigns against the Spanish, British And Guerilla Armies.

MARINES TO 95TH (RIFLES) *by Thomas Fernyhough*—The military experiences of Robert Fernyhough during the Napoleonic Wars.

LIGHT BOB *by Robert Blakeney*—The experiences of a young officer in H.M 28th & 36th regiments of the British Infantry during the Peninsular Campaign of the Napoleonic Wars 1804 - 1814.

WITH WELLINGTON'S LIGHT CAVALRY *by William Tomkinson*—The Experiences of an officer of the 16th Light Dragoons in the Peninsular and Waterloo campaigns of the Napoleonic Wars.

SERGEANT BOURGOGNE *by Adrien Bourgogne*—With Napoleon's Imperial Guard in the Russian Campaign and on the Retreat from Moscow 1812 - 13.

SURTEES OF THE 95TH (RIFLES) *by William Surtees*—A Soldier of the 95th (Rifles) in the Peninsular campaign of the Napoleonic Wars.

SWORDS OF HONOUR *by Henry Newbolt & Stanley L. Wood*—The Careers of Six Outstanding Officers from the Napoleonic Wars, the Wars for India and the American Civil War.

ENSIGN BELL IN THE PENINSULAR WAR *by George Bell*—The Experiences of a young British Soldier of the 34th Regiment 'The Cumberland Gentlemen' in the Napoleonic wars.

HUSSAR IN WINTER *by Alexander Gordon*—A British Cavalry Officer during the retreat to Corunna in the Peninsular campaign of the Napoleonic Wars.

THE COMPLEAT RIFLEMAN HARRIS *by Benjamin Harris as told to and transcribed by Captain Henry Curling, 52nd Regt. of Foot*—The adventures of a soldier of the 95th (Rifles) during the Peninsular Campaign of the Napoleonic Wars.

THE ADVENTURES OF A LIGHT DRAGOON *by George Farmer & G.R. Gleig*—A cavalryman during the Peninsular & Waterloo Campaigns, in captivity & at the siege of Bhurtpore, India.

AVAILABLE ONLINE AT **www.leonaur.com**
AND FROM ALL GOOD BOOK STORES

ALSO FROM LEONAUR
AVAILABLE IN SOFTCOVER OR HARDCOVER WITH DUST JACKET

THE LIFE OF THE REAL BRIGADIER GERARD VOLUME 1—THE YOUNG HUSSAR 1782-1807 *by Jean-Baptiste De Marbot*—A French Cavalryman Of the Napoleonic Wars at Marengo, Austerlitz, Jena, Eylau & Friedland.

THE LIFE OF THE REAL BRIGADIER GERARD VOLUME 2—IMPERIAL AIDE-DE-CAMP 1807-1811 *by Jean-Baptiste De Marbot*—A French Cavalryman of the Napoleonic Wars at Saragossa, Landshut, Eckmuhl, Ratisbon, Aspern-Essling, Wagram, Busaco & Torres Vedras.

THE LIFE OF THE REAL BRIGADIER GERARD VOLUME 3—COLONEL OF CHASSEURS 1811-1815 *by Jean-Baptiste De Marbot*—A French Cavalryman in the retreat from Moscow, Lutzen, Bautzen, Katzbach, Leipzig, Hanau & Waterloo.

THE INDIAN WAR OF 1864 *by Eugene Ware*—The Experiences of a Young Officer of the 7th Iowa Cavalry on the Western Frontier During the Civil War.

THE MARCH OF DESTINY *by Charles E. Young & V. Devinny*—Dangers of the Trail in 1865 by Charles E. Young & The Story of a Pioneer by V. Devinny, two Accounts of Early Emigrants to Colorado.

CROSSING THE PLAINS *by William Audley Maxwell*—A First Hand Narrative of the Early Pioneer Trail to California in 1857.

CHIEF OF SCOUTS *by William F. Drannan*—A Pilot to Emigrant and Government Trains, Across the Plains of the Western Frontier.

THIRTY-ONE YEARS ON THE PLAINS AND IN THE MOUNTAINS *by William F. Drannan*—William Drannan was born to be a pioneer, hunter, trapper and wagon train guide during the momentous days of the Great American West.

THE INDIAN WARS VOLUNTEER *by William Thompson*—Recollections of the Conflict Against the Snakes, Shoshone, Bannocks, Modocs and Other Native Tribes of the American North West.

THE 4TH TENNESSEE CAVALRY *by George B. Guild*—The Services of Smith's Regiment of Confederate Cavalry by One of its Officers.

COLONEL WORTHINGTON'S SHILOH *by T. Worthington*—The Tennessee Campaign, 1862, by an Officer of the Ohio Volunteers.

FOUR YEARS IN THE SADDLE *by W. L. Curry*—The History of the First Regiment Ohio Volunteer Cavalry in the American Civil War.

AVAILABLE ONLINE AT **www.leonaur.com**
AND FROM ALL GOOD BOOK STORES

ALSO FROM LEONAUR
AVAILABLE IN SOFTCOVER OR HARDCOVER WITH DUST JACKET

LIFE IN THE ARMY OF NORTHERN VIRGINIA *by Carlton McCarthy*—The Observations of a Confederate Artilleryman of Cutshaw's Battalion During the American Civil War 1861-1865.

HISTORY OF THE CAVALRY OF THE ARMY OF THE POTOMAC *by Charles D. Rhodes*—Including Pope's Army of Virginia and the Cavalry Operations in West Virginia During the American Civil War.

CAMP-FIRE AND COTTON-FIELD *by Thomas W. Knox*—A New York Herald Correspondent's View of the American Civil War.

SERGEANT STILLWELL *by Leander Stillwell*—The Experiences of a Union Army Soldier of the 61st Illinois Infantry During the American Civil War.

STONEWALL'S CANNONEER *by Edward A. Moore*—Experiences with the Rockbridge Artillery, Confederate Army of Northern Virginia, During the American Civil War.

THE SIXTH CORPS *by George Stevens*—The Army of the Potomac, Union Army, During the American Civil War.

THE RAILROAD RAIDERS *by William Pittenger*—An Ohio Volunteers Recollections of the Andrews Raid to Disrupt the Confederate Railroad in Georgia During the American Civil War.

CITIZEN SOLDIER *by John Beatty*—An Account of the American Civil War by a Union Infantry Officer of Ohio Volunteers Who Became a Brigadier General.

COX: PERSONAL RECOLLECTIONS OF THE CIVIL WAR--VOLUME 1 *by Jacob Dolson Cox*—West Virginia, Kanawha Valley, Gauley Bridge, Cotton Mountain, South Mountain, Antietam, the Morgan Raid & the East Tennessee Campaign.

COX: PERSONAL RECOLLECTIONS OF THE CIVIL WAR--VOLUME 2 *by Jacob Dolson Cox*—Siege of Knoxville, East Tennessee, Atlanta Campaign, the Nashville Campaign & the North Carolina Campaign.

KERSHAW'S BRIGADE VOLUME 1 *by D. Augustus Dickert*—Manassas, Seven Pines, Sharpsburg (Antietam), Fredricksburg, Chancellorsville, Gettysburg, Chickamauga, Chattanooga, Fort Sanders & Bean Station.

KERSHAW'S BRIGADE VOLUME 2 *by D. Augustus Dickert*—At the wilderness, Cold Harbour, Petersburg, The Shenandoah Valley and Cedar Creek..

AVAILABLE ONLINE AT **www.leonaur.com**
AND FROM ALL GOOD BOOK STORES

ALSO FROM LEONAUR
AVAILABLE IN SOFTCOVER OR HARDCOVER WITH DUST JACKET

THE RELUCTANT REBEL *by William G. Stevenson*—A young Kentuckian's experiences in the Confederate Infantry & Cavalry during the American Civil War..

BOOTS AND SADDLES *by Elizabeth B. Custer*—The experiences of General Custer's Wife on the Western Plains.

FANNIE BEERS' CIVIL WAR *by Fannie A. Beers*—A Confederate Lady's Experiences of Nursing During the Campaigns & Battles of the American Civil War.

LADY SALE'S AFGHANISTAN *by Florentia Sale*—An Indomitable Victorian Lady's Account of the Retreat from Kabul During the First Afghan War.

THE TWO WARS OF MRS DUBERLY *by Frances Isabella Duberly*—An Intrepid Victorian Lady's Experience of the Crimea and Indian Mutiny.

THE REBELLIOUS DUCHESS *by Paul F. S. Dermoncourt*—The Adventures of the Duchess of Berri and Her Attempt to Overthrow French Monarchy.

LADIES OF WATERLOO *by Charlotte A. Eaton, Magdalene de Lancey & Juana Smith*—The Experiences of Three Women During the Campaign of 1815: Waterloo Days by Charlotte A. Eaton, A Week at Waterloo by Magdalene de Lancey & Juana's Story by Juana Smith.

TWO YEARS BEFORE THE MAST *by Richard Henry Dana. Jr.*—The account of one young man's experiences serving on board a sailing brig—the Penelope—bound for California, between the years 1834-36.

A SAILOR OF KING GEORGE *by Frederick Hoffman*—From Midshipman to Captain—Recollections of War at Sea in the Napoleonic Age 1793-1815.

LORDS OF THE SEA *by A. T. Mahan*—Great Captains of the Royal Navy During the Age of Sail.

COGGESHALL'S VOYAGES: VOLUME 1 *by George Coggeshall*—The Recollections of an American Schooner Captain.

COGGESHALL'S VOYAGES: VOLUME 2 *by George Coggeshall*—The Recollections of an American Schooner Captain.

TWILIGHT OF EMPIRE *by Sir Thomas Ussher & Sir George Cockburn*—Two accounts of Napoleon's Journeys in Exile to Elba and St. Helena: Narrative of Events by Sir Thomas Ussher & Napoleon's Last Voyage: Extract of a diary by Sir George Cockburn.

AVAILABLE ONLINE AT **www.leonaur.com**
AND FROM ALL GOOD BOOK STORES

www.ingramcontent.com/pod-product-compliance
Lightning Source LLC
Chambersburg PA
CBHW031618160426
43196CB00006B/181